OXFORD MODERN LANGUAGES
AND LITERATURE MONOGRAPHS

Editorial Committee

Vincenzo Cardarelli and his Contemporaries

FASCIST POLITICS AND LITERARY CULTURE

CHARLES BURDETT

CLARENDON PRESS · OXFORD

OXFORD

UNIVERSITY PRESS

Great Clarendon Street, Oxford OX2 6DP

Oxford University Press is a department of the University of Oxford.
It furthers the University's objective of excellence in research, scholarship,
and education by publishing worldwide in

Oxford New York

Athens Auckland Bangkok Bogotá Buenos Aires Calcutta
Cape Town Chennai Dar es Salaam Delhi Florence Hong Kong Istanbul
Karachi Kuala Lumpur Madrid Melbourne Mexico City Mumbai
Nairobi Paris São Paulo Singapore Taipei Tokyo Toronto Warsaw

with associated companies in Berlin Ibadan

Oxford is a registered trade mark of Oxford University Press
in the UK and in certain other countries

Published in the United States
by Oxford University Press Inc., New York

© Charles Burdett 1999

The moral rights of the author have been asserted
Database right Oxford University Press (maker)

First published 1999

British Library Cataloguing in Publication Data

Data available

Library of Congress Cataloging in Publication Data

Burdett, Charles, 1966–
Vincenzo Cardarelli and his contemporaries: fascist politics and
literary culture / Charles Burdett
—(Oxford modern languages and literature monographs)
Includes bibliographical references.
1. Cardarelli, Vincenzo, 1887–1959—Political and social views.
2. Fascism and literature—Italy. 3. Fascism and culture—Italy.
4. Fascism—Italy. 5. Avant-garde (Aesthetics)—Italy. I. Title.
II. Series.
PQ4809.A65Z53 1999 858'.91209—dc21 98-47246
ISBN 0-19-815978-1

1 3 5 7 9 10 8 6 4 2

Typeset in New Baskerville
by Vera A. Keep, Cheltenham
Printed in Great Britain
on acid-free paper by
Bookcraft Ltd.
Midsomer Norton, Somerset

ACKNOWLEDGEMENTS

The present book derives from my doctoral thesis which I wrote mainly in the pleasant surroundings of Pembroke College Oxford between 1990 and 1993. My work at Oxford was made possible by the generosity of the British Academy. While researching for my D.Phil., I had the opportunity of spending a year at the Collegio Cairoli, Pavia. I am very grateful to the Master of the college, Marco Fraccaro, for enabling me to spend a highly productive year in the libraries of Pavia and Milan. I am also grateful to the School of European Studies in Cardiff for allowing me the time to finish my D.Phil. during my first year as a lecturer in Italian studies. I wish to thank many of my former colleagues in Cardiff both for their comment on my work and for long and valuable discussions.

I would like to thank Romano Luperini for the suggestions he made on my early research proposals. I would also like to thank Clelia Martignoni warmly for the helpful and encouraging comments she made on my early work and for the wealth of material she made available to me. At various stages I was able to discuss my work with Peter Hainsworth and I greatly valued the comments he made, particularly on my reading of Italian poetry of the 1920s and 1930s. I am also indebted to Shirley Vinall for her rigorous reading of my thesis and for the many connections she indicated between Cardarelli and other writers of his time. I wish also to thank Claudia Domenici and Claire Gorrara for the many points which they raised on reading the entire typescript of the book. I am above all grateful to John Woodhouse for the many discussions we have had on all aspects of my work and for the tireless critical attention which, as my supervisor, he dedicated to each chapter of my thesis. All the flaws which remain are my own responsibility.

CONTENTS

INTRODUCTION

Writing on Italian Fascism

A great deal has been written in recent years on the origins of Fascism. The two volumes of Roberto Vivarelli's *Storia delle origini del fascismo*[1] provide a meticulous examination of the political forces and circumstances behind Mussolini's astonishing rise to power. In *Le origini dell'ideologia fascista*,[2] Emilio Gentile has concentrated on the importance initially of the interventionist campaign and subsequently of the First World War in the formation of a recognizably Fascist ideology. In English, a number of works have looked at the rise of Fascism: among others, Zeev Sternhell's *The Birth of Fascist Ideology: From Cultural Rebellion to Political Revolution*[3] has recently been published, as has Walter Adamson's *Avant-Garde Florence: From Modernism to Fascism*.[4] Both works are primarily concerned with demonstrating that Fascism was the political descendant of the cultural revolt, promoted by avant-garde movements across Europe, against liberalism, positivism, and democracy.

During the years in which Mussolini consolidated his hold on power, Fascism developed an opportunistic ability to appropriate whole sectors of opinion. The longer he stayed in power, the more difficult it became to determine the ideological co-ordinates of the authoritarian government which he led. But the connections between the movement in its early stages and a whole range of avant-garde groupings were remarkable. The Futurists were quick to define themselves as Fascists and to participate in a number of subversive operations. Mussolini himself had contributed to a number of radical cultural journals before the First World War and when in power he was ready to acknowledge the influence that the anti-rationalist and voluntarist ideas propounded by

[1] Bologna: Il Mulino, 1991.
[2] Bologna: Il Mulino, 1996.
[3] Trans. David Meisel (Princeton: Princeton University Press, 1994).
[4] Cambridge, Mass.: Harvard University Press, 1993.

Florentine periodicals had exerted on his intellectual formation. In a speech delivered on 27 March 1924, Giuseppe
Bottai was prepared to claim that the origins of Fascism
'were exquisitely intellectual' and that Fascism was both 'a
revolution of intellectuals' and 'an intellectual revolution'.[5]
Despite the attention which has been devoted to the
examination of the ideological origins of Fascism, there
remain a number of areas that have not been fully explored.
Though Italian Futurism has been the object of a great deal
of critical comment,[6] the importance of Florentine journals
such as La Voce has not been fully acknowledged. In the
introduction to his work Adamson has observed that the
story of the Florentine avant-garde and its role in the development of Fascism is virtually unknown outside Italy.[7] It is
worth adding that this lack of attention is matched by a
more general neglect of the work of writers who began as
participants in the movement and went on to become
active proponents of Fascism. For example, the three Tuscan
writers who were most vociferous in their support for Mussolini were Giovanni Papini, Ardengo Soffici, and Curzio
Malaparte. Malaparte has been the object of an intelligent, if
journalistic, biography and some critical observations.[8] Yet
the amount of criticism that his work has attracted is in no
way commensurate with the reams of prose that he wrote.
The relative absence of comment on his work is surprising
given the positions of influence he occupied under Mussolini, and the scandal that surrounded both his writing and
aspects of his personal life. For example, the publication of
his reflections on the seizure of power by radical political
groups in Europe, Technique du coup d'État (1931), led to his
temporary imprisonment. Papini presents an interesting

---

[5] Bottai's speech is quoted in Giuliano Manacorda, Letteratura e cultura del periodo
fascista (Milan: Principato, 1974), 94.

[6] One of the most recent studies to examine the connection between Futurism
and Fascism is Andrew Hewitt's Fascist Modernism: Aesthetics, Politics and the Avant-
garde (Stanford: Stanford University Press, 1993).

[7] In Italy the scholar who has done the most important work on the avant-garde
journals of the early years of the twentieth century is Umberto Carpi. His most
authoritative work on the topic is La Voce: Letteratura e primato degli intellettuali
(Bari: De Donato, 1975).

[8] The most substantial work to date on Malaparte is Giordano Bruno Guerri's
L'Arcitaliano: Vita di Curzio Malaparte (Milan: Leonardo, 1990).

case of a committed avant-gardist who after the First World War became a fervent Catholic as well as a staunch reactionary. In Italy, Papini's early work has been the object of a number of studies that have pointed to its iconoclasm and its innovation, but the texts which he wrote after the First World War are more often than not dismissed as mere rant or used simply as a quarry from which to extract a number of fairly odious statements. The same is true for Soffici, whose early work as a Futurist has been well documented but whose writings in favour of Fascism are far less well known than the paintings he produced in the 1920s and 1930s.

In part the lack of attention that figures such as Malaparte or Papini have attracted is understandable. However, the reluctance of the critical community to examine texts written by some Fascist writers is unfortunate in the sense that it has tended to create an incomplete picture of writing in the 1920s and 1930s.[9] If the work of compromised writers does not receive adequate critical consideration, then it is easy to assume that the majority of Italian writers were either tacitly or implicitly opposed to Mussolini's regime when the reality was quite different.[10] At each stage of its political development Fascism had no difficulty in finding writers who were prepared to defend its ideals. The study of the texts which were to come out of the experience of the Florentine avant-garde reveals the degree of interventionist and Nationalist sentiment among the intellectual community. The plethora of journals which sprang up in the years after the march on Rome shows how many writers were keen to

[9] Giorgio Luti and Mario Isnenghi are among some of the critics who have written on the work of orthodox Fascist writers. In *Cronache letterarie tra le due guerre 1920–1940* (Bari: Laterza, 1966), Luti has traced the evolution of a number of cultural journals in the years of Fascist rule. Isnenghi has studied, particularly in *Intellettuali militanti e intellettuali funzionari* (Turin: Einaudi, 1979), the writings not only of pro-Fascist authors, but of officials and journalists in the years of Mussolini's regime. On the subject of Fascism and literature, the following title has recently appeared: Marino Biondi and Alessandro Borsotti (eds), *Cultura e fascismo: letteratura, arti e spettacolo di un ventennio* (Florence: Ponte alle Grazie, 1996).

[10] Isnenghi has pointed out forcefully the tendency to ignore the involvement in Fascism of a number of well-known figures. In *Intellettuali militanti e intellettuali funzionari* (Turin: Einaudi, 1979) he says: 'Cosicché, il paesaggio storico che via via si è andato definendo è quello di un fascismo senza fascisti, dove una patente di antifascismo, criptoantifascismo o, male che vada, afascismo non la si nega a nessuno' (p. 21).

establish what they regarded as a truly Fascist literature. The willingness of many writers to disseminate propaganda in favour of the regime further demonstrates the hold which Fascism exerted over the imagination of many intellectuals.

The analysis of texts by writers who saw themselves as exercising a valuable part in Mussolini's drive to transform Italy serves first of all to provide some indication of the extent to which Italian literature was deeply implicated in the history of Fascism. Some writing may have sought to remain aloof from the political realities of the time, but very few works succeeded in fulfilling that aim. Indeed, it is easy to extract from the writings of many prominent literary figures of the time a series of transparent statements either in praise of the new Italy or in support of Mussolini. But the study of the works of writers who declared their allegiance to Fascism becomes much more interesting when such texts are read as indications of the different ways in which Fascist thinking was interpreted. The Fascism of Marinetti, for example, did not coincide with that of the Florentine avant-gardists; the writers who belonged to the *strapaese* movement in the 1920s were at odds with those who declared support for *stracittà*, and yet both groups claimed to be loyal Fascists. There were, moreover, a number of strange parallels between the work of some writers who were opposed to Mussolini's regime and others who were its avowed supporters. The changing interpretation of the concept of Fascism was reflected also by the frequency with which writers united together under one manifesto but then quarrelled and disbanded.

Analysis of the textual strategies of writing published during the twenty years of Fascist rule demonstrates above all how political ideologies are experienced differently according to an individual's psychology, gender, or social position. The attempt to understand the motivation behind different stances towards a reactionary and violent political order is worthwhile because it enables us to understand the breadth of currents which together made up and sustained Italian Fascism. The analysis of the changing views of those writers who began as avant-garde Nationalists and ended as highly conservative supporters of Fascism does not in any way help to rehabilitate the reputation of those writers. Instead, the study of the texts which they wrote provides a detailed history of some of the most unpleasant aspects of their thought. The extreme depth of their masculinism emerges very clearly, as do the racist contours of their Nationalism. For example, a text like Soffici's *Taccuino di Arno Borghi*[11] was written as a serious statement of the author's views on a wide range of topics. When the book is examined today it seems like the ramblings of a madman: it indicates all the contradictions of Soffici's thought, its basis in prejudice, and its reliance on racial and sexual stereotypes.

The Case of Cardarelli

The present study does not offer a complete picture either of those elements within the Italian intellectual community which to a large extent anticipated Fascism or of the literary trends which flourished during the twenty years of dictatorship. Instead, the focus is on the development of the career of one writer, Vincenzo Cardarelli (1884–1959). Though in his time he was considered a prominent figure, few would now regard him as a great writer. Indeed, most criticism that has been written on him has attacked the formal quality of his work: for example, Eugenio Montale criticized the intransigence of his literary aesthetic;[12] Giovanni Pozzi attacked what he saw as the static and deductive sterility of his writing;[13] Piero Mauri, writing in the national daily *La Repubblica*, maintaincd that it would bc a good thing if the whole of his work could be erased.[14] However, despite such a

[11] Florence: Vallechi, 1933. Repr. as vol. iv of *Opere*, ed. E. Falqui, 7 vols. (Florence: Vallechi, 1959–68).
[12] E. Montale, 'Vincenzo Cardarelli: Una voce isolata', in *Sulla poesia* (Milan: Mondadori, 1976), 307–10.
[13] G. Pozzi, 'Vincenzo Cardarelli', in *La poesia italiana del Novecento: Da Gozzano agli Ermetici* (Turin: Einaudi, 1965), 117–30.
[14] P. Mauri, 'Il dito alzato del poeta Cardarelli', *La Repubblica*, 14 June 1979. Although the criticism on Cardarelli as a writer is in general negative, some critics have been prepared to acknowledge merits in his work. Eduardo Sanguineti, in *Poesia del Novecento* (Turin: Einaudi, 1969), casts doubt upon the usefulness of the notion of neoclassicism to define his experience as a poet. In *Ventiquattro voci per un*

weight of negative criticism, his texts are interesting because
they so closely mirror the development of Fascism. Clelia
Martignoni has written important essays on his early prose,
compiled an anthology of his writings as a journalist, and
a published collected edition of his creative work.[15] The
volumes she has edited display an impressive amount of
philological research and are indispensable for any study of
the development of his writing. Umberto Carpi has also
helped to define the historical context of Cardarelli's early
Socialist inclinations and his interest in avant-garde culture.[16]
Carpi has also pointed to the nature of the positions which
he adopted under Fascism and has indicated that the articles
which he wrote, along with those of Soffici in the 1920s
and 1930s, represent 'a highly valuable piece in our understanding of an authentically Fascist culture'.[17] In his
influential study on the history of twentieth-century Italian
literature, Romano Luperini has gone so far as to say that in
the case of Cardarelli, 'history and personal psychology
coincided to a degree that was remarkable'.[18]

Cardarelli began his career as a writer for the Socialist
newspaper *Avanti!*, shortly before Mussolini became the
paper's editor. He did, however, become disillusioned with
Socialism. In an intellectual climate dominated by anti-
positivism and an increasing hostility towards parliamentary
democracy, he became interested in avant-garde Nationalism
as it was represented in the pages of Giuseppe Prezzolini's
cultural journal *La Voce*. He wrote for *La Voce* and a number

dizionario di lettere (Milan: Il Saggiatore, 1968), 133–6, Franco Fortini suggests that
the critic of Cardarelli should attempt to go beyond the antiquated and pro-Fascist
nature of many of his attitudes and ask whether his poetry was not a continuation
of, rather than a reaction against, the expressionism of the *vociani*. Adele Dei has
produced a comprehensive formal study of his poetry in *La speranza è nell'opera*
(Milan: Il Saggiatore, 1979).

[15] Martignoni's collection of Cardarelli's early work as a journalist is entitled
Pagine sparse (Rome: Bulzoni, 1988); her edition of his creative writing is published
under the title *Cardarelli opere* (Milan: Mondadori, 1981).

[16] See in particular the chapter on Cardarelli and *Avanti!* in U. Carpi, *Giornali
vociani* (Rome: Bonacci, 1979).

[17] The observation is to be found in Carpi's article, 'Cardarelli e Péguy', *Il
Cristallo*, 2 (Aug. 1984), 17–24 (p. 22).

[18] R. Luperini, *Il Novecento: Apparati ideologici, ceto intellettuale, sistemi formali, nella
letteratura contemporanea*, 4th edn., 2 vols. (Turin: Loescher, 1994), i. 312.

of other journals, developing an interest in Bergsonian vitalism and in a cult of the genius which was central to the new morality which members of the Florentine avant-garde sought to propagate. He wrote in defence of the tenets of Nationalism, and during the First World War he published an aggressive autobiography, *Prologhi*, which displayed the extent of his reception of the thinking of Nietzsche and Weininger. His modernist work was close in style and inspiration to the unmistakably proto-Fascist autobiographies published by Papini and Soffici in the same years.

After the war, however, Cardarelli and a group of disaffected avant-gardists set up the journal *La Ronda* (1919–23). With its militaristic title and masthead, *La Ronda* overtly aimed to encourage a disciplined approach to the act of writing, to restore respect for the authority of tradition, and to promote a classically balanced form of expression. The defence of tradition promoted by Cardarelli was mirrored by other writers and painters who, after a long period of experimentation, began to defend the ideals of order and certainty. The call to order also shared obvious parallels with the Fascist implementation of a system of authoritarian political power. While claiming to be a reaction against avant-garde culture, *La Ronda* also perpetuated elements within the ideology of *La Voce*, such as the need for grandeur and the veneration of retrogressive regionalism. If *La Ronda* anticipated Mussolini's repressive imposition of order, then the sort of prose which the journal spawned reflected a variety of implicitly pro-Fascist positions. During the 'ventennio nero' Cardarelli published several collections of short prose pieces which eulogized an inward-looking rural community, demonstrated an antipathy towards the modern, and created a series of regional and national archetypes which embodied the 'heroic' virtues contemporaneously proposed by such notorious journals such as *Il Selvaggio* and *L'Italiano*. As well as writing about rural utopias, Cardarelli also showed great willingness to expound the reasons behind his unquestioning allegiance to Fascism.

At the same time as he wrote elegant prose compositions and pieces of Fascist propaganda, he also wrote poetry. His poetry, defined by an aesthetics of order and tradition, had obvious pretensions to grand art. It aimed to construct a solemn and stately image of the writer's self. If the task of Italian culture under Mussolini was to exalt the nation and to inculcate a sense of Italian power, then the works in prose which Cardarelli wrote in the late 1930s openly aimed to fulfil such a function. Writing on visits to different localities within Italy, he speculated on the ethnic identity of a given region and its folkloric traditions. Through his evocations of different regions he spoke of a sense of collective identity and he exalted what he saw as the primitive force, vitality, and vigour of the people. He was at pains to foster the nationalistic myths of Italy's past, and praised the destruction of sizeable areas of Italy's capital city in a desire to show the consonance of the Fascist revolution with the spirit of ancient Rome. After the end of the Second World War, his career as a creative writer was essentially at an end, although he continued to re-edit some of his works and in some cases removed some of his most extreme declarations in favour of Fascism. He died in Rome in 1959.

What I have attempted to do in the following study is to examine the relationship between Cardarelli's texts and the socio-political climate in which they were written. In order to show the influence of contemporary events on his writing, I have drawn on a number of works by historians which examine both the origins of Fascism and the ways in which it developed until its effective collapse during the Second World War. Chapters 1 and 2 look at the strains which appeared in the Italy of Giovanni Giolitti as radical political groupings began to challenge the legitimacy of liberal democracy. The Nationalist opposition to Giolitti's government is studied, as is the development of the campaign for Italian intervention in the First World War. Chapter 3 looks at the mechanics of Mussolini's seizure of power, while the later chapters examine the most important aspects of the regime's domestic and foreign policy, study the changes which occurred in Italy's cultural sphere, and look at major political developments. The formation of Prezzolini's *La Voce* is of particular importance, as is the role which it exerted in the interventionist campaign. The later chapters of the book also examine the role both individual writers and specific journals played in propagating the ideals of the regime.

I have pointed to various strains of thought within the Italian literary community in an endeavour to show the extent to which Cardarelli shared ideas or prejudices with other writers of his time. The examination of his reception of others' thinking demonstrates the power which certain ideas exercised on his imagination. More importantly, his appropriation of ideas of both a political and literary nature helps to show the complex implications of those ideas. Large sections of each chapter are devoted, therefore, to analysing his writing. The early chapters look at the extent to which he participated in the Florentine avant-garde and helped to perpetuate its aims. The later chapters examine his attempts to forge a form of creative writing which was not only in symbiosis with the expression of his political views, but was also in harmony with the vision of Italy presented by Mussolini's regime. In particular, his notion of literary classicism is examined in relation to Fascist politics. Although the major interest of Cardarelli's writing resides precisely in what it tells us about the intellectual climate of which it was a part, his texts gain a further interesting dimension when some of their contradictions are brought to light. He was not a simple adherent of Fascism: his texts are not only the space where certain ideological structures are reflected; they are also the space where those ideological paradigms are paradoxically challenged. The prose and poetry which he wrote both as an active member of the avant-garde and later as a self-styled literary conservative demonstrate a bizarre series of dialectics. On the one hand, his texts suggest a belief in order, discipline, and tradition, while on the other they display a decadent sensibility, a sense of contingency, and a fascination with death. Throughout this book I have concentrated on the ways in which the written self is constructed in Cardarelli's texts, since it is this which most reveals the tensions of his writing. The record of subjectivity offered by his texts, their reception initially of modernist thinking and subsequently of Fascist ideology, make them a valuable series of documents which tells us much about the relationship between literature and Fascism.

THE YEARS OF THE FLORENTINE
AVANT-GARDE (1903–1914)

Italy under Giolitti (1901–1914)

On 14 February 1901 Giovanni Giolitti (1842–1928), together with Giuseppe Zanardelli succeeded in forming a government which brought together the more progressive elements of Liberal Italy. What was known as the Zanardelli–Giolitti administration suffered a barrage of attacks from the right and lasted only until 1903. However, with the support of various sections of parliament, Giolitti was to return to power and, with brief interruptions (1905–6 and 1909–11), stay in government until the eve of the First World War. In Italian historiography, the phrase 'l'Italia giolittiana' defines the period in which he was the major political figure. The period saw the Italian Socialist Party (PSI) move from moderate support for his reforms to more radical opposition; it saw Nationalism emerge as a powerful force attracting support from both right and left; it witnessed the agitation of the revolutionary syndicalists and the rapid rise to prominence of men like Filippo Corridoni and Benito Mussolini. In intellectual circles, the period saw the birth of Futurism and the flourishing of the Florentine avant-garde. Journalists such as Giuseppe Prezzolini and Giovanni Papini successfully organized young writers around journals which noisily campaigned against Giolitti and for the cultural regeneration of Italy. Writers like Vincenzo Cardarelli, who were subsequently to feel the attraction of Fascism, were drawn towards nationalist ideas and towards avant-garde Florence.

The Liberal politicians who had held office before Giolitti's rise, Francesco Crispi (1893–6) and Luigi Pelloux (1898–1900), had supported the authoritarian suppression of working-class agitation at home and attempted colonial expansion abroad. When Giolitti assumed his post as Minister for the Interior in the Zanardelli administration, the immediate dilemma which he faced was whether to continue with the repressive legislation pursued by his predecessors. His decision was not to express unequivocal support for the country's industrialists and large landowners, but to advocate greater neutrality on the part of the state in industrial disputes. Ernesto Ragonieri has written that this move in itself was traumatic enough for the ruling classes of the time.[1]

Giolitti's advocacy of reduced state intervention in disputes was, especially during the early period in which he occupied a position of power, accompanied by increased state interest in the improvement of working conditions. Beginning in 1902, Giolitti introduced a series of policies which saw the greater regulation of non-standard working hours and of women's employment, and the protection of the rights of various categories of workers. Giolitti also granted workers in large industries greater freedom to take strike action as a means of militating for better conditions in the workplace. It was a policy clearly at odds with the view, held by the forces on the right, that repressive government was most able to reinforce the authority of state institutions. In return for the greater stability which his measures were designed to foster, he expected that the governing classes would be prepared to make a number of financial sacrifices. Although deriving his support from shifting coalitions of Liberal politicians, Giolitti believed that he could secure a parliamentary majority for his measures by attracting towards his government moderate forces on the reforming left. Although never stable, the support that the reformist wing of the PSI could offer at different stages proved an important factor in Giolitti's maintenance of power.

Crucially, however, the lengthy period in which he was the dominant force in the Italian parliament coincided with a period of sustained, if uneven, economic growth. As is well known, the newly unified Italy had been slow to industrialize, lagging considerably behind its major competitors. Under

[1] E. Ragonieri, *Storia d'Italia dall'Unità a oggi*, 3 vols., vol. iii: *La storia politica e sociale* (Turin: Einaudi, 1976), 1868: 'Il trauma provocato da questo nuovo atteggiamento fu enorme presso tutti i settori della classe dominante.'

Giolitti the country became at least partially industrialized, undergoing important structural transformations. Some of the conditions for growth had been created by previous administrations which had began to establish the infra-structure and internal market upon which any sort of growth would depend. Protectionist methods had been adopted before Giolitti came to power and his administrations suc-cessfully continued the policy. Italian banks also played an important role in allowing investment capital to fuel the growth of the economy. In his study of the period, Emilio Gentile gives figures to indicate the extent of Italy's industri-alization: in 1896 industry produced 19.4 per cent of the country's gross domestic product, while in 1908 that figure had risen to 26.1 per cent. Between 1901 and 1911 the number of people employed in industry increased by no less than 10 per cent.[2]

Valerio Castronovo, in his study of the growth of the Italian press in the years from unification to the consolida-tion of the Fascist state, lays particular stress on the effects of the economic development in the first fifteen years of the twentieth century. During this period of relative stability and impressive economic growth, the population of the Italian kingdom rose from 32 million in 1901 to 34 million in 1911, there was a significant diminution in illiteracy and a rise of around 17 per cent in the average national income. The change in social conditions and everyday living enabled, as he writes, the shopkeeper, the skilled industrial worker of the north, and the low-level civil servant to take an interest in current affairs, an interest that allowed the newspaper industry to make enormous strides.[3]

The significant upturn in the economy of the country, coupled with the alleviation of repressive measures under Giolitti, did not automatically usher in social harmony. In-deed, the more liberal policies of Giolitti towards the work-

[2] E. Gentile, *L'Italia giolittiana*, 2nd edn. (Bologna: Il Mulino, 1990), 58–9. My summary of the period of Giolitti's rule is chiefly indebted to Gentile's work.
[3] V. Castronovo, *La stampa italiana dall'Unità al fascismo* (Bari: Laterza, 1984), 129–32. Castronovo also mentions (p. 132) that in the first ten years of the twentieth century the circulation of the *Corriere della sera* rose to 200,000, more than double its circulation figures for the last years of the nineteenth century.

ing classes led to an increase in strike action. One of the principal objectives of Giolitti's governments had been to ensure social peace, but such an aim was never realized. Between 1908 and 1910 there was a decrease in industrial agitation, but after 1911 there was a wave of strike action with clear revolutionary undertones. If the rapid rise in industrial production brought with it an increase in living standards for large sections of Italian society, it was naturally also accompanied by a series of profound social problems. Only the northern and central regions of Italy had seen a marked increase in industrial and agricultural production, and the development of these regions accentuated the division between the north and south of the country. Giolitti's administrations had little effect on the inertia of the landowning classes of the south. What attempts at state intervention there were in the southern regions of Italy failed to initiate the process of transformation. Although prepared to introduce reforms which improved the lot of the more disadvantaged members of society, Giolitti was often motivated by the pressures of the moment and rarely undertook wide-ranging reforms which could have redressed some of the problems caused by rapid industrial development. Government intervention tended to be partial and inadequate.[4]

If historians have been critical of Giolitti for failing to plan and co-ordinate industrial development through effective state action, they have also drawn attention to the flaws inherent in his system of government. The period from 1906 to 1914 in which he dominated parliament is popularly known as 'il lungo ministero' or 'la dittatura giolittiana'. While such a period undoubtedly provided stability, it also encouraged widespread dissatisfaction with parliamentary politics. Giolitti did support the extension of the franchise, and in 1912 an electoral reform bill was passed which saw a rise in the electorate of 9.5 per cent. But the widening of the electorate, while it allowed the working classes a greater say

[4] Gentile, *L'Italia giolittiana*, 64: 'Lo stato giolittiano, adeguandosi meccanicamente alla dinamica sociale, non svolse un ruolo attivo di promotore, coordinatore e razionalizzatore dello sviluppo [industriale], per impedire la dispersione clientelare delle risorse finanziarie e per garantire la loro destinazione verso settori che interessavano la collettività nazionale.'

in politics, did not undermine the established parliamentary élite. Indeed by 1914 Giolitti's administration had simply become a means of holding on to power in a parliament which failed to represent the changes in society which had taken place in the wake of industrialization. The new forces in society were represented by movements such as the Nationalists or the revolutionary Socialists, movements which were united in their opposition to Giolitti's form of government and increasingly in favour of war.

The Socialist Party (PSI)

As early as 1900 Filippo Turati and the reformist wing of the PSI had put together the basic demands for which their party would militate. Such demands included universal suffrage, the right of trade unions to operate without restriction, greater welfare provision, the reduction in the number of hours in the working week and universal right to elementary education. Without becoming a recognized part of the Zanardelli–Giolitti government, the PSI was willing to support its legislative programme in parliament and thus guarantee its survival. When Giolitti returned to power in 1906, the reformist wing of the party remained prepared to react positively towards his form of Liberal government. Yet the contradictions involved in offering this sort of support ultimately proved too much for the coherence of the PSI.

Initially the support of Turati and the *riformisti* for Giolitti's programme of reform had been motivated by a fear of a return to power of the reactionary forces on the right. However, the memory of repressive government was not enough to satisfy the more radical elements within the party, who saw co-operation with Giolitti as simply a means of propping up a system of government deeply committed to protecting the interests of the ruling class. The principal representative of the radical wing of the PSI, Arturo Labriola, believed that the party should independently pursue reform and withdraw its support from a governing bourgeois regime which claimed that it was in a position to repair social evils which in reality were systemic. Labriola's opposition to the reformist line in part derived from his experience as a Socialist from the south of Italy, wary of state institutions and conscious of the enormity of the barriers separating one class from another. By 1902 he had moved to Milan to become the effective head of the revolutionary syndicalist movement in Italy and editor of its newly formed weekly publication, *Avanguardia socialista*. It was in Milan that Labriola, along with other leaders of the revolutionary syndicalist movement, was to become, like so many political activists across Europe, deeply influenced by the ideas of the French theorist Georges Sorel.

In 1906 Sorel published his most famous work, *Réflections sur la violence*, a collection of articles which had first appeared in the Italian review, *Il Divenire sociale*. The *Réflections*, inspired both by Marxist philosophy and by a conception of Bergsonian dynamism, were concerned essentially with the idea of class struggle. It was Sorel's contention that if the working classes were animated by quasi-religious myths then they would be inspired to militate not merely for better conditions but for the overthrow of the decadent bourgeois order. In the view of Sorel, it was the task of trade unions to impart to the proletariat a heroic, reforming sense of mission. The preparation for and carrying out of the general strike, meanwhile, represented the single myth most geared to mobilizing the masses. The violence inevitably generated in the course of the general strike would be the concrete expression of heroic, atavistic ideals as well as promoting collective energy and enthusiasm. Such violence would create its own morality and virtue while awakening European nations softened, in Sorel's view, by humanism, democracy and positivism.

Although Turati had been able to ensure a fair measure of reformist support for Giolitti's first administration, Socialist backing for the government remained precarious, since every violent clash between groups of workers and the forces of order weakened the position of the reformist camp within the party. By 1904 Turati's position had already suffered under the continual attack of those who regarded the strategy of co-operation as ultimately counter-productive. At the PSI conference in Bologna in April 1904, Turati's grouping failed to maintain its hegemonic status. The intransigent wing of the party under Labriola was able to forge an alliance with the other sections of the party and thereby gain the ascendancy.

The opportunity for the syndicalist section of the party to experiment with an entirely different strategy came quickly. In early September several workers were killed by police at a protest in Buggeru in Sardinia. On 14 September two workers were killed in Castelluzzo in Sicily. The Milanese Camera del Lavoro issued a call for a general strike, which began on 16 September and immediately won the support of vast sections of the country's workforce. In a sense events had overtaken the syndicalists: they found themselves supporting a mass protest which lacked co-ordination and over which it was difficult for them to assert their authority. Furthermore, if they were keen to widen the political scope of the strike action and undermine Giolitti's government, many reformist Socialists were also anxious to limit the duration of the strike. Most importantly of all, Giolitti's government did not lose its calm. The strike failed to develop a revolutionary dimension and inevitably therefore came to an inconclusive ending.

The failure of the general strike marked a diminution in the power of the syndicalist wing within the party and a corresponding strengthening of the reformists under Turati. The elections which Giolitti called in November 1904 in the wake of his successful opposition to the strike reinforced the reformists within the parliamentary PSI while reducing syndicalist representation to a minimum. Arturo Labriola himself lost his seat. In the following years the syndicalists continued their agitation outside parliament while accusing the mainstream PSI of not supporting the workers in the struggle against the repressive structures of the bourgeois state. At its congress in Rome in October 1906 the PSI officially decided that its struggle would be conducted through parliament rather than through the agitation of the trade unions. From 1906 until 1911, the party, with the reformist element in the driving seat, returned to militate, together with the Confederazione Generale del Lavoro, for better conditions and increased salaries for the working masses.

It was the Libyan enterprise of 1911 that created new problems for the Socialists. The right of the reformist wing of the party ('i destri') had been in favour of Giolitti's foreign policy. For other sections of the party the Libyan adventure seemed to make a mockery of Socialist co-operation with Giolitti's government. At the party congress in 1911 the revolutionary wing gained in strength without managing to create a rift between the reformists of the right and the left. At the party congress at Reggio Emilia in 1912, however, the ideological tensions within the party came to a head. It was Mussolini himself who led the attack against the right of the reformist wing and its major exponents, Ivanoe Bonomi and Leonida Bissolati. Despite their attempt to defend themselves, the motion advocating that 'i destri' should be ousted from the party was carried. Turati remained within the party, but his policy of reformism was at an end, with power having passed into the hands of the revolutionary faction. Costantino Lazzari became the new chairman of the party. Ambitious to participate in the victory of the revolutionary faction, Mussolini successfully fought for the editorship of *Avanti!*. As editor of a leading national newspaper, he found himself able to address a wider audience than ever before, and ideally placed to exploit the crisis that the impending collapse of the Giolittian system would create. Almost immediately after he had taken up his new position, *Avanti!* began a violent anti-government campaign.[5]

The Growth of Nationalism and the Importance of La Voce

If the early years of the twentieth century had witnessed the growing and ultimately irreparable divide between the

[5] Specifically on the situation in which Mussolini found himself after the conference at Reggio Emilia, Renzo De Felice has written: 'La crisi del giolittismo, l'acuirsi della lotta di classe, il suffragio universale, l'instabilità della situazione internazionale esigevano nuove forme di lotte, nuove soluzioni politiche che nessuno sapeva vedere bene, ma che Mussolini sapeva cogliere, sia pure nel loro aspetto più immediato, rozzo e oscuro.' R. De Felice, *Mussolini il rivoluzionario*, 2nd edn. (Turin: Einaudi, 1995), 150.

reformists and the radical wing of the PSI, another important political development that occurred in those years was the growth in Nationalism. What was to become the Nationalist movement was in reality the confluence of a number of disparate currents. It was Enrico Corradini who, more than anyone else, drew those currents together. Before becoming identified with the Nationalist cause, Corradini had been a successful writer and playwright. In particular, his receptivity to the ideas expressed in the work of writers such as Maurice Barrès undoubtedly exerted a defining influence upon the character of the political views he was later to express.[6] In 1896 Corradini moved away from the literary sphere. In that year, together with the Orvieto brothers, Angiolo and Adolfo, and the writer Mario Morasso, he had helped to set up the Florentine periodical *Il Marzocco*. The journal enjoyed the support of both D'Annunzio and Pascoli, and soon became the mouthpiece for numerous established intellectuals who were broadly anti-positivistic in outlook and who were attuned to D'Annunzio's aestheticizing ideas on the cultivation of strength and energy.

It was not until November 1903 that Corradini set up his own journal, *Il Regno*. Unlike *Il Marzocco*, *Il Regno* was born as a journal of political comment. While on specific occasions it advocated action to be taken in relation to the foreign policy of colonial powers or repressive measures to be adopted in response to working-class agitation, it was a voice which aimed to castigate the Italy of Giolitti. The journal's prefatory statement declared that the editors were united in their common purpose to rail against the degeneracy into which they believed the country had recently sunk.[7] Corradini's contempt for the present state of the Italian nation,

---

[6] In her introduction to the collected writings and speeches of Enrico Corradini, *Scritti e discorsi 1901–1914* (Turin: Einaudi, 1980), Lucia Strappini has written: 'Tutta la sua attività è segnata dalla tensione alla propaganda, vale a dire alla trascrizione della letteratura nella politica' (p. xiv).

[7] Corradini, 'Per coloro che risorgono', first published in *Il Regno*, 29 Nov. 1903, p. 1. The article is now reprinted in Delia Castelnuovo Frigessi (ed.), *La cultura italiana attraverso le riviste: Leonardo, Hermes, Il Regno*, 2 vols. (Turin: Einaudi, 1977), ii. 441. The exact words of Corradini were: 'Io e gli amici miei, fondando questa rivista, abbiamo un solo scopo: di essere una voce fra tutti coloro i quali si dolgono e si sdegnano per la viltà della presente ora nazionale.'

a nation which had failed to respond to the challenges posed by the Risorgimento and which had been humiliated in its attempt to establish itself as a colonial power, was exacerbated by the apparent stasis in the type of government which Giolitti seemed to offer. In the minds of the contributors to *Il Regno*, both Giolitti's government and the policies pursued by the reformist Socialists were indications of the contemporary state of national decline. The frequent attacks which the journal levelled against Socialism went beyond political sniping to become indictments of many of the founding principles of enlightened democracy. Concern for the weaker elements within society and the desire to promote justice and civilization were considered to be indications of bourgeois decadence.

Influenced not only by the ideas of Barrès, but also by those of Sorel, the type of political discourse in which Corradini engaged on the pages of *Il Regno* was not constructed according to the principles of rational argument, but openly appealed to the emotions and imagination of the the the journal's readership. The idea of gradual reform was not one with which Corradini or his followers had any sympathy. Indeed, they saw their movement as promoting 'the resurrection of spirituality in politics' and as furthering the cause of a moral renovation of the whole country. In the mind of Corradini an epoch of Nationalism would succeed the period in which Giolitti had allowed reformist Socialism an important say in government. In spite of their professed contempt for the Socialist movement, the Nationalists were paradoxically prepared to adopt and transform some aspects of its ideology. If the notion of the proletariat struggling against the dominance of an exploitative bourgeoisie was central to Socialism, then early twentieth-century Italian Nationalism attempted to replace the concept of one class fighting against another with that of a united national community struggling against other national communities. In Corradini's words: 'As Socialism taught the proletariat the value of class struggle, then similarly it is our duty to teach Italians the value of struggle between nations.'[8] Inherent

[8] The phrase occurs in Corradini's address to the first congress of the Nationalist Party on 3 Dec. 1910. The speech is reprinted in *Scritti e discorsi 1901–1914*, 163–75.

within such a proposition, as well as an ethics of strength and self-affirmation, is a Sorelian conception of the power of the myth to inspire wholesale revolutionary action. When reflecting in 1923 on the fortunes of Nationalism in Italy, Corradini wrote that his movement had breathed new life into 'the true myth of the nation'.[9] He suggested that the idea, which he and his followers had propagated, of a nation or imagined community which asserted its identity through violent struggle against other nations, was one that had inspired vast swathes of Italian society.

Despite its appeal to those members of the Italian middle classes who failed to identify with Giolitti's system of government and who were anxious about the growth in power of the popular masses, *Il Regno* was to cease publication in 1906. Among the contributers had been both Giuseppe Prezzolini and Giovanni Papini. In the early, and most important, parts of their careers, both were to remain strong sympathizers with the Nationalist cause, although both came to consider Corradini's ideas insufficiently forward-looking. Attracted by the philosophy of idealism, they were ardent believers in the necessity of Italy's national renewal, and regarded French avant-garde culture as the inspiration for change. From 1903 to 1907 they had printed their own journal,[10] *Leonardo*, which had loudly declared an opposition to positivism, academic forms of learning, and Giolittian versions of democracy.[11] Receptive to Vilfredo Pareto's

[9] The phrase is taken from the preface to Corradini's own collection of his political speeches. The volume was printed in 1923 and dedicated to Mussolini, 'Duce dell'Italia vittoriosa'. The piece is reprinted in *Scritti e discorsi 1901–1914*, 3–11.

[10] Of the increasing popularity among intellectuals of publishing a journal, Alberto Asor Rosa has interestingly observed: 'Si può stare certi, da quel momento in poi, che, quando un gruppo d'intellettuali non sa cosa fare (nel senso che non ha altro da fare o non vede che ci sia altro da fare), fa una rivista come atto *minimo* di organizzazione culturale.' A. Asor Rosa, *Storia d'Italia dall'Unità a oggi*, 3 vols., vol. ii: *La cultura* (Turin: Einaudi, 1975), 1149.

[11] The introduction which Prezzolini and Papini had written to *Leonardo*, their first journal, is keen to stress the youthfulness of the paper, containing affirmations about the contributors such as: 'Un gruppo di giovani, desiderosi di liberazione, vogliosi d'universalità, anelanti ad una superior vita intellettuale si sono raccolti a Firenze sotto il simbolico nome augurale di *Leonardo* per intensificare la propria esistenza, elevare il proprio pensiero, esaltare la propria arte.' See 'Programma sintetico', *Leonardo*, 4 Jan. 1903, p. 1.

assumption that political life was dictated by the succession of ruling élites, they had been eager to establish a new aristocracy. In *Leonardo* they aggressively advocated cultural renewal, conceived of in terms of an uncovering of the primal self and a defence of the regenerative potential of violence. The expression of their ideas was bolstered by a knowledge of Bergsonian concepts and Nietzschean language, and by an adoption of Otto Weininger's cult of genius and his notion of 'masculine virtues'.

In 1907 Prezzolini and Papini came to the decision that it was necessary to halt publication of *Leonardo* because the journal was failing to provide the nucleus around which an ever-growing circle of intellectuals could unite. The following year, however, the two writers brought out the first edition of the most significant of the many journals to be published before the outbreak of the First World War, *La Voce*. The *vociani*, as the contributors to the new publication were later to be known, shared with Corradini a hatred for the Italy moulded by Giolitti and a belief in the imperative that Italy should acquire a national consciousness. But whereas *Il Regno* had been an organ of political intervention, *La Voce* aimed to be the vehicle necessary for creating 'the party of intellectuals'. The very fact that *La Voce* was intended to be a new intellectual centre, attracting different currents of thought, united only in their contempt for the present state of perceived national decline, meant that the journal did not have a unified political programme.

In the second issue of *La Voce*, Prezzolini articulated the aims of the journal in a piece entitled, 'La nostra promessa' (27 December 1908, p. 5). He denounced the intellectual and literary climate of the time, accusing it of dishonesty, mediocrity, and indifference to ethical concerns. The damning criticisms made against the literary world extended to other areas of society. One of the central purposes of the newly created journal, Prezzolini argued, was to condemn perceived shortcomings in all walks of life (in his words, the journal should 'comment upon the vileness of contemporary life').[12] Towards the end of 'La nostra promessa' a

---

[12] In another article, similar to 'La nostra promessa', Prezzolini had written: 'Il nostro programma se è, da una parte protesta e critica delle deviazioni, delle

number of areas of public life which seemed to be in need of reform or improvement, such as the country's network of libraries and universities, were indicated. However, as Asor Rosa has correctly pointed out, the list of abuses which *La Voce* aimed to confront was of such a varied character that it seemed almost as if it had been compiled casually.[13]

Although the specific targets of *La Voce* initially remained vague, the journal did aim to provide an interface between the spheres of politics and culture. In the programmatic statement written on the launch of the review, there are certain indications that this is one of its chief proposals, but the point was not spelled out until 1911 with the important clarificatory article, 'La politica della *Voce*' (30 November 1911, p. 697). In this piece Prezzolini insisted that a clear split existed in Italy between culture and politics, and that such a division worked to the detriment of both. The intention of his journal was to encourage the participation of intellectuals in the political life of the nation. Simultaneously the journal set itself the task of ensuring that: 'the cultured classes, who constitute our readership, have ideas which are both balanced and well founded'. During the six years in which it was printed weekly, *La Voce* published both the work of young writers such as Scipio Slataper, Giovanni Boine, and Clemente Rebora and the views on major issues of more established figures. For example, Romolo Murri wrote on Catholic Modernism and Socialism;[14] Benedetto Croce wrote on subjects connected both with philosophy and with university life;[15] Gaetano Salvemini addressed such subjects as the parliamentary progress of Giolitti, universal suffrage,[16] and the reform of secondary schools. Beyond Italy itself, figures of the stature of Sorel and Romain Rolland published a number of pieces on the pages of *La Voce*.

The major contributors to *La Voce* shared an anxious preoccupation with the ethical character of Italian politics

meschinerie, delle viltà che guastano molti ingegni.' See 'Al lettore', *La Voce*, 11 Feb. 1909, p. 33.

[13] Asor Rosa, *Storia d'Italia dall'Unità a oggi*, ii. 1257.

[14] See e.g. the article 'Modernismo e Socialismo', *La Voce*, 4 Feb. 1909, p. 29.

[15] See e.g. the article 'Il caso Gentile e la disonestà della vita universitaria italiana', *La Voce*, 4 Mar. 1909, p. 45.

[16] See e.g. 'Suffragio universale e clericalismo', *La Voce*, 27 Apr. 1911, p. 558.

and culture. It was no coincidence that they called themselves (and are now commonly referred to as) 'i moralisti
vociani'. To a degree the ideals to which the *vociani* declared
it their intention to adhere to were simple. In 'La nostra
promessa' the editor promises, on behalf of his journal,
honesty ('we promise to be honest and sincere'), seriousness ('we intend to grapple with what matters'), hard work
('we want to work'), and plain-speaking ('we intend to
use a rough-edged language, necessary to restore a bit of
honesty'). Underlying such straightforward precepts are
more interesting notions concerning standards of personal
and collective behaviour. In the view expressed most co-
gently by Giovanni Amendola,[17] but endorsed by the other
vociani, a hoped-for regeneration of Italy could occur only if
there were to be an increase in the individual's moral awareness. By publishing articles on religious and social questions
which could attract the interest of a wide body of individuals,
the journal hoped to encourage a regenerative movement of
ideas. There is no doubt that such a project was inspired to a
degree by Sorelian theories on social change. Although
reformist Socialism, involved in Giolitti's system of government, was anathema to both Papini and Prezzolini, both
were prepared to accept that the syndicalists, already able to
organize widespread popular action, offered the possibility
of real change.

Nevertheless, for the *vociani* the agent of change remained
the individual. No revolution, they believed, could take place
without a transformation in the moral outlook of those who
could go on to form a new ruling élite. Writers such as
Papini, Amendola, and Ardengo Soffici derived a harshly
voluntarist moral code from the work of such thinkers as
Nietzsche, Weininger, and Carlyle. Amendola, in the widely
influential text revealingly entitled *La volontà è il bene* (Rome,
1911), acknowledged that his notion of the identity of

[17] In his article, 'Il convegno nazionalista', *La Voce*, 1 Dec. 1910, p. 446, Amendola had written that a 'higher concept of individual morality' inspired both him
and his associates to despise those who occupied public office without in any way
feeling the 'terrible seriousness of every individual action'. He went on to write
that the lack of responsibility and energy among public officials, coupled with their
widespread dishonesty, was the result of the 'weak and backward moral life of the
individual'.

goodness with the will's potential to inhibit the instincts of the subject had its basis in the philosophy of Nietzsche. Papini described Weininger's *Geschlect und Charakter*, with its misogynous emphasis on the cultivation of the masculine psyche, as 'a true masterpiece . . . the most important theoretical work that Germany has produced since the last books by Nietzsche'.[18] The urge to forge a new morality, a new society, and even 'un uomo nuovo' is a feature which recurs both in the articles and in the written correspondence of most of the younger and most fervent contributors to *La Voce*. Writing to Prezzolini in May 1908 Papini had declared, 'I feel compelled to change things. I feel within myself . . . that intolerance of the present state of affairs and that mania to change them which makes missionaries and apostles.' Clemente Rebora, never the most prolific of the *vociani*, wrote to a friend in terms which convey the extent to which *La Voce* had captured the imagination of a generation of young writers. He spoke of having met and talked to Prezzolini, whom he described as the standard-bearer of 'a moral renewal . . . which will be the preparation for a vast renaissance for both men and God'.[19]

Both Prezzolini and Papini stated that the cultural renewal of Italy for which their journal militated could be attained only if examples of European avant-garde culture were introduced to as wide an Italian audience as possible. In 'La nostra promessa' the editor had undertaken to inform his readership about 'the best of what is happening abroad', and in many of the editions of *La Voce* translated extracts were published from the work of modern European writers, frequently with critical comments and appreciations added by the *vociani* themselves. In particular, French thinking as represented by Rolland, Paul Claudel, Daniel Halévy, and

[18] Otto Weininger's *Geschlect und Charakter*, was first published in Germany in 1903. It seems that Prezzolini discovered Weininger's work on a trip to Munich in 1906. It was first translated into Italian in 1912 (*Sesso e carattere*, trans. G. Fenoglio), and was reviewed by Italo Tavolato in *La Voce*, 10 Oct. 1912 p. 924. Papini's reaction to the work is reported in Adamson, *Avant-Garde Florence*, 122.
[19] The letter is quoted by Umberto Carpi in *La Voce: Letteratura e primato degli intellettuali*, 202. Rebora's letter was written on 1 May 1911 to Daria Banfi Malaguzzi, and is now contained in the work by the same Daria Banfi Malaguzzi, *Il primo Rebora* (Milan: Mondadori, 1964), 44.

Charles Péguy was received enthusiastically, while the impact exerted by the discoveries of Bergson was enormous. Prezzolini himself, an accomplished scholar of German culture, was responsible for encouraging interest in thinkers such as Weininger, while writers from Trieste, such as Slataper and Carlo Stuparich, were particularly well placed to appropriate the experiments of German expressionism. The receptivity of the *vociani* to works of foreign culture did not imply contempt for the Italian tradition. Indeed, in one article, 'L'Italia risponde' (20 December 1908, p. 1), Papini drew attention to great Italian writers of the past. But the opening towards contemporary European culture betrayed a return to their deep-seated dissatisfaction with what was regarded as the stale intellectual atmosphere of 'l'Italia giolittiana' as well as an essentially avant-garde craving for the new.

The Libyan War

During the years in which it was published, *La Voce* drew together writers and thinkers from wholly different areas of the country: Rebora was from Lombardy, Piero Jahier from Piedmont, Stuparich and Slataper from Trieste, Boine from Liguria, Renato Serra from Cesena, Amendola from Naples. Moreover, the extremely broad-based notions which had motivated its creation permitted a whole range of applications and/or adaptations which, as will be seen, were to lead to very different responses to Fascism. The single most important idea which united the *vociani* was the belief in the necessity of the national renewal of Italy. If the disparate grouping of intellectuals which had gathered around *La Voce* had found common cause in this issue, then the Nationalists and radical syndicalists, although coming from very different directions, were similarly able to find common ground. Both groups shared an aversion to the existing political system, unified in their belief that the Liberal parliamentary democracy personified by Giolitti represented a kind of debilitating illness from which the country must recover. Since its inception, the Nationalist Party had fought for a colonial war which would erase the humiliation of Italy's defeat at

Adowa in 1896 and affirm the country's presence as a major power in Europe. More surprisingly, by 1910, Labriola himself, together with other prominent radical syndicalists, had begun to maintain that the concepts of war and of nation were not antithetical to those of syndicalism and Socialism. Angelo Olivetti, writing in the review *Pagine libere*, had affirmed in 1911 that Nationalism and syndicalism were similar in that they were both doctrines which exalted energy and willpower. He went on to state that a further similarity drawing the two movements together was their hatred for all that was 'flat, weak and soft' both within the bourgeoisie and within the concept of democracy.[20]

By 1910 a considerable number of political factions were united in pressing noisily for a greater affirmation of Italian colonial power. In the early years of the twentieth century, the French had received Italian political support for their expansion in Morocco. The Agadir crisis of July 1911 made it clear to Giolitti and his government, however, that if they did not impose an Italian presence on Libya then they would be leaving the French a space in which to extend their influence. Well aware of the extent of Nationalist sentiment in Italy, Giolitti made the single most decisive move in his career as a politician: in September 1911 Italy invaded Libya. Ostensibly, the decision was motivated by the fear of the French taking over Tripoli, but the invasion owed much to the desire to placate the increasingly important Nationalist lobby at home. The majority of Italian political parties, the Futurists, and the Nationalists were all in favour of the conquest of Libya. *La Voce*, initially at least, opposed the enterprise, maintaining that it was simply a Giolittian strategy to deflect attention away from more serious problems affecting Italy.

The Libyan campaign encountered a number of serious difficulties, including the unforeseen extent of the Arab population's hostility, but victory was finally gained in October 1912 when Turkey, weakened by war in the Balkans, officially ceded the country to Italy. Giolitti might reasonably

[20] 'Sindicalismo e nazionalismo', *Pagine libere*, 15 Feb. 1911. The article is partially reproduced in Mario Isnenghi, *Il mito della grande guerra* (Rome: Laterza, 1973), 20-1.

have expected that the successful conclusion of a colonial war would strengthen his power-base, but neither he nor his allies were to prove the beneficiaries of the conflict. It was the Nationalists who emerged greatly strengthened from the enterprise. An uncompromising campaign for Italian intervention in the First World War would be the direct result of their enhanced standing. By contrast, the reformist wing of the PSI, having been superseded by the revolutionary faction, no longer constituted a force on which Giolitti could draw for support. By 1913 it was proving more and more difficult for him to arrange the various groupings within his coalition into a viable parliamentary majority and, after his pact with Vincenzo Gentiloni's Catholics ran into trouble, his resignation became imminent.

Cardarelli's Contributions to Avanti!

To follow the progress of Vincenzo Cardarelli as a struggling writer and journalist in the early years of the twentieth century is to follow an ideological itinerary representative of the changing character of Italian politics. He moved away from an allegiance to the PSI of Turati and towards the enthusiastic adoption of the ideas which were being circulated by Prezzolini and the *vociani*. The way in which his political outlook changed indicates the power of attraction which *La Voce* exerted over young writers anxious to become known and to define a role for themselves. Cardarelli's eagerness to gain acceptance by the *vociani* and the degree to which he was prepared to alter his style in order to do so testify to the power that a collective organization could exert on the individual writer. Further, while the principal purpose of *La Voce* was to encourage national renewal, the journal also advocated a stream of associated ideas. Many of these ideas are reflected in the writings of Cardarelli as he moved from columnist in *Avanti!* to aspiring *vociano*. It is through the consideration of these ideas, together with the peculiar form of their expression, that it is possible to attain a more complex picture of what *La Voce* stood for.

It was as a Socialist that Cardarelli began his career. In

1905 he had left his home town of Tarquinia to move to Rome. He was 18, had little money, and little formal education. He did, however, have a few contacts in Rome's PSI, and these proved invaluable in helping him to find work as a reporter. Initially he was compelled to supplement the income he gained as a journalist by working as a secretary, an accountant, and even a night-watchman. The first short articles and book reviews he wrote were published in papers with a radical orientation. In 1907 he published, for example, a series of short pieces on union organization for the paper *L'Azione sindicalista* and in 1908 he contributed to the radical newsheets *Il Germoglio* and *La Vita*.[21] By 1909, however, he had begun to work as a columnist for *Avanti!*

There is no doubt that his position as a journalist for a leading national daily newspaper facilitated his introduction to some of the capital's political and cultural circles. It was while he was working for *Avanti!* that he began his relationship with Sibilla Aleramo[22] and deepened his association with the critic Emilio Cecchi. During the time in which he was employed by *Avanti!*, that is until 1911, the editorship of the paper passed from the hands of Bissolati to Claudio Treves, but the newspaper remained the mouthpiece for the reformist wing of the PSI. Cardarelli was too young and his political training too slight for him to occupy a position in *Avanti!* as a political commentator or theorist. The subjects on which he wrote included politics but covered mainly home news, theatre, and literary criticism. Those Socialist sentiments and ideas which he did express remained generic and confined to a relatively circumscribed number of themes. Indeed, the interest of his Socialism lies not in its political sophistication but in its ideological frailty. The reasons for his imminent switch to the Nationalist camp,

[21] Many of the articles which Cardarelli wrote for various newspapers and periodicals in the early stages of his career have been collected and commented on revealingly by Clelia Martignoni in her edition, *Pagine sparse*. As well as providing a critical commentary on the articles, the introduction to the volume gives an excellent account of the biographical details of Cardarelli's life at the time.

[22] The reasons, as yet not adequately explored, why two temperaments as radically different as those of Aleramo and Cardarelli should have become for a time intimately associated would prove extremely interesting, particularly in the light of Cardarelli's unmistakably misogynous leanings.

moreover, are to be traced to the very nature of his early allegiance to the PSI.[23]

The adoption of a recognizably Socialist point of view is most apparent when Cardarelli writes on the effects of rapid industrialization and on the poverty endured by both a rural and an urban underclass. On his own initiative he wrote a piece for *Avanti!* charting the activities of the Socialist-inspired group, whose members included Sibilla Aleramo and Andrea Cena, which established a number of itinerant schools in the Agro Romano, a seriously deprived area to the south of the capital. One of his articles, 'Germogli di civiltà sulla deserta terra dell'Agro' (26 September 1909), takes the form of an interview with Aleramo in which she reveals the logistical problems encountered by the schools project and its lack of state funding. In another article, 'Tra i villaggi di paglia' (9 February 1910), Cardarelli visits the same area to reveal the degrading conditions of the inhabitants of the half-constructed village of Colledifuori. As well as exposing the plight of sections of the population of the Agro Romano, Cardarelli also wrote a series of articles on aspects of an underclass living in Rome itself. These articles, each entitled 'Malinconie romane', begin with elaborate evocations of Rome's beauty, and then explore areas, often close to the centre of the city, to which that beauty does not extend. The articles chart the physical reality of the squalor suffered by different groups, such as the homeless who sleep outside Palazzo Massimo ('Sotto il portico di una casa insigne', 28 November 1909), the prostitutes who inhabit the side streets beyond Ponte Sant'Angelo ('Sotto la luna', 25 September 1910) or the destitute living in caves near the Arco di Costantino ('Beniamino e i suoi compagni', 30 October 1910).

However, none of these articles is an example of simple factual reporting. Comparisons are made throughout between the ancient splendour of Rome and the present state of degradation suffered by its less fortunate inhabitants. Although Cardarelli is keen to convey precise details about living conditions, he also emphasizes the lurid aspect of the

[23] For an authoritative discussion of the ideological elements which constituted Cardarelli's early Socialism, see U. Carpi, *Giornali vociani*, 165–81.

localities he visits. His prose becomes the vehicle for frequent expressions of indignation and is coloured by rhetorical phrases and examples. To emphasize the shocking quality of the sights he sees, he conjures up a world that has remained untouched by the process of civilization, a world with supernatural, Dantesque overtones. The ability to describe aspects of the daily existence of groups of destitute individuals within or close to Rome indicates a commitment to revealing particular social evils or articulating the plight of a given minority. For example, the article 'Tra i villaggi di paglia' contains the statement: 'The hapless inhabitants of Colledifuori are alone, [they live] beyond the town council, beyond the state, beyond civilization.' Also prominent within such writing is a self which is prepared to attack institutions or belief systems and which seeks to establish patterns of sympathy with the marginalized figures who are described.

Underlying this kind of documentation there is an attack on the effects of industrialization unaccompanied by state intervention. It is in fact remarkable how rarely Cardarelli misses an opportunity to denigrate the move towards greater industrial productivity which was such a feature of Giolitti's Italy. He objects to any alteration of the urban landscape of Rome, he is contemptuous of the growing importance of the Italian Stock Exchange, and he prophesies that the goals of an increasingly industrialized civilization will ultimately prove to be nothing more than a set of illusions. Above all, he points to the disorganization that a significant change in a country's means of production inevitably brings with it. Such disorganization is evident materially in the displacement or even destitution suffered by various elements of society in and around Rome. The disorientating course on which the country was embarked also entailed, 'una formidabile disorganizzazione di spirito' ('La nuova follia', 11 January 1911). The very emphasis on the problems of industrialization and the nostalgia for the rural would be one of the factors which motivated Cardarelli's migration from the Socialist newspaper (with its close concern for the realities of the world of industry) to La Voce (many of whose contributors remained closely attached to provincial or rural centres).

Accompanying the pronounced distrust of Italy's rapid industrialization, there is in Cardarelli's writing for *Avanti!* a parallel tendency to idealize the figure of the industrial worker or the *contadino*: both types are seen as embodying a set of values which have deep roots in Italian culture. Both types, moreover, are ennobled by the inevitable physical suffering that their lifestyles involve. In this idealization of the worker, Carpi has accurately detected an echo of and a comment on D'Annunzio's concept of *superomismo*: it is not the dashing aesthete of bourgeois or noble extraction who carries on the essential struggle for life, but the worker. In Cardarelli's characterization of the worker, there is a clear emphasis on moral appreciation and a need to identify figures capable of offering an example for emulation. In one piece entitled 'Il sermone' (25 December 1909) he describes the worker as 'the most moral and perfect type of man' and locates this moral perfection in the 'chastity of work' and the 'profundity of suffering'. The values of the industrial/agricultural worker are seen as antithetical to the capitalism of the successful classes of Giolitti's Italy, and Cardarelli implies that they are more enduring. In the article, 'L'ultimo sacrificio' (6 January 1910), he polemically affirms: 'We need to return to the soil and begin to work it with the wisdom which we will have attained during our lengthy and painful exile. . . . On the ruined castles of the new [industrialized] world the ancient Latin spirit still has a mission to fulfil.'

In the majority of his articles for *Avanti!* the progressive concern for the disadvantaged is balanced by the retrogressive vision of an ahistorical past. The conceptual weakness of the model of the past, presented as a possible solution to pressing urban problems, points to the nature of Cardarelli's journalism. His articles do not offer sophisticated political comment. Instead, they represent the ground for the author to explore a personal and often imaginative reaction to a series of concrete realities or problems. It is no coincidence that the articles for *Avanti!* were written at a time when he was defining his techniques as a writer and moving towards an interest in matters of cultural, rather than strictly political, importance. The degree to which the writing self

becomes the object of its own discourse can be appreciated
by looking at one piece, entitled 'Tre momenti' (19 January
1911). The article is constructed around Cardarelli's memory of three separate encounters with Andrea Costa, one of
the founding figures of the Italian Socialist movement. It
describes the enthusiasm with which the author first heard
Costa address a crowd of supporters, it then evokes the
powerful effect produced by Costa's visit to Cardarelli's
home town of Tarquinia, and finally it describes the third
meeting, which occurs as the author's belief in the idealist
message of Costa is beginning to wane. The article thus
provides a sketch of Costa at different moments in his
campaigning career, but it also provides an implied history
of the writer's own belief in the Socialist cause. This belief is
founded upon an initial, passionate enthusiasm for the
powerful ideas of a great figure: 'because the voice of Andrea
Costa vibrated with sincerity'. But the allegiance to Costa's
brand of Socialism becomes gradually weaker, partly because
it is motivated by an initial onrush of enthusiasm rather than
by any profoundly examined ideology.

In 'Tre momenti' the extent to which Cardarelli uses an
important figure as a means of defining his own ideas is at
best only implicit. However, while employed as a journalist
for *Avanti!* he also wrote a number of reviews on recently
published or translated works. These reviews are interesting
in the way that they use another figure or text as a means of
defining the ideas of the reviewer. By 1910 Cardarelli had
already written lengthy pieces on some of the writers most
admired in Socialist circles, including Zola and Gorky. But it
is worth looking more closely at two of the articles which he
wrote in 1910, one on the recent translation of H. M.
Stanley's memoirs ('Un esempio', 12 July 1910) the other
on a production of Ibsen's *Brand* ('Il pastore Brand', 15
August 1910).[24]

Little attention is paid in these two articles to the exam-

[24] Like many of the writers who were at one point to be connected with *La Voce*,
Cardarelli responded with boundless enthusiasm to certain literary works. Like
Slataper he was mesmerized by the gravity of Ibsen's theatre and wrote to Emilio
Cecchi on 24 July 1911: 'Tu non puoi credere, quale educazione sia per me la
lettura di Ibsen! È un fatto che diventa qualche volta mania.' Cardarelli, *Epistolario*,
ed. Bruno Blasi, 3 vols. (Tarquinia: Ebe, 1987), i. 162.

ination of the dramatic properties of Ibsen's work or the narrative structures of Stanley's autobiography. Instead, all is focused upon the analysis, or better, the exaltation, of the character of the central protagonist. Brand and Stanley emerge as the exemplars of an uncompromising voluntarist code of action, and the reviews read not so much as conventional pieces of literary criticism but more as orations. Even in the exposition of the action of Ibsen's play a terse and assertive style is employed, one which insists rhythmically upon the uniqueness of the character's endeavour to stamp his will upon the events which befall him. Concerning the figure who stands out from Stanley's autobiography, a similarly spare style characterizes the writing, a style which consistently foregrounds words indicative of power and physical prowess, 'and which incorporates numerous injunctions to the reader to take heed of the example offered by the memoirs. Cardarelli writes: 'Stanley rises from these pages with all his stark, moral strength: with his troubles and his claws, he is a man of willpower who has a mission to fulfil. Without a cradle, a family or a home, he is thrown against ever worse dangers and yet he remains undaunted. . . . Behold the man!'[25]

In reviews such as these, the role Cardarelli assumes is that of echoing ideas extracted from the text. If, however, the text seems to be animated by ideas which do not accord with his own, then he sets out to denigrate it instead. While working for *Avanti!* he wrote two reviews on the poetry of the *crepuscolari* Marino Moretti and Guido Gozzano ('I nostri decadenti', 27 August 1910; 'L'arte di fingersi'; 26 March 1911),[26] each of these reviews takes the form of a sharp verbal attack. In his article on Moretti he detects the expression of apparently trivial emotions; he manifests his dislike for the emotional range of the collection by first comparing Moretti to a precocious adolescent and then

[25] In the original Italian the quotation reads: 'Stanley oggi si solleva da queste pagine nella sua diritta nudità morale, con le sue pene e i suoi artigli, uomo di volontà e di missione, senza culla, senza famiglia, senza patria, lanciato traverso tutti i pericoli sempre più forte, sempre più indomo . . . Ecce homo!'

[26] Carpi has usefully compared Cardarelli's appraisal with Slataper's discussion of the same subject, 'Perplessità crepuscolari', *La Voce*, 16 Nov. 1911, p. 689. See Carpi, *Giornali vociani*, 178.

subjecting the poet, together with other members of his school, to a series of insulting diminutives. At the same time, adopting an angered tone, he levels a series of accusations, couched in morally laden terminology, against the verse. He speaks of it being obscene and pretentious, and at one point proclaims: 'And this they have called poetry. It is an artificial combination of a few names and a few small phonetic effects masquerading as melancholy and regret. Hardly poetry!'[27] In precisely the same way Gozzano is judged and found to be wanting what is termed 'a robust moral seriousness'. The image of the poet which emerges from the printed volume is berated and undermined by the critic with the same type of abusive vocabulary. Rather than serving an expository function, Cardarelli's review provides a platform for him to air, through a series of fiercely mocking comments, some of his prejudices about the proper form which verse should take. The fierceness of the commentary was indeed such that Emilio Cecchi, with whom Cardarelli had corresponded on a friendly basis since 1908, accused him of being excessively vituperative. Cardarelli, in reply, did not attempt to conceal that the article had provided him with the opportunity of setting forth his own theories on writing and the self, but argued that within his review there had circulated 'a certain moral passion'.[28]

What is perhaps most interesting in his contributions to *Avanti!* is the movement away from a compassionate interest in the plight of the excluded and the beginnings of an appreciation for the expression of force and voluntarism. Such a movement is in part explained by his impatience with Socialist ideals and his attraction towards Nationalist and avant-garde thinking. In his reviews of Ibsen, Stanley, or the *crepuscolari*, his critical vocabulary works by setting up polarities between weakness and strength, renunciation and conquest, resignation and willpower. The same reliance on

---

[27] In the original Italian the observations read: 'E questa l'hanno chiamata poesia. È una combinazione artificiosa di certi nomi e di certi piccoli effetti fonici mascherata di malinconia e di rimpianto, altro che poesia! . . . È falsa perché pare fatta di sentimento e non è in fondo che il prodotto di piccole raffinatezze estetiche.'

[28] The letter was written to Cecchi and dated 2 May 1911. See *Epistolario*, i. 145.

binary oppositions, coupled with a cult of energy, is shared by Corradini's Nationalists, the Futurists, and a number of the leading *vociani*. Corradini himself, for example, had expressed views essentially similar to those which animate Cardarelli's ethical evaluation of literary works.[29] But the real object of all Cardarelli's early writing is an enquiry into his own beliefs. His articles are evidence of a series of encounters with the various philosophies, movements, and figures which were to constitute the points of reference of avant-garde culture. Indeed, in his hands a particular event or work becomes nothing more than the pretext for an introspective enquiry. He wrote, again to Emilio Cecchi, that his work as a journalist revealed the drama of his 'inner development' and that he felt compelled to examine everything he came across through the subjective prism of his own conscience.[30]

Cardarelli's Movement Towards La Voce

During the years in which he was a contributor to *Avanti!* Cardarelli had become conscious that his emphasis on the 'personalità etica', his anti-decadent polemics, and his search for his own identity through the process of writing naturally impelled him towards the group of writers which had gathered round Prezzolini's *Voce*. He felt he would be more at home writing for *La Voce*, or at least for *Il Marzocco*. He was certainly dissatisfied with working for *Avanti!* and the direct engagement in daily political matters which that involved. He had in fact spoken in his letters of his work for the paper having become 'an ugly, sterile torture'. As early as September 1909 he wrote letters to both Orvieto and Prezzolini urging them to publish his work. Eventually his

[29] In the article 'La guerra' (*Il Regno*, 28 Feb. 1905, p. 2) Corradini had written that for him 'the beauty of art' and 'the aesthetic life of the world' were born of the 'spasm of force, of conquest and of the desire to overcome oneself'. The article is reprinted in *Scritti e discorsi* 1901–1914, 110.

[30] He writes in his letter to Cecchi of 2 May 1911: 'Basta leggere un mio articolo per capire l'esasperazione e la drammaticità dei miei interni sviluppi. Io sono uno spietato con me: uno sperperatore: un suicida. Non so e non voglio rinunziare a nulla. Voglio tutto infilare dentro la cruna del mio ago.'

entreaties to Orvieto succeeded in gaining him the regular hospitality of *Il Marzocco*. Prezzolini, on the other hand, was a good deal more wary of his Socialist connections and the value of his critical contributions. In his early and suppliant letters to Prezzolini he expresses both his enthusiasm for the ideals of the journal[31] and his hope of contributing his own voice. The letters he wrote in 1910 and at the beginning of 1911 again contain proposals for possible articles and yet express disappointment at the reluctance of *La Voce* to receive his work. Moreover, his protestations of faith in the rightness of *La Voce*'s cause were not confined to his private correspondence with Prezzolini.

In April 1911, when Italy was gripped by the question of what action Giolitti would take in Libya, he published an important article in *Avanti!*, 'Polemiche di gioventù'. With the Nationalist camp baying for intervention, but the *vociani* taking a more sceptical line, his article was a defence of *La Voce*. Indeed, so unequivocal were the views expressed in the article that the editorship of *Avanti!* felt impelled to distance itself from them. The article begins by characterizing the Nationalists as *letterati* who had become politicians; it then attacks the need for politics in general to find concrete solutions to specific problems. It goes on to make a distinction between the Nationalists and the *vociani*: if the former are 'uomini politici' the latter are 'uomini morali'. Cardarelli contends that the proposal of *La Voce* to create the conditions for a 'moral revolution' by encouraging the formation of a new governing class imbued with a strong sense of personal morality is a more radical and far-reaching proposal than the Nationalist endeavour to improve Italy's standing with regard to the European colonial powers.[32] In the concluding section of the article, he appropriates Prezzolini's appeal to the Nationalists for 'a more ardent exercise of moral virtues'. He ends by admiring the way in which *La*

---

[31] Of particular interest are the letters Cardarelli addressed to Prezzolini in 1909. See *Epistolario*, i. 25–7.

[32] In her introduction to the collected articles of Cardarelli, Martignoni reports his description of the Nationalists in the piece, 'L'italiano all'estero ha la parola', *Avanti!*, 25 June 1911: 'gagliardo nucleo d'italiani che vogliono ridestare nel paese il senso della sua dignità nazionale e di suoi interessi nel mondo.' See *Pagine sparse*, 58.

Voce encourages its readers to become disciplined 'men of action and reflection'.[33]

Despite such affirmations, the distrust which Prezzolini felt towards him meant that he published only one, albeit important, article ('Charles Péguy', 7 September 1911, p. 644), in the pages of *La Voce*. Yet, for a number of reasons, it is natural to see his early work as a writer as belonging securely to the *vociano* movement. First, his collected letters show him to have been in correspondence not only with the founder of the journal but with many of its more prominent members, including Boine, Slataper, and Papini. Many of the observations which he made in his letters to Cecchi in this period clearly indicate a reading of all the writers most esteemed by the *vociani*. But it was above all the articles he wrote on literary and cultural matters before and during the years of *La Voce* which marked him out as close in temperament to the moralists of Prezzolini's journal.

Already, in the reviews of Stanley's and Ibsen's works, it is easy to see a harsh moralistic code being sketched out. From the publication of his first review, moreover, Cardarelli seems conscious of the potentially political or Nationalist dimension of certain literary texts. Significantly, when Italy began its military operation in Libya he published an article in *Il Marzocco* ('La letteratura che presentì l'azione',26 November 1911, p. 3) which looked at the way in which the works of D'Annunzio and Carducci had prepared Italy for imperialist action. In his article 'La politica della *La Voce*' (30 November 1911, p. 697), Prezzolini had attacked academic literary criticism, claiming that it was 'pointless' and indicative of a 'national illness'. In opposition to established forms of criticism, *La Voce* had from the beginning aimed to cultivate an

---

[33] The declaration in support of the aims of *La Voce* in Italian reads as follows: 'Si appagano [i vociani] di un programma modesto, di cui si potrebbe anche fare a meno, e intanto corrono l'Italia infaticabilmente a scoprire, col giornale, col libro o di persona, gli spiriti vergini e timidi, vogliosi di vivere e di sapere, e li disciplinano, cordialmente li incuorano, li aiutano a diventare uomini d'azione e di riflessione.' The article is quoted in full in Carpi's *Giornali vociani*, 179–80. In his discussion of Cardarelli's early writings Carpi makes the correct observation: 'E riduttivo cercare il vocianesimo di Cardarelli sulla *Voce*: esso, implicito ed esplicito, va cercato proprio là dove Cardarelli collabora meno episodicamente e dove politicamente più si compromette, sulle pagine dell'*Avanti!* e negli articoli di cultura e di critica letteraria' (p. 177).

aggressive type of analysis which focused on the ethical importance of a given work. Cardarelli certainly agreed with such an imperative. In one letter to Cecchi he affirmed that 'criticism served a moral purpose',[34] while in another he announced that a critic without 'ethical intentions' could not be considered 'complete'.[35] But it was not until 1912, with the article entitled 'Metodo estetico' (triggered by the publication of Alfredo Gargiulo's monograph on D'Annunzio and published by *Lirica* in October 1912),[36] that he made a detailed exposition of his own method of reading a literary text. The method which he polemically outlined accorded on most points with that adopted by the *vociani*, and it usefully illuminates many of the ways in which they set out to examine literary texts.

In 'Metodo estetico' Cardarelli aligns himself with the practitioners of the 'critica morale' against those who sought to adhere to principles proposed in Croce's *Estetica*. As Martignoni has pointed out,[37] he makes a number of distorting simplifications of Croce's arguments and the piece provides an early indication of a hostility towards Croce which was later to become xenophobic and *strapaesano*. In the course of his discussion, he accepts that the critic who enquires only into the formal characteristics of a work may attain a measure of analytical objectivity. Yet, in his view, if the 'metodo estetico' succeeds in objectifying the process of criticism it also succeeds in sterilizing it. By treating the literary work not as a living presence, but as an object or machine, the method concentrates not upon the essence of a text but upon its shell, or what he describes disparagingly as the 'formal chrysalis'. He maintains that the necessary corollary of only analysing formal qualities is that the critic

[34] The letter was addressed to Cecchi and dated 14 July 1911: *Epistolario*, i. 159.
[35] See the letter addressed to Cecchi of 2 May 1911: *Epistolario*, i. 145.
[36] From the evidence provided by the *Epistolario* it seems that Cardarelli had prepared a series of observations on the *Estetica* of Croce in the hope of finding an obliging publisher. In March 1911 he wrote to Prezzolini, asking, 'Pubblicheresti alcune osservazioni *pensatissime* sull'*Estetica* di Croce?' *Epistolario*, i. 141.
[37] See *Pagine sparse*, ed. Martignoni, 66. For a further discussion of the relationship between Croce and Cardarelli see Luigi Baldacci, 'Movimenti letterari del Novecento italiano', in *Dizionario della letteratura italiana contemporanea* (Florence: Vallecchi, 1973), 19.

accomplishes a superficial task, ending up either by duplicat-
ing elements of the text or merely indicating some of what
are deemed to be its noteworthy features. If purely formal criticism is a superficial mode of enquiry then, in his
opinion, it leaves itself open to the charge of self-indulgence
or, to use his word, 'hedonism'. Its apparent indifference to
matters of moral importance in turn justifies the dismissive
comments to which he exposes it throughout the article. He
asserts that it is necessary to distrust those who concentrate
on the linguistic shell of a work, since they are not critics but
merely 'degustatori di effetti'. The significance of a literary
text lies beyond formal considerations and any judgement
must be formulated solely on the basis of a work's content.

   While making his slighting observations on 'il metodo
estetico' Cardarelli indicates what he regards as a more
meaningful method of literary appraisal. He does not advocate an empirical approach, or one which cultivates scientific
objectivity by analysing the sophisticated verbal forms of the
text. Indeed, he makes the remarkable proclamation: 'Criticism should be carried out from a distance, when the book is
closed.' He proposes a methodology which does not proceed
so much by analysis as by intuition, and one which is based
upon the contention that a work of literature is an ethical
rather than an aesthetic expression of consciousness. If, like
many adherents of the *vociano* movement, he believed that
the act of criticism should be geared towards forming moral
judgements, then he also believed that such an aim could be
realized only through considering the text as a manifestation of the author's philosophy, psychology, and, to use a
key word of the *vociani*, his personality. Elsewhere in the
article he states, 'we must see the artist simply as a man', and
'we must moralize aesthetics'.

   The extent to which Cardarelli's thoughts on the function
of criticism coincided with those offered at around the same
time by other writers in *La Voce* can be appreciated by
considering a couple of examples. With minimal variation,
Slataper had expressed the same view in his study of Ibsen,[38]
writing: 'In ethical criticism [*la critica morale*] it is necessary

---

[38] Scipio Slataper, *Ibsen* (Florence: Sansoni, 1944), 345.

to focus the analysis on the personality of the artist: to look at the power of his will, his tone and his individuality.' Equally, Boine in the pages of *La Voce* had launched two polemics against Croce's *Estetica*[39] and, reviewing the work of Adolfo De Bosis for *Riviera ligure*, had affirmed a faith in the same line of enquiry as Cardarelli: 'My business is to sound out contemporary Italian literature; I go in search of human substance, in search of men and of life.'[40] The notion of the text as personality was elaborated upon by Cardarelli when he wrote a survey of the work of Charles Péguy for *La Voce*. In his article he attributes to the French writer, consciously or unconsciously, all the major elements which constitute his own critical method. He writes that when Péguy criticizes the work of an author he takes on the role of the 'moral judge': if he discovers within the work the will and the world-view of the author, then an impassioned dialogue becomes possible, because Péguy has discovered the man behind the text.[41]

In his endeavour to produce an image of the personality of the writer, Cardarelli explores his subjective response to the text. He uses the words on the page to illuminate his own intellect and emotions. At the same time he employs his own belief-system and his sentimental inclinations as the criteria with which to assess a book. Again the method has obvious similarities with that adopted by Boine, who in his review of De Bosis had affirmed: 'I am bold enough to declare that I judge things, using myself as my own yardstick [*pigliando me medesimo a metro*].'

[39] Giovanni Boine, 'Un ignoto', *La Voce*, 8 Feb. 1912, p. 750; id. 'L'estetica dell'ignoto', 29 Feb. 1912, p. 766.

[40] Boine, *Il peccato. Plausi e botte. Frantumi. Altri scritti,* ed. by Davide Puccini (Milan: Garzanti, 1983), 107–11.

[41] In Cardarelli's exact words: 'Si pone dinanzi l'artista, come uomo morale, in istato di assoluta responsabilità. Se egli scopre nell'opera una ragione di essere che si deve ricercare nella segreta volontà direttrice dell'artista, in una sua generale e armonica concezione del mondo, di cui l'opera non è che sintesi e frammento; allora egli si accende, si esalta. Ha trovato l'uomo.' It is interesting and revealing to compare the observations which are made on Péguy's methods of approaching a literary text with those which Cardarelli says he himself employs in a letter to Cecchi, 5 July 1911: *Epistolario,* i. 155, 'Quando mi accosto a un libro o a un uomo non sono preoccupato del giudizio ch'io ne dovrò dare. Ho qualche istinto. Se un suono è sordo, l'avverto. Se un uomo è falso,—nel senso più innocente, di quella falsità che consiste in simulazione cerebrale e deficienza di sensi—io l'avverto. Così è il libro.'

Another important feature of this type of criticism, and one which indicates its intellectual misogyny, is the way in which it posits writing as an exclusively masculine pursuit. The critic looks for an encounter with another 'uomo'. The encounter may lead to an unqualified expression of admiration, but more frequently it is staged as a clash of antagonists, with the critic attacking the figure of a writer which a particular text may project. Further, whether the encounter proves positive or negative, a notion of maleness is used as a standard of judgement. For Cardarelli, as for the majority of writers associated with *La Voce*, the idea of maleness implies the possession of a combative temperament, the aspiration towards an unreachable goal, the ability to impose the will and to provide an example for emulation. Behind such a construction of masculinity are to be found Nietzschean ideas of the self's duty to surpass its present state, a Carlylean fascination with great men, and, above all, the thinking of the Austrian philosopher Otto Weininger. In Weininger's treatise *Geschlect und Charakter*, the concepts of male and female are presented oppositionally as different sets of archetypal characteristics: among the psychological features associated with the male principle are logicality and the aggressive impulse to assert individual identity. If maleness, conceived of in such terms, becomes an essential critical criterion, then it follows that the sort of text most likely to win praise is that which most directly represents a forceful writing self.

Looking at the criticism Cardarelli wrote in the years before the First World War, it is remarkable how many times words carrying connotations of masculinity are used as expressions of admiration. For example, he says of Stanley, 'Ecce Homo'; concerning Ibsen's work he writes of the 'the will to assert violently his faith'; of D'Annunzio he enquires: 'I need to know who this poet is . . . And if he expresses emotion I need to know if it is the emotion of a proud form of masculinity [*una maschiezza orgogliosa*] which has smashed against stronger forces.' The emphasis upon a paradigm of masculinity is central to the criticism of all the major contributors to *La Voce*. Reflecting on his own work, Slataper explained to Prezzolini how he endeavoured to find the man rather than the artist.[42] In the introductory section to his review of Claudel's *Partage du midi*, he described the literary text as the representation of a victory of the will over passionate disorder and announced, 'a criterion of greatness graduates our response towards other men'.[43] In his polemical article 'Un ignoto', Boine spoke of criticism being the recreation of the writer, of 'the concrete man, the living man, the man as giver of life'. In 1915 Papini published a collection of his reviews on literary subjects under the title of *Maschilità*. The obvious susceptibility to the mystique of leadership helps to explain why so many *vociani* were to become convinced supporters of Fascism. Moreover, the affirmation of the authoritarian self, so much a part of the *Voce*'s *critica morale*, is essential in the metaphysical and clearly proto-Fascist autobiographies which the *vociani* were to write.

Beyond its political implications, the elevation of a notion of maleness to a standard of judgement inevitably leads to an inflexible critical methodology. On his system of bestowing credit or apportioning blame in literary matters, Boine wrote in *Plausi e botte*: 'I have here only two stamps, two clean, round stamps, one is used for marking praise, the other is used for marking contempt.'[44] The same dramatic polarization of praise and denigration is a striking feature of many other of the young critics in some way connected with *La Voce*, and Cardarelli is no exception. His critical inflexibility is most evident in the articles, such as those on the *crepuscolari*, which he wrote for *Avanti!* Equally, his articles for *Il Marzocco* consistently show an inability to appreciate texts which do not seem to support his own ethical assumptions. In his review of Cecchi's *Studi critici* ('Critica e critica', 25 August 1912, p. 2) he censures the collection's excessive attention to form and complains of Cecchi's lack of 'ethical intuition'. If some texts appear to trangress moral precepts derived from the writings of Nietzsche or Weininger, other

---

[42] The letter is dated 30 Apr. 1911 and is to be found in Slataper, *Epistolario*, ed. Gianni Stuparich (Milan: Mondadori, 1950), 218.

[43] Slataper, *Scritti letterari e critici*, ed. Gianni Stuparich (Milan: Mondadori, 1956), 213.

[44] Boine, *Plausi e botte*, 134.

writers seem guilty of an ignorance of the teaching of Henri Bergson, another of the philosophers most esteemed by the *vociani*. In an appraisal of three works by Julien Benda ('Tre briciole d'oro', 13 August 1911, p. 2), Cardarelli makes the sustained observation that Benda speculates intellectually about emotion rather than conveying a convincing impression of the flux of the internal life of his protagonists. The implication is that such a tendency induces inert and mechanical conclusions. In another article ('Inquietudini contemporanee', 3 March 1912, p. 3), ostensibly dedicated to the discussion of a recent work by Jean Schlumberger, *L'inquiète paternité*, but which considers also the work of the Tharaud brothers, André Gide and, once more, Julien Benda, the same kind of accusation is voiced. At one point in the article, Cardarelli, adopting the exclamatory and ironic style which he invariably relies upon to express disapproval, voices the following criticisms: 'God how unBergsonian [*poco bergsoniana*] these young French writers are! . . . They don't understand anything about the immediate and continual flux of emotions. Although they write with intelligence, that intelligence is cold and calculating. They don't rely on intuition, but on deduction.'

The Work of Charles Péguy

If Cardarelli was critical of a large number of recent French publications he reserved his unqualified admiration for Péguy, and the article he wrote for *La Voce* on his work remains his most significant critical review. By the time the essay appeared, Péguy was already well known to the readership of the journal. Prezzolini had twice written on the *Cahiers de la Quinzaine*, the editorial project which Péguy had started from his own bookshop in 1900 and which had, with some intervals until the outbreak of the First World War, published essays, criticism, and creative writing by a generation of French writers. Indeed, the *Cahiers* had been an inspiration for *La Voce* itself, and in his comments on the project Prezzolini had spoken of his appreciation for the French writer's success in drawing together intellectuals from all areas of France. In his article 'Il risveglio dell'anima francese' (*La Voce*, 14 April 1910, p. 303) Georges Sorel had attributed to Péguy an essential role in redefining through *Les Cahiers* the notion of nationalism for the whole of his generation, and he had interpreted Péguy's massive *Le Mystère de la charité de Jeanne d'Arc* as a compelling manifestation of French patriotism. In other words, Péguy had succeeded in becoming the object of veneration of intellectuals as different as the neo-idealist Prezzolini, the theorist of revolutionary syndicalism Georges Sorel, and Vincenzo Cardarelli, himself a reformed Socialist.

Beyond the immediate vicinity of *La Voce* the reception of Péguy had even wider implications. In October 1910 Paolo Orano began publishing the syndicalist journal *La Lupa*, and the editorial staff of the new publication included the names of both Sorel and Péguy. In *The Birth of Fascist Ideology*, Zeev Sternhell has charted Mussolini's move from the left of the PSI to the ranks of the revolutionary syndicalists. He has also convincingly shown how, for Mussolini, Péguy provided an inspiring example of a Socialist who, disillusioned by the parliamentary party, graduated towards Nationalism and towards a violent hostility to the reformism of Jean Jaurès. In support of his argument, Sternhell quotes Mussolini's own reflections on his intellectual formation in the years leading up to the First World War:

> In the great river of fascism you will find currents that go back to the Sorels, to the Péguys, to the Lagardelles of the *Mouvement Socialiste*, and to that group of Italian syndicalists who, thanks to Olivetti's *Pagine Libere*, Orano's *La Lupa* and Enrico Leone's *Il Divenire sociale*, between 1904 and 1914 introduced a new note into Socialist circles emasculated and chloroformed by the Giolittian fornication.[45]

For Mussolini, Sternhell writes, Péguy was the 'object of an interest bordering on admiration'. Cardarelli's interest in Péguy involved both hero-worship and self-recognition. To begin with, Péguy was an enemy of positivist scholarship and a follower of Bergson. He distrusted the modern industri-

---

[45] Sternhell, *The Birth of Fascist Ideology*, 34. Sternhell is quoting from Mussolini's *La Doctrine du fascisme*, vol. ix of the *Édition définitive des œuvres et discours de Benito Mussolini* (Paris: Flammarion, 1935), 76.

alized world and looked nostalgically upon a pre-capitalist past. In his autobiographical work *Notre jeunesse* (first published in 1910) he had described his youthful Socialism as part of a generational effort to combat the ills of 'this modern world completely orientated towards money',[46] and had attacked the workings of capitalism in a way that was clearly similar to Cardarelli's writing in *Avanti!*. The values which his work upheld, such as an emphasis on austerity, pride in manual work, integrity of thought, and belief in the renewal of society by the people, all accorded with the judgements Cardarelli had come to formulate, whether independently or in association with other *vociani*. In many of his works, but particularly in *Notre jeunesse*, Péguy makes a clear distinction between 'la mystique' on the one hand and 'la politique' on the other. He affirms that it is the duty of those who understand 'la mystique', or the true values of the French people, to oppose the mediocrity and corruption of politicians from whatever party. A similar distinction lies at the heart of the *vociano* project to reform Italy. The distinction also accounts for Péguy's move from being a committed member of the Socialist party towards a brand of Nationalism which remained aloof from any organized political grouping. This ideological change of direction was similar to Cardarelli's detachment from the PSI and his allegiance first to *Il Marzocco* and then *La Voce*. Writing to Prezzolini in 1911 Cardarelli had gone so far as to confess: 'In all modesty I presume to have some degree of mental affinity with Péguy.'[47]

Péguy is represented in Cardarelli's essay for *La Voce* both as an object of veneration and as a figure of the self. The essay sets up a dialectical relationship between critic and writer, a relationship that can best be illustrated by looking closely at one passage. After having spoken of Péguy's autobiographical works and the elements of the ideology of which they are the reflection, Cardarelli affirms:

Avvinto alla vita, alla terra, all'opera sua, al suo lavoro, duramente, come s'egli dovesse campare tutta l'eternità—ecco il fondo granitico, la non

---

[46] Charles Péguy, *Notre jeunesse* (Paris: Gallimard, 1957), 170.
[47] *Epistolario*, i. 160.

fallace gravità del suo spirito. Egli sa che si vive una volta sola, che ogni
tempo della vita è destinato a qualcosa di assoluto che scade, e guai a
lasciarlo passare senza integrarlo; sa che la divinità è sulla terra, l'eternità
è nel tempo; e colui che non avrà vissuto sulla terra e nel tempo non avrà
mai posseduto nei suoi sensi il divino e l'eterno, come il germe della
parabola che essendo caduto sulla zolla senza inserirvisi è morto invece di
mutarsi a poco a poco in fiore. Perciò egli ripercuote entro di sé,
vivacemente, nelle sue circostanze, gli esempi immortali della sua religione—non li imita. Imitano o negano gli insufficienti: coloro che ador-
ano di una religione le forme e le lettere, e coloro che pretendono di
giudicarle, mancando del primo dei requisiti necessari al giudizio; e
voglio dire l'intuito della fede. Gli altri, gli intelligenti, i consapevoli,
confermano in *atti*.[48]

[Ruggedly attached to life, to the earth, to his own work, as if he had to
survive for eternity—that's what makes up the solid basis, the authentic
gravity of his spirit. He knows that we only live once and that every
moment of life is something absolute which passes. Beware of letting that
moment pass without appropriating it fully! He knows that divinity resides
within the earth, and that eternity resides within time; and he knows that
whoever does not live solidly on the earth or in time will never gain a
sensation of the divine or the eternal, just as the seed of a future action, if
it fails to penetrate the earth, will wither instead of blooming. It is for this
reason that he [Péguy] enthusiastically imbibes the immortal examples
offered by his religion—but he doesn't imitate them. Imitation is for
incomplete people: people who adore the forms and the letters of religion and who claim to be able to judge them, without having the first
requisite of judgement, namely the intuition of faith. But others, those
who are both intelligent and conscious, confirm their faith through
action.]

The first sentence of this extract elevates the writer to a
level of high esteem; the adverb 'ecco' introduces a clause
expressing veneration. But as the passage proceeds we witness a display of how distinctions between critic and writer
can be broken down; the two subject positions interchange.
When speaking in the second sentence of temporal limitations and the need to bring one's personality to fruition,
Cardarelli refers to thoughts expressed in Péguy's work, and
to that extent he acts as the medium through which the
writer expresses his message. But the message is not

[48] 'Charles Péguy', *La Voce*, 7 Sept. 1911, p. 713.

delivered simply as a piece of information: it is added to and altered. At a lexical level an impression of emotion on the part of the critic is suggested by the way that certain terms are afforded a privileged position. The first clause of the second sentence and the two sub-clauses which follow enunciate different aspects of the same fundamental truth, each emphasizes words denotative of the uniqueness of the experience of life and the brevity of its passing. The sense of urgency implied by the lexical choices is heightened by the way in which the sentence is ordered grammatically into a series of short and tense statements, all in the present. The moral seriousness of the enunciation is underlined by its admonitory tone and by the biblical resonance of both its vocabulary and of the parable with which it ends. If, at the beginning of the extract, the critic has assimilated the meaning of the author and rendered it in an expressive form which is clearly his own, in the latter part of the passage it appears as though the work of the writer is used to support or provoke the assertions and moral reflections of the critic.

The deliberate failure to establish a dividing-line between the enquiring subject and the object of his enquiry, allowing appropriation and attribution to flow together, is a way of reproducing on the written page an impression of the effect which the reading of Péguy has produced. In passages such as this the association between critic and writer comes close to identification, while at other points in the article Péguy is presented from a distance as the hero of French Nationalism. Péguy is admired for his ability to animate a religious sense of national identity through his portrayal of figures such as Joan of Arc and through his literary evocation of the lives of his rural ancestors. At one point Cardarelli exclaims: 'He is a countryman, a Frenchman and a Christian, as his tenacious forefathers were, and as one is a countryman, a Frenchman and a Christian in the land of Orléans.'

In its appreciation of Péguy's religious faith in the traditions of his place of origin, the article expresses one of the central elements in the ideology of La Voce. To a large extent La Voce was the mouthpiece of those sections of society which felt threatened by Italy's rapid industrialization. It actively sought to promote awareness of particular problems faced

by various rural communities. The number of articles in the
journal which draw attention to problems faced by specific
regions is indeed surprising: for example, Boine wrote on
his native Liguria, Slataper on the Carso, and Papini and
Soffici on Tuscany. Aside from voicing or defending the
interests of an extensive number of regional centres, *La Voce*
addressed itself to the 'giovani intelligenti' who belonged to
the small rural communities of the provinces, rather than to
an urban élite. Meanwhile, as Walter Adamson has written, it
was a fundamental assumption on the part of the *vociani* that
the spiritual revolution for which they militated 'would use
the dormant sensibilities and energies of regional, peasant-
based cultures to overthrow the false and hypocritical' values
promoted by Giolitti.[49] In his own article on Péguy, Prezzolini had spoken of his appeal to the serious and honest
community within France, the community which was 'solid
in both its virtues and its outlook, highly moral and convinced that it had a mission to fulfil in the world'. Within
such an observation there is an evident sense of identification with Péguy's project in *Les Cahiers de la Quinzaine*.
Writing to Prezzolini on the progress of his article, Cardarelli
had described how he wanted the latter part of the essay to
reflect not only his personal appreciation of the French
writer but the significance which Péguy held for his entire
generation: 'I'd like to end the article on a choral note
stressing our own youth and our own religious sense. I'd like
to say that we are the true contemporaries of Péguy rather
than those who share his own age.'[50]

Within Cardarelli's elevation of Péguy to the status of
guiding model there was a strong current of reactionary
sentiment. Hatred for the compromises of capitalism, a
nostalgia for pre-industrialized communities, and a faith in
'mystique' rather than in active political engagement were
an intrinsic part of the belief-system which he formulated in
the years of the Florentine avant-garde. Such sentiments
represent the ground from which his pro-Fascist ideas would

---

[49] Adamson, *Avant-Garde Florence*, 161.
[50] The letter was addressed to G. Prezzolini and dated 10 July 1911: *Epistolario*, i.
157. Péguy was some ten years older than the majority of the young writers who
contributed to *La Voce*.

grow in the 1920s and 1930s. In his poetry and prose Péguy attempted to articulate the national spirit of France or in his words 'the qualities of the French, the virtues of the race'.[51] In his later 'prosa d'arte' Cardarelli would equally set out to find a form of expression which would serve to exalt what he regarded as the authentic traditions and qualities of the Italian people. Such a form of expression would go hand in hand with explicit declarations in favour of Mussolini's regime, and would indeed be defined theoretically to accord with official Fascist ideology.

[51] Péguy, *Notre jeunesse*, 135.

2

THE INTERVENTIONIST CAMPAIGN, THE AESTHETICS OF *LA VOCE*, AND CARDARELLI'S *PROLOGHI*

The Campaign for Intervention and Avant-Garde Aesthetics

There is little doubt that the war in Libya served as one of the principal markers in Italy's path towards intervention in the First World War. As indicated, it led indirectly to the decline of Giolitti's hold on power and a corresponding weakening of the reformist Socialists. When war broke out between the major European powers in the summer of 1914, both Giolitti and the majority of the reformists favoured Italian neutrality. Unfortunately, by that stage Antonio Salandra had formed a conservative government disposed to listen to elements within the interventionist camp. Together with the irredentists and the Nationalists, a good deal of right-wing Liberal politicians were in favour of intervention. Many revolutionary syndicalists, who had failed to achieve substantial change through strike action, looked to war as the opportunity to provide the conditions for radical change. They believed that the war would not simply be another struggle between nation-states for minimal advantages, but a conflict which could overturn social structures and radically alter the position of whole sections of the societies involved. In previous years the revolutionary syndicalists had attacked those Socialists who had advocated gradual change. With the outbreak of hostilities, they attacked all those who supported a neutralist line.

The power of suggestion which a major European war could exert on the individual and collective imagination was certainly immense: Sorel saw the war as the opportunity for the breaking of bourgeois humanism and for a working-class revolution; for Corradini war represented the chance for Italy to renew its governing élite and for 'a more courageous, more lively and more intelligent ruling class'[1] to come to the fore. After some initial hesitation, Mussolini converted to the cause of intervention. On 18 October 1914 he published an article in *Avanti!* attacking the PSI's advocacy of neutrality. As he no doubt expected, his article immediately led to an open rift with the party leadership. His reaction was to resign from the paper and found his own journal, the *Popolo d'Italia.* A belief in the ability of war to foster widespread change, the moral renewal of Italy, and such virtues as discipline, courage, and a love of daring was common to all the avant-garde movements which had flourished in Italy since the turn of the century. *La Voce* strongly advocated Italian intervention in the conflict, while Papini and those closest to him set up the journal *Lacerba* (1913–15) first as a vehicle to pursue their bellicose ideas and subsequently to conduct a relentless interventionist campaign. But it was the Futurists who represented the movement which most unequivocally glorified the virtues of war.

Marinetti's first Futurist manifesto had appeared in February 1909. It had made clear its opposition to the staleness of institutionalized forms of culture. The manifesto was inspired by a desire to widen the appeal of new forms of art and literature beyond restricted, élitist circles. Marinetti and the predominantly Milanese group of writers, painters, and architects who shared his ideas were united in their admiration for the physical properties and potentialities of machines. As a movement they championed the aesthetic properties of noise and action, while preaching freedom from past traditions. They produced 'propaganda for the modern world',[2] and, underlying their veneration for speed, power, and the properties of the mechanized world, it is not difficult to detect Sorelian ideas on the regenerative power of violence. In literary terms, their cult of dynamism led to a radical disregard for syntax and codified vocabulary, while

---

[1] Isenghi, *Il mito della grande guerra*, 11.
[2] Martin Clark, *Modern Italy 1871–1982*, 7th edn. (London: Longman, 1991), 174. A useful introduction to the Futurist movement is provided by Judy Rawson's 'Italian Futurism' in Malcolm Bradbury and James McFarlane (eds.), *Modernism: A Guide to European Literature 1890–1930*, 2nd edn. (London: Penguin, 1991). A more theoretical approach to the subject is provided by Andrew Hewitt's *Fascist Modernism*.

in painting (particularly in the work of Balla and Carrà) it led to the exploration of fundamentally new methods of representing movement.

The Futurists, with their deliberate iconoclasm, were never aloof from politics. Marinetti's publication of the Futurist manifesto in 1909 had been accompanied by a statement of political ideals, the *First Futurist Political Manifesto*. In 1911 the *Second Futurist Political Manifesto* was published, and in 1913 Marinetti, together with Boccioni, Carrà, and Russolo, published *The Futurist Political Programme*. Broadly speaking, the political line of the Futurists differed from that adopted by other avant-garde groupings (such as the *vociani*) in the emphasis it placed on the need for rapid agricultural and industrial modernization. But in other respects the Futurists adopted Nationalist political assumptions. Bitterly opposed to reformist Socialism and in favour of an aggressive foreign policy, they played a prominent role in promoting support for Italian action in Libya. After the First World War, the Futurists, so far as they became a political organization, fused with the Fascists and no doubt contributed important elements to the latter's ideology and rhetoric.

The exaltation of the tremendous power that modern machines could wield was linked with a cult of war, and the Libyan enterprise exerted a significant effect on the Futurist imagination. In December 1911, Marinetti's narrative 'La battaglia di Tripoli' appeared in the French periodical *L'Intransigent*. As Isenghi has revealed, the narrative presents an idea of war as a form of ecstatic pleasure with echoes of D'Annunzian vitalism. In Marinetti's piece the aesthetic aspect of machines in motion is so overpowering as to exclude any concession to humanistic sentiment. Instead, war breeds its own ethics. The publication of 'La battaglia di Tripoli' was followed by two polemical pieces by Marinetti which defended Italy's action in Libya and which pointed with unmistakable clarity to the role which the Futurists believed that both their aesthetics and their campaigns had played in changing attitudes towards the concept of war in Italy:

In fact, while noting that our Futurist campaign in favour of militarism and war, the world's only hygiene, and against pacifist and utilitarian cowardice, has served to prepare the great bellicose atmosphere which at present is raging through Italy, I have also to admit that our propaganda has not yet rid the Italian spirit of those other antiquated vices which are called: sentimentality, morbid compassion and love for the feeble.[3]

The Futurists and the *vociani* shared a degree of common ground concerning nationalist notions about the need for Italian regeneration and expansion, but the relationship between the two groups was by no means a simple one. If there was an obviously ludic and deliberately, though frighteningly, irresponsible side to Futurist polemics and actions, then by contrast the *vociani* tended to adopt a more serious tone when advocating solutions to Italy's problems. In his piece, 'Il Futurismo' (*La Voce*, 31 March 1910, p. 295) Slataper had produced a swingeing criticism of Marinetti's movement. In his view, the Futurist revolt against traditional aesthetics lacked any serious motivation and was bereft of 'a true spiritual content'. It was instead a series of clownish manifestations which, while they could momentarily grab the attention of the public, ultimately signified very little. Slataper went further to suggest that the movement, while pretending to anticipate future technological developments, was in fact rooted in the past. In his article he pointed to the symbolist derivation of some of Marinetti's ideas and saw Futurism as a later strain of 'a decadent Romanticism'. The admiration of the material objects of modern life was interpreted by Slataper as camouflage, and he castigated the Futurists for failing 'to examine the interior process of the individual subject'. He wrote: 'But Marinetti's Futurists have no conception of the internal drama of the mind; indeed, they shout and scream so as not to hear it.' Equally Cardarelli, writing in *Avanti!* ('Il passatismo dei futuristi', 22 January 1911), attacked what he perceived as the old-fashioned qualities of the Futurists and, like Slataper, he linked the movement both to the French symbolists and, perhaps more surprisingly, to the writings of poets such as Gozzano and Corazzini. His contention that Futurism represented an

---

[3] The passage is quoted in Isnenghi's discussion of the Futurists' veneration of war in *Il mito della grande guerra*, 30.

essentially tame phenomenon, by no means beyond the
boundaries of tradition, was supported by his caustic assertion that Futurism was merely a piece of 'puerile exhibi-
tionism'.

The reactions of both Slataper and Cardarelli represented
only one side of the initial *vociano* response to the noisy
appearance of Futurism. To begin with, Papini and Soffici
were equally dismissive. Indeed, the mocking statements
which Soffici made in his article on Futurism, 'Arte libera e
pittura futurista' (*La Voce*, 22 June 1911, p. 597) led to
Marinetti and his friends travelling from Milan to Florence
to assault him physically.[4] Despite this initial enmity, however,
Futurism did come to exert a powerful effect on Papini
and Soffici, both of whom came to see analogies between
Marinetti's appropriation of French avant-garde culture
and their own. Both Tuscans were attracted, moreover, to
the aggressiveness with which the Futurists went about de-
bunking established institutions and conventions. The link
between some leading *vociani* and the Futurists became
strongest when Papini set up *Lacerba* and both groups began
to campaign enthusiastically for Italy to assume an interventionist stance. In 1914 Papini explored his own concept
of the movement in the work *Il mio futurismo*, while between
1913 and 1915 Soffici, as both painter and writer, began to
experiment with techniques inspired by the Futurists.

The partial adoption of elements of Futurism by such
figures as Papini and Soffici represents a later development
of *La Voce* and one which was to prove short-lived. The type
of literary practice which most inspired the *vociani* was
theorized along very different lines and the only common
element it shared with Futurism was the attack it made on
certain existing and, in their view, antiquated traditions. In
the criticism of the *vociani* published in *La Voce* there was a
dissatisfaction with, or a contempt for, existing models of
literary composition. Papini, for example, wrote: 'We can
eliminate paths that have already been followed in directions
that are perfectly well known' ('Le speranze di un disperato',
15 June 1911, p. 589); Slataper expressed the uncompro-

---

[4] The story of the relationship between the *vociani* and the Futurists is well
documented in Adamson, *Avant-Garde Florence*, 143–52.

mising opinion that 'A whole world needs to be thrown into the dustbin' ('Ai giovani intelligenti', 26 August 1909, p. 149); and Boine affirmed: 'The usual formulae of literary expression are like arid and rigid mummies' ('Un ignoto', 8 February 1912, p. 750).

Of the genres which irritated writers such as Boine or Slataper, the novel was singled out as deserving the most severe attack.[5] With the collapse of positivism as a convincing philosophical system, the realist novel seemed to have been robbed of its status as a meaningful mode of sociological or cognitive enquiry. The convention of the third-person narrator, upon which the genre so often depended, no longer constituted a quasi-scientific device by the aid of which the writer could better penetrate the workings of society and the human mind. Instead it seemed a sterile contrivance which obstructed the writer from delving into the hidden psychological mysteries of the individual. Further, the *vociani* believed that the novelist, by inventing a set of fictitious characters whose lives interlocked according to the determinist requirements of plot, necessarily portrayed human existence as a logically ordered and rationally explicable sequence of events; in other words, in a way that the *vociani* found entirely fallacious. Concluding a characteristically pugnacious review of a now forgotten work by the novelist Clarice Tartufari, Boine exorted his fellow Italian writers to abandon the novel: 'Enough, enough of the novel . . . Do we have to spend eternity writing fables to amuse the public? Do we have to sell our souls packaged in rhetorical formulae? . . . Do we have to make our minds dance on a fictitious stage so that the ignorant public applauds?'[6]

---

[5] It is not difficult to find sarcastic remarks directed against the novel in the writings, both private and public, of many of the writers associated with Prezzolini's *Voce*. Cecchi, for instance, in a review of Benda's *L'Ordination* (see below) made the following point which summed up the feelings towards the novel of many of his contemporaries: 'Non possiamo sempre accettare le ragioni empiriche che vogliono dare le assolute motivazioni psicologiche dei vari personaggi, come poteva accettarle, per esempio, un lettore di cinquant'anni fa.'

[6] Later in the same article Boine wrote: 'Io piangerò. Starò con, [*sic*] dirò la mia anima nuda. Non scriverò romanzi.' See Puccini's edition of Boine's works, pp. 137–9. Clelia Martignoni, in her study of the reasons behind the *vociani*'s disdain for the novel, 'Per una storia dell'autobiografismo metafisico vociano', *Autografo*, 2 (June 1984), 32–47 (p. 34), goes so far as to suggest that Boine's views may indeed

Intensely aware of the deficiencies of the realist novel of nineteenth-century derivation, the *vociani* regarded autobiographical writing as a genre which better corresponded to their anxious desire to affirm subjective perceptions of themselves and of external reality. Piero Jahier, referring in *La Voce* ('La salute', 25 July 1912, p. 861) to the new methods of composition employed by his colleagues, had declared: 'Our art has to be autobiographical: we await at a crossroads, full of solitude and expectancy.' Boine, in another of his reviews for *Riviera ligure*, made the important and now often cited remark, 'I don't know what one can talk about except oneself.'[7] The type of criticism which Cardarelli wrote for *Il Marzocco* and *Avanti!* was overtly self-exploratory; many of the works which he admired, such as Péguy's *Notre jeunesse* or Benda's *Mon premier testament* (published, like Péguy's work, in 1910) belonged to an autobiographical strain of writing, and most of his reflections on literature implied a strong belief that the function of a work was to represent the consciousness of its author. In the early work of the critic and close associate of Cardarelli, Emilio Cecchi, the inclination towards the revelation of the self is much less obvious.[8] Yet, although Cecchi remained unconvinced by elements of 'la critica etica', he fully acknowledged the reasons which impelled his fellow contributors to *La Voce* to experiment with the devices of autobiography. Indeed, in one of his letters to Boine he spoke of the need to undertake the task of writing a long introspective work.[9] In his notebooks, he mentioned 'our aspirations towards a literature of internal

have been influenced by those of Cecchi: 'Non v'è dubbio che il giudizio di Cecchi sulla scrittrice [Clarice Tartufari] e sul genere [the novel] influenzò Boine, che ancora non conosceva l'opera della Tartufari e ne chiedeva copia all'amico.'

[7] The review is of Soffici's *Giornale di bordo* and is again included in Puccini's edition of Boine's works, p. 187.

[8] Reflecting on the different degree of self-exposition in their respective works, Cardarelli once wrote to his friend: 'Tra te che celi virilmente i tuoi processi interiori ed io che li mostro al modo di certi romantici che disistimo quanto te, la differenza è esterna e può riguardare tutt'al più la nostra indole.' The letter is dated 5 July 1911.

[9] The letter is dated 28 Feb. 1914 and contained in Giovanni Boine, *Carteggio: G. Boine–E. Cecchi (1911–1917)*, ed. M. Marchione and S. E. Scalia (Rome: Edizioni di Storia e Letteratura, 1972), 85.

events, of consciousness',[10] and at one point he confided the following ambition: 'I have often had the idea of patiently elaborating, exclusively for myself, a critical moral biography of myself.'[11]

His remarks are revealing in the emphasis that they place upon analysis of the internal functioning of the self, since it was this, rather than the documentation of the events of a life, which interested the *vociani*. Their experiments in this direction were intended, to use the terminology of Papini, to trace 'un'arte interna' in contraposition to the 'arte esterna' exemplified by the realist novel. Their ideal writer would not look outwards at the workings of society but inwards to examine his emotions and thought processes; he would not use his imagination to invent fictional characters and events upon an unreal stage but employ his intellect to analyse his ideas, meditations, and reflections as they appeared upon the screen of his consciousness. The depiction of the external world would be either excluded or confined to the minimum. The protagonist of a work would be the centre of his own idealistic world, not part of a larger social construction. Boine, in his polemical piece on Tartufari, declared in a way that left no doubt that the *vociani* were obsessed with an exclusively masculine self: 'We have to be men [*Bisogna esser maschi davvero*]. Being men means casting aside the caresses, the tinted softness of the material world and harshly reducing ourselves to our inner essence.' Cecchi, reviewing Benda's lyrical novel *L'Ordination* (*La Tribuna*, 12 October 1911), admired the way Benda had excluded any concession to the traditional necessity of a social setting for the action of his work. He praised the absence of any description of towns, movements, faces, or people. He ended his article with an earnest appeal to the reader which amounted to a declaration of faith in the creative efforts of the writers associated with *La Voce*. He asked his readers to consider the importance of the fact that 'the new literary forces are inspired not by the masters of fine style . . . but by ascetics, by thinkers, by artists who look inwards'.

[10] Emilio Cecchi, *Taccuini*, ed. N. Gallo and P. Citatii (Milan: Mondadori, 1976), 80.
[11] Ibid. 84.

If the *vociani* had lost any residual belief in the ability of a literary genre such as the novel to encompass or account for the complexity of reality, then they valued those works which did not adhere to a narrative logic and therefore did not portray the world as an ordered succession of events, actions, and thoughts. The works of writers such as Pascal or Amiel were held in favour,[12] while the psychological introspection and self-examination of Rimbaud's *Saison en enfer* enjoyed enormous esteem. It was, in fact, Soffici who in 1911 introduced Rimbaud to a wider Italian audience with an enthusiastic introduction and translation of parts of the *Saison*. In Cecchi's notebooks there are several important references to Rimbaud. In one instance we find, next to a series of musings on his autobiographical project, the transcription of parts of a letter written by Rimbaud, the opening sentence of which reads: 'La première étude de l'homme qui veut être poète est sa propre connaissance, entière; il cherche son âme, il l'inspecte, il la tente, l'apprend.'[13] More strikingly still, Cardarelli, writing to Cecchi in May 1914, confided that he had read and reread the *Saison en enfer* and that he found in Rimbaud and Baudelaire 'his 'spiritual fathers'.[14] Rimbaud's *Saison*, like Pascal's *Pensées*, is above all a fractured and disjointed work, and it was the fragment of prose or poetry which the writers of *La Voce* proposed in opposition to the ordered narrative scheme of the nineteenth-century novel. The style which they cultivated was neither rich nor elegant, nor even visual, but trenchant and terse. It was a style which inclined naturally towards the enunciation of the moral truth or what Boine called 'the living aphorism'.

Aside from the influence exerted by Rimbaud's example, there is a further reason why self-exploratory writing should have appealed so strongly to the writers of *La Voce*. The *vociani* were, and prided themselves on being, *moralisti*. In

---

[12] Later in his article on Benda's *L'Ordination*, Cecchi had specified: 'I romanzi che leggiamo più volentieri, quelli le cui avventure ci commuovono . . . sono *Les Pensées* di Pascal, magari, o il *Journal* di Amiel.'

[13] 'The first object of study for any man who wishes to become a poet is his own consciousness; he must look for his soul, inspect it, feel and apprehend it.' Cecchi, *Taccuini*, 168. The letter is that addressed to Paul Demeny contained in Arthur Rimbaud, *Œuvres complètes* (Paris: Bibliothèque de la Pléiade), 269–74.

[14] The letter is dated 26 May 1914, and reprinted in the *Epistolario*, i. 359.

their opinion, to write a spiritual or metaphysical autobiography was in itself to accomplish a morally uplifting
action since the writer of an autobiography was someone
who, through merciless introspective enquiry, had necessarily accentuated his awareness of his moral self. In the
ethical importance attributed to the practice of self-examination and in the particular accent on 'l'esser maschi', the
theories of both Nietzsche and of Weininger are to be found.
It is well known that Nietzsche's ideas exercised enormous
power not only over the Florentine grouping but over avant-
garde movements all over Europe, and in the works of
Papini, Boine, and Soffici echoes of *Ecce Homo* and *Thus
Spake Zarathustra* reverberate continually.

Consonant with the philosophy of Nietzsche and underlying to an equal degree the structure of much autobiographical writing associated with Prezzolini's *Voce* were
Weininger's dualistic conception of personality and his notion of morality. In the psychological scheme which he had
advanced in *Geschlecht und Charakter*,[15] the human personality
is divided into two distinct elements: the 'empirical ego', the
part of the self that responds automatically and instinctively
to external stimuli and which is, therefore, perpetually
in a state of chaotic disorder, and the 'intelligible ego',
the constant element of human character, responsible for
formulating motivation and dictating action. Morality was
conceived by Weininger, and by extension by many of the
vociani most attentive to the central tenets of his work, as the
incessant attempt of the 'intelligible ego' to inhibit the
amoral and dispersive drives of the 'empirical ego'. The
vociani considered their autobiographies to represent an
ethically orientated literary genre precisely because they
aspired to portray the struggle of the individual to overcome
his instinctive desires by the action of his will. Slataper

---

[15] The majority of the writers who contributed to the *Voce* were familiar with
Geschlect und Charakter. In *La Voce: Letteratura e primato degli intellettuali*, Carpi, when
speaking of the thinkers who most influenced the *vociani*, speaks of 'quella vera
scoperta vociana che fu Otto Weininger' (p. 12). There are certainly a great many
elements about Weininger's work which are disturbing. Although both his parents
were Jewish, his text is notorious for the number of overtly anti-Semitic statements
which it makes. His distinction, meanwhile, between the male and female principles is one that strikes the modern reader as both irrational and offensive.

defined the autobiographical fragment as 'the psychic struggle of the modern soul'[16] and, in much of the work connected in some way with *La Voce*, aggressive and combative
language accompanies images of internal strife.

Papini's Un uomo finito *and Soffici's* Lemmonio Boreo

Roughly between 1910 and 1915 the writers associated with
La Voce produced a number of autobiographical texts: in
1912 Papini published his *Un uomo finito*; in the same year
Slataper published *Il mio Carso* and Soffici *Lemmonio Boreo*;
Rebora's *Frammenti lirici* appeared in 1913 and Bacchelli's
Poemi lirici in 1914; Boine's *Frantumi* were published post-
humously in 1917. All these texts obey their own laws of
construction and some, especially those of Slataper and
Boine, remain important examples of expressionism. Yet all
these texts emerge from a common matrix of ideas and
theories concerning writing about a specifically masculine
self. The detailed study of Cardarelli's own metaphysical
autobiography helps to reveal some of the techniques which
the writers of *La Voce* relied upon as well as some of the
theoretical assumptions which both motivated and structured their work. Equally the self which emerges from Cardarelli's work cannot be understood without looking at the
first-person protagonists who form the centre of other autobiographical experiments belonging to the culture of *La
Voce*.

The authorial figures of Papini's *Un uomo finito*, Slataper's
diary,[17] and Soffici's *Lemmonio Boreo* are possessed of 'a mania
for greatness'.[18] Each text is in some way similar to Cardarelli's work, but Papini's text is particularly close.[19] Struc-

[16] Slataper, *Appunti e note di diario* (Milan: Mondadori, 1953), 103.

[17] In one entry to his diary, for example, Slataper writes: 'Tu non sai che io ho
letto tante vite di santi, e ho sognato tante volte di diventare un maestro e apostolo;
apostolo della vita.' Ibid. 124.

[18] The phrase occurs in the chapter of Papini's *Un uomo finito*, entitled 'Il mondo
sono io'. The edition I am quoting from is Giovanni Papini, *Un uomo finito*
(Florence: Vallecchi, 1960). Subsequent page references are given in the text.

[19] Clelia Martignoni has carefully documented the borrowings which Cardarelli
made both from Nietzsche and from Papini in 'Alle radici della prosa d'arte
cardarelliana', *Letteratura italiana contemporanea*, 5 (Jan.–Apr. 1984), 161–87.

turally, Papini's *Un uomo finito* does not rank among the most experimental of the works produced by the *vociani*. The text follows a fairly clear, linear pattern which traces the history of the protagonist's life from childhood to adolescence and then through a series of formative friendships and experiences, such as the setting up of or participation in various journals. However, the text is not about the material details of the protagonist's life, but about his intellectual development. With few exceptions, details such as dates, names, and places remain unspecified. Papini's intellectual autobiography is principally concerned with the protagonist's wish to rise above others, to fulfil his desire for individual greatness or, to use his phrase, to satisfy his 'malattia di grandezza'. The style in which the work is written is relentlessly egocentric and awash with extreme adjectives and uncompromising exclamations. The implied analogy throughout is that the protagonist's ambition is to raise himself to the level of God. He writes: 'I needed the eternal, the grandiose, the totality of things, the fullness of time, the procession of centuries and of great works' (p. 27).

At least the first half of *Un uomo finito* is made up of the narration of one absurdly ambitious project after another. Inspired by the Nietzschean imperative to re-examine all values, the protagonist sets out to write a new and definitive compendium of knowledge, a new history of the world from ancient Egypt onwards, a new history of religion and of world literature. Other, madder, proposals include a project for universal suicide. Yet the dynamics of the work remain simple. Each individual project encounters different obstacles leading to the adoption of another enterprise, while Papini's addiction to a notion of personal greatness remains strong. If the first half of *Un uomo finito* documents the conquest of the self, then the latter half documents the conquest of others: that is, the protagonist changes from becoming a god in his own image to becoming an apostle of his own law. He inspires others to reach the same heights which he believes himself to have attained, although he notices: 'In none of my new friends did I discover the passion for pure thought, the habit of hard reasoning and the appreciation of and skill in skirmishing with ideas' (p. 69).

The literary journal becomes the tool through which the protagonist makes an assault on the contemporary world. The desire to propagate his new discoveries is nevertheless accompanied by a contempt for people deemed to be less exceptional, or, to use Papini's phrase, for 'i piccoli vivi'. We witness an attitude which insists on berating others for failing to achieve an arbitrary level of intellectual freedom, a continual attempt to assert the superiority of the protagonist and a spate of specifically misogynous asides. Despite the aggressiveness that Papini vents against whole swathes of humanity, the latter part of the text is characterized by a sense of failure. The protagonist admits to a consciousness of personal failings, a fear of incipient physical decline, and acknowledges that he has not attained the Weiningerian status of genius. The frenetic embrace of different philosophies leads finally to the renunciation of any single philosophy, and the book ends with a polemical statement of defeat:

I present myself to your cold eyes with all my scars, all my hopes and all my weaknesses. . . . If after having listened to me you believe . . . that I am really a finished man you must at least confess that I am finished because I wanted to begin too many things and because I wanted to be everything. (p. 327)

In *Un uomo finito* Papini's unrestrained cultivation of the self feeds on the protagonist searching for and then overcoming any obstacle which stands in his way. In its depiction of confrontation the text is symptomatic of the avant-garde culture from which it arose. It both anticipates and helps to explain the reasons behind the *vociani*'s interventionism. It is also easy to draw a parallel between the aggressiveness with which the protagonist affirms his own views and the brutal assertion of a given set of values which was to occur under Fascism. The violence with which Papini sets about his opponents within the text does, however, remain purely intellectual. The same is not the case in Soffici's unquestionably proto-Fascist *Lemmonio Boreo*.[20] The text is written in a more

---

[20] Writing on Soffici's *Lemmonio Boreo*, Isnenghi has observed: 'È un vero condensato di fascismo *ante litteram*': *Il mito della grande guerra*, 37. Quotations from *Lemmonio Boreo* are from Soffici, *Opere*, ed. E. Falqui, 7 vols. (Florence: Vallecchi, 1959–68), vol. ii.

fantastic and allegorical register: the writer does not identify himself explicitly with the eponymous hero, although auto-biographical elements are clearly perceptible. The text's principal protagonist functions as a medium through which the writer can articulate his own intellectual aspirations and direct his polemics.

After a period spent abroad, Lemmonio returns to his native Tuscany. He has an intense hatred of all that is sub-standard, frivolous, or mediocre and he decides to embark on a crusade to alter what he perceives to be the prevailing climate of degrading torpor. The dynamics of the book are to a degree similar to those that dictate the structure of *Un uomo finito*: Lemmonio isolates a series of situations or figures which he thinks should be changed, he then sets to work, and the book moves from one picaresque episode to another. In each episode Lemmonio acts as the instigator of change, but he quickly realizes that his intelligence and nationalistic sentiments are not enough on their own. He therefore recruits a kind of bodygurad, Zaccagna, to whom he explains: 'I'm going about the world trying to put things right . . . But it's not enough to have a strong sense of justice, do you understand? You need force' (pp. 100–1). Lemmo-nio's next realization is that 'reason and a strong stick' are not enough and that he and Zaccagna, to be truly successful, must enlist the support of the artful character, Spillo. The three friends are then able to administer successfully a number of lessons to a series of groups or individuals, all of which are symbolic of one institution or another: they admonish a hypocritical priest; overturn a malfunctioning railway carriage; provoke a riot as a reformist Socialist is addressing a crowd in public; chastise a group of arrogant foreigners; renew the fervour of a dormant writer. In its representation of a nationalistic intellectual intervening effect-ively with the support of figures emblematic of other social classes, the text reads like a Fascist allegory. It is all the more disturbing in that each of the changes which it sees intro-duced are brought about through the use of violent action. There is no reflection on the legitimacy of violence; its usefulness in affirming the principles of renewal is presented as self-evident.

Cardarelli's Prologhi

Cardarelli's own autobiography, *Prologhi*, was not published until 1916. But he was keen to assert on the title-page of the book that its period of composition dated back to 1913–14, during the years when the *vociani* were most insistently advocating Nietzschean notions of the 'superuomo' and a literary form antithethical to the realist novel. The work certainly belongs to the aggressive climate of thought which characterized the Florentine avant-garde and, as will be seen, Cardarelli makes a number of identifiable borrowings directly from *Un uomo finito*. However, unlike the texts of Papini or Soffici, *Prologhi* does not follow a narrative framework and it carries the process of abstraction to more extreme limits.

Prologhi is a collection comprising sixteen short prose pieces and fourteen lyrics, some of the latter no longer than an epigram.[21] The fragmentary quality of the work hints at an underlying notion of disorder and the impossibility of conceptualizing the self except through disconnected pieces of information. In the original text, the prose and poetry were divided into seven further subsections, each with a separate title. The self-exploratory themes of the collection are common to both the prose and the poetry.[22] The principal interest of the text lies in the complex manner in which it articulates a typically domineering protagonist and yet at the same time hints at the way in which the self

[21] *Prologhi* (Milan: Facchi, 1916). The prose pieces bear the following titles or opening words: 'Dati biografici', 'Commiato', 'Impressioni', 'Nuovo addio', 'Se oggi ritornasse Gesù Cristo . . .', 'Ringraziamento', 'Le parole', 'Constatazioni', 'Accorgersi che quel . . .', 'Pausa', 'Trasformazioni', 'Temi dell'addio', 'Psicologia', 'Lamentazione di chi rimane', 'Saggezza', 'Silenzio della creazione'. The lyrics are entitled: 'La speranza è nell'opera', 'Saluto di stagione', Tempi immacolati', 'Amicizia', 'Stanchezza', 'Fuga', 'Passaggi', 'Estiva', 'Arabesco', 'Adolescente', 'Incontro notturno', 'Tristezza', 'E ora in queste mattine', 'Ispirazione'.

[22] Martignoni, writing on the avant-garde implications of Cardarelli's choice of the fragmentary form in *Prologhi*, has observed: 'La scelta del frammento significa adesione a disgregazione e caos epocali; unione rivoluzionaria di prosa e poesia in un continuum. Si mescolano, nell'assenza del flusso narrativo, i livelli diversi e tradizionalmente disgiunti.' 'Vincenzo Cardarelli tra mito e moralità', *Poesia*, 3/26 (Feb. 1990), 35–42 (p. 35).

becomes a prisoner or victim of its own assertive paradigm of individual greatness. It is both an example of and a comment on the construction of the *vociano* self at a time when Italy was lurching towards intervention, in part because of the campaigns undertaken by nationalist journals like *La Voce*.

For the sake of simplicity it is worth looking first at those prose fragments of *Prologhi* which affirm the superiority of the protagonist and then at those poems which problematize the apparently straightforward self-image. As I have implied, the work is not intended to give a comprehensive explanation of the author's personality; it simply provides an indication of how the subject perceives himself, others, and external reality. The lyrical and discursive fragments which together make up the collection are, as their title suggests, a selection of prologues to articulate the personality of an authorial presence, or, to use an apposite phrase which Cardarelli employed in his critical appraisal of the work of Charles Péguy, they are: 'lyrical perceptions of a larger autobiographical reality'. *Prologhi* opens with the bellicose prose passage 'Dati biografici', a piece in which the narrative voice sets out the dominant traits of his personality. He gives himself neither an age nor a name, he gives no indication of his physical appearance and makes not the slightest reference to his material environment. He does not attempt to describe how he came to be by pointing retrospectively to events and encounters which may have exercised a formative effect upon his character. Instead, as if he were consciously following Boine's injunction to 'reduce ourselves to the inner essence', he has distilled his character to its finest psychological core, and he supplies biographical data of a uniquely abstract kind:

Non ho mai potuto compiere un atto che non fosse ostacolato da un'immancabile contrarietà. All'innocenza ci son dovuto arrivare. Mi son sempre alzato da una disfatta. . . . La mia forza è quando mi ripiego. La mia massima musicalità quando mi giustifico. Non sono vittorioso che in certe fulminee ricapitolazioni. . . . Il segreto delle mie conoscenze è l'insoddisfazione. Di ogni cosa vedo l'ombra in cui culmina. Affermo il limite, principio dalla negazione: la realtà è l'eterno sottinteso.

[I have never been able to accomplish an act that has not been opposed
by inevitable hostility. I have had to arrive at innocence. I have always had
to raise myself from a defeat. . . . My strength resides in thought. I achieve
my greatest musicality when I defend myself. I'm only victorious in certain
rapid recapitulations. . . . The secret of my knowledge is dissatisfaction. I
see the shadow in which everything culminates. I affirm the limit and
work out from negation: reality is what is eternally implied.]

In this passage the narrator is not depicted as a part of a
larger social system, but as an independent moral and logical
entity. External reality is merely, 'l'eterno sottinteso'. The
style of the piece asserts the egocentricity of its speaker; it is
an accumulation of abrupt and formally repetitive sentences
all announcing the exceptional mental attributes of the
speaker. In the very means in which the passage, like the rest
of the prose piece, is syntactically ordered, there are further
indications of the narcissistic drive of the speaker to define
the patterns of his mind. It is noticeable how the predicate
of each phrase seems to contradict, or at the least oppose, an
idea which is implicit within the subject of the sentence: thus,
the innocence of the speaker is something which has been
reached, the notion of creativity is associated with that of
error, strength resides in retreat, and so forth. Reflecting
on Cardarelli's literary endeavour at self-presentation in
Prologhi, Cecchi spoke tellingly in his journals of someone
who expressed himself through 'vehement psychological
asides'.[23] It is certainly the case that the figure projected by
'Dati biografici' is proud and agonistic: he presents himself
as a creator, a man whose excessive talent and metaphysical
strength put him above more ordinary men. Often in the
above passage, but particularly in the second paragraph,
words denotative of power are directly associated with others
connotative of introspective enquiry. It progressively becomes clear that the author considers his strength, his talent,
and the very core of his personality to reside within the force
of his intellect.

In his article for *La Voce*, 'Le speranze di un disperato' (15
June 1911, p. 589), an article which was among the many
which proposed an autobiographical form of composition,

---

[23] Cecchi, *Taccuini*, 262.

Papini had observed: 'We need to switch the centre of interest from the normal to the theoretical, from the animal-esque to the angelic, from the pictorial to the philosophical.' 'Dati biografici', with its presentation of the mental structure of a subject who in every sentence affirms his exceptionality, evidently works in this direction. In another of his articles, 'Inno all'intelligenza' published in the volume *Maschilità* (1915), Papini had eulogized the destructive power of the intellect, writing: 'You destroy everything Intelligence. Your breath is poisonous . . . You consume, annihilate and destroy everything.' Again this positive evaluation of the potential of the intellect to dissolve the phenomenal world is something which emerges strongly from the final lines of the above extract from 'Dati biografici'.

If the desire to dominate through the action of the intel-lect is central to the subject's initial act of self-definition, then the theme is reinforced by other prologues which represent the interaction of self and others. In these com-positions the subject's relationship with others is explored in two distinct, if complementary, ways. The prose may take the form of the internal monologue similar in many respects to the self-expository writing of 'Dati biografici'. Such solilo-quies begin either with a maxim of possible general applica-tion upon the flaws inherent within all kinds of human contact, as in 'Constatazioni', or with an observation on the effects that contact with the other exercises upon the self, as in 'Impressioni'. The prose of the second type takes the shape of an address, often an extended and embittered farewell,[24] to an unspecified group of listeners.

It is in the manner in which the addressee is confronted in *Prologhi* that the prose most reveals a debt to Nietzsche's *Thus Spake Zarathustra*. The very fact that the subject har-angues a group of figures implies a relationship between unequal partners: they are present only as recipients of the protagonist's message. The acts of communication further accentuate the difference between addresser and addressee, not only in the way in which they posit the existence of the other, but in the manner in which they explicitly, and

[24] The prose pieces 'Commiato' and 'Nuovo Addio' are examples of this type of composition.

sometimes didactically, express disapproval or disappointment. In the valedictory piece 'Commiato', for example,
Cardarelli writes:

Le ferite più stridenti me le avete fatte senza saperlo; questo è il male. Io
mi posso vantare d'aver sempre saputo bene dove sarei riuscito più
doloroso quando vi battevo; voi no. Voi non vi siete curati di me; neppure
per assestarmi un bel colpo. . . . Ma voi non sapete quello che giova alla
vita. La vostra parola non testimonia. I vostri silenzi che cosa dicono? Non
c'è sistema nei vostri silenzi e nelle vostre parole. Non si sa mai con chi si
discorre, con voi.

[You have inflicted the most painful wounds upon me without knowing;
that is the problem. I can at least boast that I always knew where to hurt
you most when I attacked you; but you didn't. You didn't care about me;
not enough even to prepare a heavy blow. . . . But you don't know what
life's all about. Your word is meaningless. And what does your silence say?
There is no system in your silences or in your words. One never knows
what to speak about with you.]

In this passage the addressees are accused principally of
ignorance and indifference, but within that accusation there
are further suggestions of ineptitude, even cruelty. The
narrator assumes an imperious and reprobative tone
which divests his interlocutors of any reputable qualities. An
intense antagonism[25] towards others is expressed implicitly
in the number of verbs and nouns connotative of physical
injury and more explicitly in the way in which all the
phrases which have the addressee as their subject express the
absence or negation of a quality. In other prose pieces
belonging to the same collection, the subject represents
himself as the victim of others' malevolence. In 'Impressioni'
he casts a backward reflective glance on past encounters,
and enumerates those occasions when he has discovered,
lurking under a deceptively welcoming mask, a series of
hostile sentiments. In 'Trasformazioni' he represents himself
as a wounded animal, profoundly suspicious of the inten-

---

[25] The reflections which Cecchi makes in his notebooks concerning Cardarelli
often usefully illuminate aspects of the latter's literary practice. On the subject of
antagonism Cecchi writes: 'Concepire bisogna la vita come un continuo antagonismo: . . . quello solo fra i miei vicini che concepisca questo antagonismo adeguata-
mente è Cardarelli, malgrado tutti i suoi difetti, tutte le sue caricature.' Cecchi,
Taccuini, 134.

tions of others and continually prepared to protect himself. But the register and syntactical organization of the above extract from 'Commiato' perhaps most calls to mind elements of the early literary criticism of Cardarelli, especially those articles in which the outraged critic conducts a verbal assault upon what he perceives as the deficiencies of a writer's style and philosophy. If the diatribes against the poetics of such writers as Moretti and Gozzano allowed Cardarelli to advocate his own vision of the function of literature then, in an analogous fashion, the denigratory passages of *Prologhi* serve to emphasize further the set of characteristics which distinguishes the speaker from the mediocre. The speaker defines himself relationally, and thus the very absence of qualities in the group of addressees serves to enhance his own superior quality. The same process is used throughout *Un uomo finito*. At one stage Papini writes: 'And what about other people! Passing shades on the screen of my sensibility, ghosts evoked at will' (p. 86). The speaking voice of *Prologhi* asserts in 'Dati biografici': 'Those who wish to have my company have to prepare themselves to be annihilated.'

In its concentrated and aggressive attempt to define the ethical character of its speaker, *Prologhi* exemplifies important aspects of the 'moralismo vociano'. In the prose of the collection the protagonist is depicted as a figure who, acutely aware of the composite elements of his character, strives to govern his instincts by the exercise of his will. If the speaker endeavours to subject his instinctual drives to the uncompromising power of his intellect and if he clearly dominates the undefined figures of the other protagonists who appear in his prose, then he also seeks to gain an ascendancy over reality. He is at war with himself, the Other, and his surroundings. In the prose pieces of *Prologhi* there is, as I have already remarked, a striking absence of social setting, but another noteworthy feature the collection's depiction of reality is the manner in which the speaking subject does not perceive the objects of the external world but struggles to identify the laws by which they are governed. The two prose pieces which are placed at the end of the collection, 'Riposi' and 'Silenzio della creazione', are combative meditations upon the structure of the cosmos. In the uncompromising manner in which these two compositions pronounce a series of metaphysical observations, one can detect the tone of the Nietzschean 'superuomo', who enquires through assertion. Further, the cosmic principles which the speaking voice indicates reflect the patterns of the mind which perceives them. In *Un uomo finito* Papini declares: 'The world is my representation—the world is my spirit—I am the world. . . . The whole world was nothing but a part of my being; its existence depended on me, on my sensations and on my mind' (pp. 85–6). Likewise the prose of *Prologhi* creates an ethical universe in the absence of a phenomenal world, and that ethical universe is the extension of the protagonist's moral system.

In 'Dati biografici' the speaker equates the notion of personal identity with intellectual power. In the statements of poetics offered by the collection and in several of its major poems, the same equation between force and intellect is propounded. Above all, the protagonist affirms his rationality. A striking feature of the order of the universe as it is perceived in *Prologhi* is that, like the personality of the speaking subject, its defining characteristic is its logicality. Towards the beginning of 'Temi dell'addio' the speaker refers to his 'unalterable faith in that which is logical'. Later in the same prose piece, making an unstated but nevertheless unequivocal connection between the self and its surroundings, he observes: 'Ultimately what I recognize as most conclusive in the world is its order and its unchangeability'. If in 'Dati biografici' the destructive potential of the intellect has been laid bare, then in the final prose compositions of *Prologhi* reality appears as menacing or frightening not because it is chaotic but because it is ineluctably and logically ordered.

So far what we have seen in the defamatory prose of *Prologhi* is an act of self-definition which proceeds at one level through the annihilation of the other while at a secondary level it represents the external world as an extension of the speaking subject. The overpowering egocentricity of the subject gains a further dimension when we consider the collection's recurring statements of poetic intent. In the same assertive manner with which the speaker defines the central aspects of his character, he proposes, towards the end of 'Dati biografici', the essential elements of his poetics:

La mia lirica non suppone che sintesi. Luce senza colore, esistenze senza attributo, inni senza interiezione, impassibilità e lontananza, ordini e non figure, ecco quel che vi posso dare.

[My lyrics suppose only syntheses. Light without colour, existences without attributes, hymns without emotion, impassibility and distance, orders not figures, that is what I can give you.]

This statement should be read in conjunction with another, untitled, fragment in verse:

> Ispirazione per me è indifferenza
> Poesia: salute e impassibilità.
> Arte di tacere.

[Inspiration for me is indifference | Poetry: health and impassibility | The art of being silent.]

In both these concise formulas it is clear that the dominant traits of the author's temperament reappear, a fact which is obviously meant to imply that the art of poetical composition is intended to be a means of self-definition. There is, in other words, an identity between poetic subject and poetics. The author is not a figure within the text, he is the text, or, as Cardarelli himself had written in his article, 'Il metodo estetico': 'My form is my spirit.' If the author we know from the prose prides himself upon his incisive intelligence, then his poetry, compared to light, is equally penetrating; if he demonstrates a propensity to capture the essence of a thing or being, then his lyrics betray a similar quality, they are syntheses which reduce rather than amplify the object they portray ('esistenze senza attributo'); if the author claims to possess the temperament of a cynic, then his work, in like manner, is characterized by its measured form, its impassivity ('indifferenza', 'impassibilità'). The cynic is propelled by an imperative desire to see clearly beyond external appearances even to the extent of distrusting sensory perception, and so the poetry does not offer 'figure' but 'ordini'.

From the declaration of poetics we also learn, although this point is made less overtly, that the author does not consider poetry to be the appropriate site for the outpouring of emotion but rather the medium to represent its suppression ('inni senza interiezione'). It is in the rational power of his mind rather than in his sentimental orientation or in his imaginary processes that he locates the source of his identity. In a singularly fitting definition Contini has referred to Cardarelli's poetic persona as the 'high priest of rationality'[26] and one of the most revealing affirmations of 'Dati biografici' is the line: 'My strength resides in thought. I achieve my greatest musicality when I defend myself.' The lyrics of *Prologhi* are all structured as intense acts of intellection, a point which can be made by looking closely at one of the most abstract fragments of the collection, 'Passaggi':

> Le voglie trattenute
> mi stemprano in languide inedie.
> E il riso spunta sulle fissità.
> Amori senza connubio
> passano
> come frutti sul ramo.
> Il più frettoloso figliolo
> del tempo, il Disinganno,
> che si nutre di sottigliezze
> acerrime e conclusive,
> ancora intatti li uccide
> i sogni della mia indecisione.

[Inhibited desires I wear me down to languid exhaustion. I And laughter flickers on [my] immobility. I Unconsummated love I passes I like fruit on the branch. I The most hasty child I of time, Disappointment, I which feeds off unripe but conclusive subtleties, I while they are still intact kills I the dreams of my indecision.]

In 'Passaggi' we witness a consistent endeavour to allow the metaphysical to achieve so absolute a form of dominance that empirical objects are almost entirely banished from the composition. Cardarelli declines to indicate the physical consequences of a given feeling, electing instead to record a succession of closely related psychological states in purely abstract terms. Thus the exhausting effect of continual repression is conveyed simply by the words, 'languide inedie'.

---

[26] The definition is to be found in the article, 'La verità sul caso Cardarelli', now contained in Gianfranco Contini, *Esercizi di lettura* (Turin: Einaudi, 1974), 34–42.

When speaking of love, there is no lyrical elaboration of the cause of the feeling and no delineation of the object or objects of desire responsible for stimulating 'inhibited desires'. In the final line of the poem the idea of dreaming is evoked and yet the source of images potentially contained within that notion is not the subject of any exploration. The verse remains resolutely within the mental sphere of its speaker, or, to use Cecchi's words, it constructs 'Landscapes of the will, pictures of time; architectural structures made of scruples, remorse and resentment'.[27] In the lyric a protracted emotional experience has been condensed to its rational core. Even within the imagery of the poem there is no relief from its intellectual essentiality. The line, 'E il riso spunta sulle fissità' contains the suggestion of an image, but one which cannot readily be visualized. In the construction which follows, the metaphorical transfer is weak to the point of unobtrusiveness and the force of the subsequent personification is diminished by the abstract quality of the adjectives ('acerrime e conclusive') qualifying the action of 'il Disinganno'. If, like many of the compositions in verse of *Prologhi*, 'Passaggi' cultivates rationality by avoiding the imaginative luxuriance of the image, it also does so by steadfastly maintaining a reflective unity of tone. The lyric traces repression, unfulfilled desire, and disillusionment over an unspecified period of time but without ever gaining the force of lament or objection capable of disrupting its tonal and metrical regularity.

If, for the most part, the prose pieces of the collection are assertive statements which define the self in opposition to what surrounds it, then a different and more complicated process of self-definition begins to operate in the lyrics. A poem like 'Passaggi', instead of affirming the strength of the subject's clarity of mind, offers a reflection on its limits. The self in the verse is not, as is almost invariably the case in the prose, the subject of each enunciation, rather it is confined to the grammatical category of the object. The self is not an agent but something which is acted upon. Furthermore, the compression of emotion and imagination into the

---

[27] 'Testimonianze classiche', *La Tribuna*, 18 Oct. 1916.

intellectual affirmation is not only a significant formal com-
ponent of the verse but also one of the major semantic
concerns of the collection as a whole. The reduction of the
objects of the external world to abstractions in the mental
sphere of the perceiving subject induces an inhumanly bare
level of intellection.[28] Within sections of the prose the subject's attested ability to see beyond the surface forms of the
external world provokes statements of the kind: 'I hear time
collapsing noisily in my mind. At my back I have nothingness. I lean against my errors' ('Nuovo addio'). In the lyrical
compositions the frequency of expressions evoking the self's
intuitive or philosophical recognition of the emptiness of
time or of life is even more noticeable. In 'Tempi immaco-
lati', for example, he writes: 'Time is behind us, | but like an
invisible backcloth | to this which is life | a play of contrasts |
in nothingness.'

The more the self in *Prologhi* asserts its will, the more it
seeks to define its most essential features, then the more it
becomes aware of the desolating evidence of its own susceptibility to the destructive agency of time. The drive towards
self-dominance is thus profoundly ambivalent. The theme of
exhaustion, present in poems such as 'Passaggi', is the main-
spring of a lyric like 'Stanchezza'. However, interspersed
with intuitions of an inimical cosmic order bearing down
upon the individual human subject, there are indications of
possible solutions to existential problems. In one four-line
verse fragment, the author declares the persistence of a faith
in a cult of personal fame:

> La speranza è nell'opera.
> Io sono un cinico a cui rimane
> per la sua fede questo al di là.
> Io sono un cinico che ha fede in quel che fa.

[Hope is to be found in work. | I am a cynic who retains | in return for his
faith, a notion of this afterlife. | I am a cynic who has faith in what he
does.]

The final prose piece of *Prologhi*, entitled 'Silenzio della

---

[28] In his review of Cardarelli's first collection of prose and poetry, 'Testimonianze
classiche', Cecchi wrote on this point: 'La materia spogliata fino al disumano, dà
uno smarrimento, un'angoscia di funebre e gelato petrarchismo.'

creazione' amounts, like the initial composition, to an assertion of the value of stoicism. It implies that man may attain a dominant faith in the future if he is able to achieve a mental attitude which is defined in the following terms:

Distrutti gl'idoli e smesso di chiederci le ragioni; abbandonata in un'esperienza indiscutibilmente amara ogni innocenza carnale; . . . esaurite le impossibilità, provocati tutti i limiti; pieni d'ironia verso ogni promessa, diffidenti contro ogni suggestione.

[When we have destroyed our idols and stopped looking for reasons; when we have abandoned, in what is an undeniably bitter experience, every carnal innocence; . . . when we have exhausted all the impossibilities, and tried all the limitations; when we are full of irony towards every promise, and distrustful of every suggestion.]

The conspicuous occurrence of semantically similar verbs such as 'distruggere', 'abbandonare', and 'esaurire' makes it clear that if a certain acceptance of man's condition can be reached then it is at the cost of shedding the most basic elements of human motivation. The solution that is proposed is in itself, therefore, pessimistic and of appeal only to the Nietzschean figure of the superman. But the blank assertions which typify the message of 'Silenzio della creazione' are reworked in a more complex and subtle form in the two seasonal lyrics of *Prologhi*, 'Saluto di stagione' and 'Estiva', poems which should be read as hymns to an ideal of indifference.

Particularly in 'Saluto di stagione' the seasons of the year form symbolic representations of clearly identifiable psychological states. Beyond its literal significance, spring acts as a metaphor for a restless and changeable condition of mind, one which the speaker is anxious to distance himself from:

Lascio la primavera
dietro di me
come un amore insano
d'adolescente.

[I leave spring | behind me | like an unwholesome | adolescent love affair.]

By contrast, in the terms of its metaphorical transfer,

summer stands for an idealized mental attitude of the stoic,
one which subsumes clarity, maturity and above all serenity:

> Benvenuta estate.
> Alla tua decisa maturità
> m'affido.. . .
> che amo i tempi fermi e le superficie chiare.

[Welcome summer. | To your decisive maturity | I entrust myself . . . | I
love still time and clear surfaces.]

Yet if the notion of summer provides the medium through
which an inner state of being can be communicated that
medium is deliberately ambiguous. Earlier I mentioned the
way in which the subject's excessive tendency towards rati-
ocination promotes a funereal awareness of nothingness. In
'Saluto di stagione', and to a lesser degree in 'Estiva', the
mental state of which summer is the symbol is close in its
attributes to a condition of non-being. The adjectives which
are employed to evoke the presence of the season do not
suggest warmth, colour, or activity but the absence of such
properties. Summer in the two poems is imbued with a
tomb-like quality: its dawns are 'noiseless', its days 'equal' or
'identical', its moments static. The season brings with it 'the
rhythm of eternity' ('Estiva'). Summer like death is a silent
force to which the speaking voice consciously decides to
yield and the verbs in the opening section of 'Saluto di
stagione', all placed in the first person ('I entrust myself . . . I
shall rest . . . I shall exchange . . . I shall leave') express, with
varying degrees of explicitness, a desire to relinquish personal identity. It is, however, in the final lines of the lyric that
the dual nature of the tenor of the metaphor of which
summer is the vehicle attains its greatest level of prominence:

> Ai punti estremi, alle stagioni violente,
> come sotto il frantoio dei pericoli
> dove ogni inquietudine si schianta
> prendo le sole decisioni buone,
> la mia fuggiasca fecondità
> ritrovo.

[At points of extremity, in violent seasons, | as if under the press of danger

| under which every preoccupation is crushed | I take only the right decisions, | and find again | my fleeting productivity.]

When these lines are placed securely within the context of the speaker's overriding desire to achieve and affirm self-mastery, then the reading which they suggest is that im-passivity, metaphorically communicated as the season of summer, dissipates illusion, fear, and concern, while simul-taneously performing a function like that of death. Acting with implicit violence at 'a point of extremity', summer promotes the imposition of an unalterable silence. As is the case with many of the other pieces, whether in prose or in poetry, the self is the unstated yet willing victim of its own mental processes.

The nihilist tension regarding death is by no means unique to 'Saluto di stagione'; other lyrics play upon notions of extinction: 'Stanchezza' concludes with the expression 'my exhaustion is mortal', and the prose fragment 'Pausa' ends with the declaration: 'It is necessary that I do not hear, that I do not see and that I do not exist any longer.' Yet, the poem which, although not included in *Prologhi*, bears the greatest resemblance to 'Saluto' is 'Homo sum'.[29] The lyric, addressing notions of retribution and expiation, is con-structed almost entirely of fiscal language and similes: the concept of spiritual atonement is represented by the mater-ial act of settling an account; divine justice comes in the form of a visit from the bailiffs of God, and the preventative act of self-castigation is symbolized by the anticipatory act of payment. The speaking subject of the poem does not lead the worried and precarious existence of the debtor, for he scrupulously pays what he owes, recognizing the justice of the charge. Yet 'Homo sum', despite its opening, does not function as a robust affirmation of moral autonomy: the defiant sequence of declarations which constitutes the first part of the poem is undermined by its concluding simile:

> Talvolta infatti io mi vedo come uno
> di quei poveri santi
> che sulle tele delle sacrestie

---

[29] 'Homo sum' was first published in the journal *Lirica* in December 1913.

> stanno in adorazione della Vergine,
> inutilmente aspettando
> un suo sguardo.

[Sometimes I see myself as one | of those poor saints | who on paintings in sacristies | kneel in adoration of the Virgin, | uselessly waiting for a glance from her.]

The total appeasement of conscience elevates the self to an exalted ethical station, and yet that exaltation entails the suppression of its vital but dispersive instincts. The final lines of 'Homo sum', in common with those of 'Saluto di stagione', evoke a character who, by force of will and a punishing moral code, has deprived himself of his vitality and, fixed in a gesture of propitiation, has achieved a permanent state of immobility. Again the parallel can be made with the movement towards death which seems the inevitable result of Papini's ambition to attain the status of genius. He writes in *Un uomo finito*: 'Everything or nothing! And I wanted always everything—nothing should escape or be excluded! Completeness and totality—with nothing left to desire. And afterwards, the end, immobility, death!' (p. 23).

In the prose pieces of *Prologhi* the drive towards an idealization of the self is relatively uncomplicated, but the more the poems are exposed to scrutiny the more troubled and problematic that drive becomes. The cultivation of properties which transcend an ordinary range of emotional experience leads ambiguously towards perceptions of sterility, even annihilation. The essentially contradictory nature of the psychical workings that motivate the poetry is succinctly foregrounded by the two lines which alone form the substance of 'Psicologia': 'If there is something which I respect it is limitation. If there is something which I do not know it is limitation.' The opening towards the possibility of adventure or sensual experience together with a subsequent reimposition of the inhibiting power of the intellect provides the structural framework for the two poems of the collection which most regularly find their way into anthologies of twentieth-century Italian verse, but which cannot be understood unless they are placed in the specific self-obsessed climate of *Prologhi*, 'Adolescente' and 'Incontro notturno'.

More descriptive of striking aspects of the external world than any other composition within *Prologhi*, the two lyrics occupy a somewhat anomalous position within Cardarelli's abstract, cerebral autobiography, and in their original edition were both placed in a subsection of the work, 'Fonti nascoste', the title containing an implicit acknowledgement of the diversity of the two poems with regard to the others in the collection.

Both lyrics begin with a rhetorical figure upon which many of the prose pieces rely, namely the apostrophe. But while the rhetorical device, when used in the prose, invariably introduces a barrage of accusations, in the two poems its function is to convey an appreciation of the other which is as unqualified as it is uncharacteristic. The reverential tone of the initial stanzas provides an absolute contrast with the aggressive and denigratory style of those prologues in prose where another protagonist is the object of the narrator's discourse. More importantly, in the prose any other figures which appear beyond the narrator remain at the level of pure abstraction, while in 'Adolescente' and 'Incontro notturno' two sharply and physically delineated creations stand out from the verse. In 'Incontro notturno' the romantic figure of an outcast, nonchalantly living on the margins of society, initially implies the awe of the speaker:

> Ah, vagabondo, gli esseri come te!
> Con le tue scarpe di tela bianche,
> i vasti pantaloni di velluto,
> e un sigaro spento che pende
> fra le tue labbra
> come un proposito dimenticato, . . .
> tu sei capace di aver visitato
> tutti gli scali del mondo.
> Hai fatto non una, ma dieci
> e dieci spedizioni di Colombo,
> tu, per il Globo.

[Ah, vagabond, beings like you! | With your white canvas shoes, | and your wide velvet trousers, | and a cigar hanging | from your lips | like a forgotten remark, . . . you've probably visited | all the ports of the world. | You've made not one but tens | of expeditions like Columbus | across the globe.]

But as the poem progresses the initially striking outcast is

gradually worn down to become a pathetic character, unable
to sustain the depth of his solitude and craving comfort from
those whom he encounters.

In 'Adolescente'[30] the relationship between the figure
and the speaking subject is that between a physically self-
possessed individual and a more meditative observer:

> Su te, vergine adolescente,
> sta come un'ombra sacra.
> Nulla è più misterioso
> e adorabile e proprio della
> tua carne spogliata. . . .
> Se ti veggo passare
> a tanto regale distanza,
> con la tua chioma sciolta
> e tutta la persona astata,
> la vertigine mi si porta via.

[Over you, adolescent virgin, I hovers a sacred shadow. I Nothing is more
mysterious I and adorable and appropriate I than your bared flesh. . . . I If
I should see you pass I at such a regal distance I with your hair let down I
and your whole person held erect, I I should be overcome with dizzi-
ness].[31]

In the opening stanza of the lyric, the mythical aura sur-
rounding the figure hints at the powerful effect that is
exerted on the observer. Yet what justifies the inclusion of
the composition, with its voyeuristic overtones, in so abstract
and egocentric a collection as *Prologhi* is that the real subject
of the poem is not the 'adolescente' at all but the corrosive
nature of the rational speculations to which she is progressively subjected. If the strong sensuousness of the language
in the first part of the poem indicates the intrusion of a
startling figure from the physical world into the consciousness of the narrator, in the second and third stanzas the

[30] Luperini has compared this lyric interestingly with Montale's famous composition 'Falsetto'. Romano Luperini, *Il Novecento: Apparati ideologici, ceto intellettuale, sistemi formali nella letteratura italiana contemporanea*, 4th edn., 2 vols. (Turin:
Loescher, 1994), i. 317.

[31] The translation of 'Adolescente' is by the Irish poet Desmond O'Grady and
was orginally published in the volume *Off Licence* (Dublin: Dolmen Press, 1968).
The translation, together with other translations of Cardarelli's poems, is included
in the article by Alessandro Gentili, 'Per un ritorno alla "parabola" poetica di
Cardarelli', *Tuttitalia*, 7 (June 1993), 26–36.

cerebral processes of the speaker sadistically reassert themselves. The tone of the lyric shifts from reverential to rati-
ocinative, as the authorial presence which is known to us
from the other prologues sees through the phenomenal
world to an invisible logical order. Sensory experience is
raised to an evaluative plane and the status of the figure is
reduced from that of an object of desire to that of an abstract
entity. In *Un uomo finito* the narrator becomes increasingly
aware of a trajectory which is leading inevitably towards
nothingness: 'I know that nothing will come of our efforts; I
know that the end of everything is nothing; I know that the
recompense for every work, at the end of the progression of
centuries, will be nothing, absolutely nothing' (p. 296). In
the latter part of 'Adolescente' the richness of the outside
world is transformed into a series of lapidary statements all
of which insist upon the destructive passage of time and the
nearness of an encounter with nothingness which will involve both the observer and the observed. As the speaker in
'Dati biografici' informs his reader, in his lyrics he produces
'ordini e non figure':

> E tutto è così.
> Tu anche non sai chi sei.
> E prendere ti lascerai,
> ma per vedere come il gioco è fatto,
> per ridere un poco insieme.
> Come fiamma si perde nella luce
> al tocco della realtà
> i misteri che tu prometti
> si disciolgono in nulla.

[And everything is like that. | You too do not know who you are. | And you
will allow yourself to be taken, | just to see how the game is played, | in
order to laugh a little together. | Like a flame that is lost in the light | at
the touch of reality | the mysteries that you promise dissolve into noth-
ingness.]

The writings of *Prologhi* begin to define a personality which
conceives of morality, not in terms of responsibility to others
but of conflict and self-affirmation. The writings define a self
which seeks to gain mastery over its surroundings and over
others, even to the extent of annihilating both. Any external

object is transformed into an aspect of the self. The more aggressively the self seeks to attain power over that which lies beyond its boundaries, the more enhanced is its sense of self. Like the majority of metaphysical autobiographies associated with *La Voce*, *Prologhi* aims to represent the acquisition of intellectual greatness. It sets out to create patterns of dominance and subordination in a way that is closely analogous to Papini's *Un uomo finito*, and despite the level of abstraction which it attains, the work does offer some uncomfortable similarities with Soffici's *Lemmonio Boreo*. But there are paradoxes in the self which is articulated through *Prologhi*. The aggression which is its defining principle becomes the force which most threatens its being. The protagonist's drive towards self-expression through affirmations of intellectual domination tends on the one hand to enforce the self's dependency on a concept of relationality, while on the other it encourages a sense of self-annihilation. In its striving to assert the autonomy of the speaking subject, *Prologhi* betrays the extent of Cardarelli's reception of Nietzsche's and of Weininger's thinking.[32] At the same time the text indicates a certain nihilism inherent within the theories which it has appropriated. After the war Cardarelli, in his attempt to define a more classical kind of literary composition, was to renounce his attachment to Nietzsche and to other thinkers admired by the *vociani*. But what is interesting about many of the texts which he was to write under Fascism is that they are equally preoccupied with the psychic drives of a domineering self, only in a less overtly aggressive form.

[32] As indicated, Martignoni has looked at the borrowings which Cardarelli made from Nietzsche's *Thus Spake Zarathustra*, but more could be said on the dependency of Cardarelli and of other *vociani* on the theories of Weininger.

3

THE RESTORATION OF POLITICAL AND LITERARY ORDER

Italy after the War: The Rise of Fascism

The First World War ended for Italy on 4 November 1918. Although victorious, the country emerged from the conflict facing enormous economic, social, and political problems. Those groups which had militated for Italian intervention, believing that participation in a major conflict would by itself produce a radical and irreversible change in the way in which society operated, were to be proved correct. To begin with, the post-war government of Vittorio Emanuele Orlando (who had become prime minister in the wake of Caporetto) faced the task of changing the country's economy to accommodate the new realities of peace despite Italy's massive budget deficit. The end of the war meant the immediate and drastic reduction in demand for the products which heavy industry had been geared to produce. Such a reduction inevitably entailed the laying off of workers who had previously been regularly employed. Further, enormous numbers of men who had seen service in the trenches and who had been encouraged by promises of a brighter future after the war found themselves demobilized but unemployed and with few prospects of changing the situation in which they found themselves. In November 1919 the number of people unemployed reached 2 million. To add to the country's problems, inflation was increasing alarmingly, destroying savings and reducing the value of wages.

During the brief period in which he held office, Orlando failed to tackle successfully any of the major problems facing Italy: in the words of Roberto Vivarelli, his 'inaction was almost total'.[1] But surprisingly it was not domestic but

---

[1] 'Di fronte agli aspetti economici come a quelli psicologici del problema della smobilitazione . . . l'inazione del gabinetto Orlando fu pressoché totale.' Vivarelli, *Storia delle origini del fascismo*, i. 404.

foreign policy which led to Orlando's downfall: he resigned when he failed to secure Italy's claims in the Adriatic at the Paris Peace Conference. The refusal of the Allied powers to respect Italy's claims served to encourage the belief among many important sections of Italian society that the country's hard-earned victory had partly been in vain.[2] The Nationalists spoke of a 'mutilated victory', and D'Annunzio's personal and highly problematic annexation of Fiume in September 1919 was a direct result of the perceived failures of Italy's post-war government. In June 1919 Orlando was replaced by Francesco Nitti, who was prepared to take a more compromising line over Italy's ambitions in the Adriatic, aware that the country depended on continuing aid from Britain and the United States to avoid economic collapse. Indeed, Nitti made a more serious attempt than his predecessor to deal with the problems which arose in the wake of mass demobilization. He was able to make considerable reductions in military spending, even if in the process he incurred the hostility of many sections within the army. He was, however, unable to gain the support of the Socialists for his programme of moderate and progressive reforms, and proved himself inept at forming the coalitions which were necessary to steer legislation through parliament. His failure in this area was to pave the way for a return to power of Giolitti.

As well as failing to implement a set of urgent economic reforms, the governments of the immediate post-war period also failed to deal adequately with the social unrest generated by the economic crisis and by the widespread feeling of popular resentment against those classes who were considered to have profited from the war. The year 1919 witnessed a spate of demonstrations which by no means involved only the urban working classes. The increase in the cost of living provoked even schoolteachers and elements within the clergy to demonstrate in favour of improved conditions. In the same year, demobilized soldiers returning to agricultural jobs, especially in Lazio, began to stage

---

[2] In the words of Adrian Lyttelton, 'Italy acquired the psychology of a defeated nation'. *The Seizure of Power: Fascism in Italy 1919–1929* (London: Weidenfeld & Nicolson, 1973), 30.

occupations of property belonging to the landowning classes. There were riots at the increase in prices, in particular the price of food. Many disputes resulted in violence or renewed unrest. If many demonstrations occurred locally as a result of problems faced by specific groups within society, then other disputes were planned more centrally. Although the PSI did not instigate many of the clashes between demonstrators and the forces of order, it did play an active role in protesting against the institutions and policies of the post-war Liberal governments. During this period the intransigent wing of the PSI asserted its command over the party, the democratic interventionists among the reformist Socialists having lost a lot of ground when Italy failed to gain either Fiume or Dalmatia at the Peace Conference. The PSI continued its attack on those parties which had supported intervention, and continued to expose the idea of 'patria' as a bourgeois myth which had encouraged ordinary workers to participate in a struggle between imperial powers. The party militated for the appropriation by the workers of the means of production and for goods to be distributed through workers' co-operatives. The struggle for radical reform in which the Socialists were engaged was lent particular impetus by the example of the successful Russian Revolution. Under its editor Giacinto Menotti Serrati, *Avanti!* continually exalted the achievements of Lenin and his followers while making a series of declarations of war against the prevailing bourgeois order in Italy.

Already in early 1919 the revolutionary propaganda of the PSI was serving as a focal point for the forces of reaction. The Nationalist Party had emerged greatly strengthened from the war: while having seen some of its aims fulfilled it was in a position to castigate the government for failing to pursue other objectives. It had witnessed the development of industries whose owners were well disposed towards its cause, and it had seen the dramatic rise of militarism. Major exponents of the Nationalist Party such as Enrico Corradini and Alfreddo Rocco, while advocating an imperialist foreign policy, emphasized the value of discipline and the need for the individual to submit to the needs of the collective. In favour of authoritarian government and a repressive internal policy, the Nationalist Party, to use Vivarelli's terms, presented itself as 'the ideology of permanent counter-revolution'.[3] Adopting positions close to those of the Nationalist Party and sharing many of its points of cultural reference was Mussolini. He had emerged from the war with a degree of uncertainty as to what course of action to follow. Both the death of Filippo Corridoni and the adoption by the PSI of a *massimalista* position meant that radical syndicalism no longer functioned as an autonomous political force after the war. Moreover, Mussolini had began to adopt a political stance which was geared more towards the defence of the rights of the bourgeoisie. From August 1918 his newspaper, *Il popolo d'Italia*, officially dropped its pretension to be a leftist publication and became the mouthpiece of 'combatants and producers'.

In part the change in direction of Mussolini's politics was motivated by the fierceness of his opposition to the Socialists, guilty in his opinion both of having opposed Italy's intervention in the war and of having militated against the concept of national solidarity. In part also Mussolini was concerned to make himself the interpreter of the 'hopes of the war' and to exploit popular nationalistic sentiment. In his desire to remain receptive to changes in the popular mood, he was careful to avoid too close an association with any one group or set of ideas, and willing to be flexible.[4] On 23 March 1919, in a building in Piazza San Sepolcro in Milan, Mussolini founded his own political movement, the Fasci di Combattimento. The association, as its name indicated, was largely a continuation of the groups or *fasci* which had been formed to agitate for intervention. The core of the movement's membership was initially made up of former Arditi (shock troops) and of Futurists. The new grouping set out with a political programme which was very broad but at the same time unmistakably reactionary. The Fasci di Combattimento would militate for an aggressive foreign policy; they

    [3] Vivarelli, *Storia delle origini del fascismo*, i. 297.
    [4] As he was to write on 11 Aug. 1918 in *Il popolo d'Italia*: 'Un uomo intelligente non può essere una cosa sola. . . . Deve mutare. Non si può essere sempre socialisti, sempre repubblicani, sempre anarchici, sempre conservatori. Lo spirito è soprattutto "mobilità".' The statement is discussed in Vivarelli's *Storia delle origini del fascismo*, i. 299.

would defend the interests of those who had fought in the war, but above all they would sabotage the progress of those parties which had advocated Italian neutrality.

With the intent of presenting an armed resistance to the Socialist threat, *fasci* were formed in Rome, Turin, and many of the major towns of Italy. In the first half of 1919 they had attracted an impressive body of support including Nationalists, veterans, and militant students. The readiness with which anti-Socialist gangs were prepared to use violence was shown when on 15 April 1919 an improvised demonstration headed by Marinetti and others had successfully confronted a Socialist march and had then gone on to burn down the offices of *Avanti!* It was the use of violence, or more specifically the formation of para-military 'squads', which allowed the Fascist movement, whose electoral results were initially poor, to develop with astonishing rapidity. In late 1920 in north and central Italy squads of local Fascists, with the support of small leaseholders and ordinary agricultural workers, made countless violent attacks against the Socialists, their local party headquarters, councils, and labour leagues. During such actions, the civil authorities, whose loyalties to the Liberal state could reasonably be questioned, either abstained from intervening or acted with 'gross partiality'.[5] In the words of Martin Clark: 'the red provinces of Po Valley and of Tuscany were transformed, sometimes in only a few weeks, from being the home of the most powerful peasant unions in Europe to being the main strongholds of the Fascist squads'.[6]

Mussolini was able to watch the surge in support for the reactionary violence of the Fascist squads. The persistent fear of a Bolshevik-style revolution, inspired in the middle classes by the prolonged occupation of the factories in September 1920, helped to ensure such support. In response to the *squadrismo* of the Fascists, the PSI was neither able to organize its own defensive strategy nor to form an effective alliance with other groups in parliament. The position of the Socialists was further weakened when the Communist faction seceded at the Livorno party conference in

[5] See Lyttelton, *The Seizure of Power*, 40.
[6] Clark, *Modern Italy 1871–1982*, p. 216.

January 1921. Strengthened by the tacit support of elements within the Liberal establishment and more explicitly by the Liberal press, the Fasci di Combattimento were becoming a mass movement. Fascist syndicates rapidly began to take over defeated Socialist unions and the Partito Nazionale Fascista (PNF) was formed. The governments which were in office in the period leading up to the march on Rome were unable to stem the tide of Fascist violence. In the wake of Nitti's failure to gather support for his reforms, Giovanni Giolitti had returned to office in June 1920. Unable to secure the support of the reformist Socialists and at odds with Don Sturzo's Popolari, he resigned as prime minister after the elections of May 1921 left him with no realistic possibility of forming a viable coalition. His successors, the reformist Socialist Ivanoe Bonomi (prime minister from June 1921 to February 1922) and the Liberal Luigi Facta (prime minister from February to October 1922) were not decisive enough leaders with strong enough followings in parliament to attempt the suppression of the lawless activities of the Fascist squads.

During the months in which the campaign of terror against the PSI was at its height, Mussolini was able to present himself as the only politician able to restrain the spate of reactionary violence. In autumn 1922, when a new governmental coalition was in the process of being formed, he made it clear that the PNF, with its means of exerting pressure and its depth of popular support, could not be excluded. Indeed, he was confident that by assuming the role of the saviour of the nation he could form his own government. What he feared was that both the king and the forces of parliament might unite around Giolitti to impede his achievement of power. It was in part to obviate that danger that the PNF decided on 16 October 1922 to mobilize its forces and, with the support of sections within the army, march on Rome and occupy public offices and buildings. Rivalries between different Liberal politicians, the procrastination of Giolitti, and Mussolini's ability to play one parliamentary faction off against another through a series of deceitful negotiations meant that by the time that the Fascist insurrection was imminent, no concrete measures of

resistance had been put in force. On the night of the 27–8
October organized bands of Fascist militants, who encountered varying degrees of resistance, took over public buildings and telegraph offices in provincial towns throughout
north and central Italy. In Rome, the king initially seemed
prepared to oppose Fascist pressure by signing a decree
establishing martial law. However, doubting the loyalty of
the army, he failed to act in time and by 28 October the
march on Rome had effectively proved successful. Mussolini
was invited by the king to form a new government.

The War and the Vociani

Along with other Nationalist and avant-garde groups the
vociani had done their utmost to ensure Italian intervention
in the First World War. With the country's entry into the
conflict in 1915 it seemed to many of them that at last the
changes for which they had militated would become realities. The complacency and mediocrity which they believed
were fundamental characteristics of Giolitti's Italy would be
replaced by a new mentality as a new ruling class emerged
from the war. The 'moral revolution' for which the *vociani*
had worked both directly through their journalism and
indirectly through their more literary texts would finally be
accomplished by the myth of war. Yet it is a curious paradox
that the war, while in one sense it marked the triumph of
La Voce, also coincided with its demise. The war years witnessed the disappearance of some of the more prominent
vociani: Scipio Slataper, Renato Serra, and Carlo Stuparich
were killed in action; Giovanni Boine, whose *Discorsi militari*
(1915) had been distributed among Italian soldiers as a
potential source of inspiration, died of tuberculosis in October 1917. For some writers associated with *La Voce*, the first-
hand experience of death and destruction marked a
profound change in direction. The poet Clemente Rebora,
whose work *Frammenti lirici* (1913) had been described by
Boine as expressing more powerfully than any other 'the
intense moral seriousness of the new generation',[7] retreated

---

[7] Boine's review of Rebora's *Frammenti lirici* is now contained in the collected
works of Boine, ed. Puccini, pp. 115–20.

into Roman Catholicism after the war and subsequently wrote verse of an exclusively religious character.

Prezzolini had been quick to enrol and to move up to the front, but his experience of life in the trenches was soon to lead to a sense of disillusionment. He became aware that the majority of Italian soldiers were not eager participants in the war: many were in fact keen to return home, while others were actively hostile to those who were known to have played an important role in the campaign for intervention. In his letters to his friends from the front Prezzolini began to express his growing lack of faith in the sort of intellectual movement that he had once inspired.[8] Although he was later to write for Mussolini's *Il popolo d'Italia*, he was not to prove a staunch supporter of Fascism. Indeed, he argued increasingly for an attitude of disengagement. In one article ('Per una società degli Apoti', *La Rivoluzione liberale*, 28 September 1922, p. 103) he argued for the establishment of a society for those intellectuals who were able to stand back from the turbulent political situation and not fall victim to those proposing facile solutions. In 1925 he moved to Paris, and four years later he moved to New York to take up a teaching post at Columbia University.

The disappointment that Prezzolini experienced was certainly shared by some of his former colleagues, many of whom began to re-examine beliefs that had once seemed fundamental. Serra, for example, wrote a subtle but critical assessment of the intellectual climate which had prevailed before the war. In his *Le lettere* (1915) he claimed that the ethically charged form of writing which the *vociani* had cultivated in their aggressive autobiographies had led to an impasse. Referring to the title of Papini's work, *Un uomo finito*, he claimed that a feeling of exhaustion was common to all the writers of his generation.[9] In his *Esame di coscienza di un letterato* (1915), written shortly before his death, he expressed his scepticism that the war, so ardently desired by

---

[8] For a good discussion of the development of Prezzolini's thought at this stage in his career see Adamson, *Avant-Garde Florence*, 204–9.

[9] At one stage in *Le lettere* Serra wrote: 'Qualcuno parla addirittura dell'uomo finito, e tutti sentono che c'è del vero; qualche cosa è finita, se non nello scrittore lontano, certo nelle coscienze nostre che hanno superato anche questi.' R. Serra, *Scritti*, ed. M. Isenghi (Turin: Einaudi, 1974), 257.

many of his associates, would produce any kind of positive change: 'What will have changed when the tired earth has drunk the blood of so many sacrifices; when the dead, the wounded, the tortured and the abandoned will sleep together under its surface and the grass above will again be tender and new, full of silence and richness under the sun of spring which never changes?'.[10]

In 1915 Prezzolini ceded the editorship of *La Voce* to the writer and critic Giuseppe De Robertis. With the change in editorship, the journal effectively lost its impetus as a vehicle for the rejuvenation of Italian society and it began to publish only critical and creative writings. While the newly constituted journal, or *La Voce bianca* as it became known, never printed a programmatic statement, it was clear that it favoured a form of literary composition which concentrated less upon the revelation of a writer's self and more upon exquisite technical refinement. In one editorial piece, De Robertis expressed his impatience with the moralistic language that most writers associated with *La Voce* had adopted, and with the uncompromisingly autobiographical character of their works. He declared that the first duty of modern writers was not to indulge so often in washing what he called their dirty linen in public.[11] It is possible, from the very tone of such remarks, to gain an impression of the extent to which *La Voce* had become a shadow of the combative journal that Prezzolini and Papini had set up in 1908. De Robertis's comments also usefully indicated a tendency among a certain group of intellectuals to turn away from the dramatic political realities which the country faced both during and after the war.

Among the most regular contributors to the literary *Voce*

---

[10] 'Che cosa è che cambierà su questa terra stanca, dopo che avrà bevuto il sangue di tanta strage: quando i morti e i feriti, i torturati e gli abbandonati dormiranno insieme sotto le zolle, e l'erba sopra sarà tenera lucida nuova, piena di silenzio e di lusso al sole della primavera che è sempre la stessa?' *Esame di coscienza di un letterato* (Milan: Treves, 1915); the quotation is taken from the edition by B. Tonzar (Pordenone: Edizioni Studio Tesi, 1994), 30.

[11] 'Ma psicologia e confessione non sono arte. E i poeti che veramente realizzano, uccidono queste sostanze greggie in forme vive. Anche se in pochi segni e linee a cui gli altri disperano di arrivare. Prima moralità oggi sarebbe di non risciacquare tutti questi panni; troppi panni; fuori di casa.' G. De Robertis, 'Primavera agra', *La Voce*, 15 Apr. 1915, p. 302.

were Arturo Onofri, a symbolist poet, Carlo Linati, a writer
of elegantly crafted impressions of country scenes, and,
surprisingly, Giovanni Papini. Papini had been one of the
most noisy and most irresponsible advocates of military
action: in one of his articles for *Lacerba* he wrote that a 'hot
bath of black blood was necessary' and that 'brothers have
always been good at killing brothers'.[12] Because of his poor
eyesight, however, he did not participate in the conflict. A
perception of the disparity between the role which he had
assumed before and during the war led him to publish an
article explaining the paradoxes of his situation: the piece
he wrote was entitled 'La mia vigliaccheria' ('My Cowardice').[13] The awareness of his unenviable position was accompanied by a more profound reassessment of the values which
he had advocated while one of the most prominent figures
of the pre-war avant-garde. Such a reassessment led first to a
disengagement with both politics and the business of cultural organization. Instead of writing inflammatory rhetoric
as he had done on the eve of the war, Papini began to devote
his attention to writing poetry, a good deal of which was
published in the *Voce* of De Robertis. As the war reached its
final stages, he made a further move towards an acceptance
of the established order which he had earlier done so much
to challenge. In the spring of 1918 he converted to Roman
Catholicism. His conversion made it abundantly clear that
he deemed the avant-garde's attempt to create a new faith
and a new man to have failed. In 1921 he published a
lengthy and well-received work on the life of Christ, *La storia
di Cristo*. While engaged in the writing of his new book he
explained to Prezzolini: 'it has become increasingly difficult
for me to become impassioned about what is generally called
politics'.[14] It was not until the 1930s that he began to regain
an interest in politics and to align himself strongly with
Fascism.

[12] G. Papini, 'Amiamo la guerra!', *Lacerba*, 1 Oct. 1914, p. 274.

[13] The article appeared as the preface to the collection of articles published
under the title of *La paga del sabato* (Milan: Studio Editoriale Lombardo, 1915).

[14] Papini's letter to Prezzolini was dated 4 Oct. 1919. It is included in the
collection of their correspondence, *Storia di un'amicizia*, 2 vols. (Florence: Vallecchi, 1966), ii. 317–18. The letter is quoted in Adamson, *Avant-Garde Florence*,
239.

Together with Prezzolini and the majority of the Futurists, Soffici saw action in the First World War. His experience as an officer, unlike that of Prezzolini, did not engender a sense of futility or dissatisfaction. Both during and after the war he wrote positively about the life of Italian soldiers facing the Austrian enemy. The two works he published were *Kobilek* (1918) and *La ritirata del Friuli* (1919). In the aftermath of the war he did not withdraw temporarily from the world of politics as Papini had felt compelled to do. He wrote a number of articles for Mussolini's newspaper *Il popolo d'Italia* inveighing against the 'cowardice' of the Socialists and the corruption of the Liberal politicians. In one article, 'Sfogo naturale', he wrote of the need for a violent reaction which would once and for all dissipate the Socialist menace.[15] The sort of language which he used in this article together with the sort of solution which he posited recalled his earlier *Lemmonio Boreo*. Indeed, from the beginning Soffici lent his support to the Fascist reaction, and he seemed to have no qualms about the violence with which it set about achieving its goals. However, he did fall short of becoming its most vociferous apologist (a role that fell to Curzio Malaparte), and he did not participate in the march on Rome. At the same time, moreover, that he was writing articles explicitly in support of Mussolini's movement, he was also claiming a certain detachment from some of the more subversive statements he had made as a contributor to both *La Voce* and *Lacerba*.

In March 1920 he began to publish, without the aid of any other contributors, the quarterly journal, *Rete mediterranea*. In the 'Dichiarazione preliminare' of his new journal he declared that he had emerged from the war a different man. He argued that his experience with other common soldiers in the trenches, at all times facing death, had made him aware of the pretentiousness of some of the attitudes which he and others had assumed before the war.[16] He claimed to

---

[15] He wrote: 'Un giorno, qualcuno o qualcosa verrà che, con un soffio violento o un atto fiammeggiante, spazzerà via tutto questo sterco; farà sparire tutte queste vergogne, queste uniliazioni e stupidità.' The article was contained in *Battaglia fra due vittorie* (Florence: La Voce, 1923). It is reprinted in Soffici's *Opere*, vi. 334–40.

[16] He wrote: 'La morte presente e permanente nella zona delle battaglie, l'atmosfera di morte in cui si muove, che si respira, e dove tutto acquista un

have rid himself of a belief in his own grandeur and of a desire to achieve novelty at all costs in his work as both artist and writer. In place of youthful arrogance he claimed to have discovered 'maturity' and a renewed appreciation of traditions which he had earlier dismissed. At the same time that Soffici was expressing views of this kind, other artists were moving to similar conclusions. During the war Carlo Carrà had begun to dissociate himself from Futurism and to develop an appreciation of the painting of Giotto and the Renaissance. Likewise Giorgio de Chirico became interested in the technical methods of the Italian classical tradition. In November 1918 Mario Broglio founded the art journal *Valori plastici*, which became both the vehicle for the theory of metaphysical painting and the expression of a classical reaction against the preceding avant-garde experimentalism.

Whatever the extent of the correspondence between Soffici's post-war thoughts on composition and those of other leading artists, it is clear that he saw support for violent political reaction as entirely consonant with a new-found respect for order and tradition in artistic and literary matters. As he became more involved in Fascism he began to articulate more elaborate theories on the extent to which modes of composition could reflect political ideologies. In his article 'Il fascismo e l'arte',[17] for example, he contended that nothing would be more sterile than an art form which slavishly set out to convey the message of one political party. He argued instead that political and aesthetic principles were motivated by the same philosophical and moral impulses, and that literary movements could act to further the aims of political groupings without being placed at their service. He expressed his dislike for any movement which drew its inspiration from foreign ideas, and suggested that if the 'parties of order' wanted a state that was 'architecturally solid, strong and disciplined, hierarchically ordered and respectful of every good Italian tradition' then it was their

carattere grande di serietà, di purezza, di terribile austerità, fu per la mia anima come un bagno salutare dal quale uscii purgato e rinfrescato.' 'Dichiarazione preliminare', *Rete mediterranea* (Mar. 1920), 3.

[17] The article is contained in the volume *Battaglia fra due vittorie*, now in Soffici, *Opere*, vi. 353–60.

duty to promote cultural movements which advanced such ideals in their aesthetic theory and practice. He chose to characterize such movements with one word, 'classical'. Important as Soffici's early support for Fascism and his surprising advocacy of traditionalism were, it was not his journal, *Rete mediterranea*, which succeeded in defining a post-war climate of literary reaction. The role of uniting intellectuals with an avant-garde past in the pursuit of a renewed sense of order fell to the understandably maligned journal that Cardarelli and his associates set up in 1919, *La Ronda*.

La Ronda *and Cardarelli's Return to Order*

Like Papini, Cardarelli did not take part in the First World War owing to health problems. In common with many other writers who had been associated with *La Voce*, he was nevertheless profoundly affected by the war. In one of his letters to Cecchi he described the sensation of living under a malevolent spell, not knowing which of his friends would be wounded or killed.[18] The second-hand experience of the war caused him to reconsider some of the assumptions which he had made in the years of the Florentine avant-garde. To begin with, he began to object to examples of the morally committed criticism prized by the *vociani* and which he himself had earlier aspired to write.[19] Equally, he began to express his dissatisfaction with his metaphysical autobiography, *Prologhi*. In a letter to Soffici dated 17 January 1916[20] he voiced his fear that the text was associated too closely with the culture of Prezzolini's *Voce* ('That book is already too far behind') and therefore out of touch with a literary climate radically altered by the reality of war. What is striking about

---

[18] In a letter dated 4 Aug. 1917 he wrote: 'Ma chi resterà? Io ho l'impressione di essere sotto un incanto malefico. È l'influsso della guerra a distanza. È la morte che non impunemente può passarci accanto': *Epistolario*, ii. 601.

[19] Commenting to Cecchi on a copy of Slataper's monongraph on Ibsen, he disparaged what he considered the simplistic and moralistic nature of Slataper's critical lexicon: 'E poi c'è l'eterno dramma, il linguaggio etico, le solite tirate patetiche e sentimentali sui grandi. Queste cose non mi vanno.' Letter dated 9 Apr. 1917: *Epistolario*, ii. 570.

[20] *Epistolario*, ii. 479.

many of his appraisals of his own recent work is their uncompromising severity. In a letter to Antonio Baldini, for instance, he expressed the melancholy he felt about having a past in which he no longer believed and his desire not to talk about his former sympathy for avant-garde writing.[21] Assertions like these occur time and again in his letters to his closest friends, suggesting that he was not merely disappointed with his recent past as a *moralista vociano*, but ashamed of it.

The idea of setting up a literary journal is one that he had entertained since 1913. It is clear from his private correspondence that he spent a large part of that year discussing with friends what the aims of the proposed new periodical should have been and which writers should have been encouraged to contribute. Although few records of the original aims of the journal survive, Cardarelli provides some indication of the purpose of his journal in a letter dated 29 October 1913 and addressed to Giovanni Boine:

Immaginate il massimo del rigore e della spregiudigatezza commisti; e una profonda fiducia lirica in tutto, una seria fede nella grandezza, un inquieto bisogno di stile. . . . Si tratterà appunto di lavorare in un'atmosfera di riflessioni, di esitazioni e di virilità. Tutto ciò non ci impedirà naturalmente di essere giovani. Insomma, io, voi, Cecchi potremmo fare oggi in Italia qualcosa di assolutamente nuovo e non privo di necessità storica.[22]

[Imagine the highest degree of rigour together with the maximum amount of freedom; with a profound lyrical faith in everything; a serious faith in grandeur; an unquiet need for style . . . It will be a question of working in an atmosphere of reflection, hesitancy and virility. All that naturally won't stop us from being young. Indeed, me, you, Cecchi we can do something absolutely new today in Italy and something not without historical necessity.]

What is interesting about this brief sketch of the intentions of the journal is the extent to which those aims clearly provide an echo of some of the most characteristic elements of Prezzolini's *Voce*: witness the proposition of virility and grandeur, concepts which indicate the theories of Nietzsche and Weininger; the abiding faith in the power of literature;

[21] Letter dated 18 Sept. 1917: *Epistolario*, ii. 607.
[22] *Epistolario*, i. 325.

the passionate seriousness of the undertaking; the need for novelty and youth; the typically *vociano* desire to combine a subversive impulse with a need for order. But aside from providing programmatic statements of this kind, Cardarelli's private correspondence also indicates that the contributors to his review would not only have included Cecchi and Boine but other *vociani* such as Serra and Amendola. Given the names of those writers who were willing to contribute to the journal, it is relatively safe to assume that had it seen publication it would have shared a number of obvious similarities with *La Voce*. It would certainly have published *Prologhi*, Riccardo Bacchelli's *Poemi lirici*, and the early poetical fragments of Cecchi and Boine. Although he seems to have succeeded in drawing together a set of possible contributors, Cardarelli did not secure financial backing for his venture and in early 1914 he decided to shelve his project.

Despite its initial failure, the endeavour to found a periodical had succeeded in forming a small but potentially significant group of writers. In his correspondence with De Robertis, Renato Serra seems to have appreciated that both Cecchi and Cardarelli were attentive to the more conservative message of the *Voce bianca*, and talked of them being 'on the same road' as himself and De Robertis.[23] When Giuseppe Raimondi brought out the short-lived journal *La Raccolta* (March 1918–February 1919), the names of Cardarelli and Bacchelli figured prominently in its list of contributors, while Cecchi was involved in its editorial decisions.[24] However, it was not until 1919 that Cardarelli's plan to publish a periodical of his own finally succeeded, largely because he managed to persuade the wealthy publisher Aurelio Saffi to provide the necessary money for the enterprise. The first issue of *La Ronda* was printed in April 1919 and the review appeared monthly thereafter until November 1922 (although a special issue was printed as late as December 1923). The review's editorial staff naturally

[23] The quotation is taken from a letter addressed to G. De Robertis and dated 20 March 1915. The letter is now contained in R. Serra, *Epistolario*, ed. L. Ambrosini, G. De Robertis, and A. Grilli (Florence: Vallecchi, 1934), 556.

[24] Raimondi's memories of *La Raccolta*, a journal which he explicitly saw as the precursor of *La Ronda*, are contained in the volume *I tetti sulla città* (Milan: Mondadori, 1977), 95–102.

included Cecchi and Bacchelli, but also the lesser-known writers Antonio Baldini, Bruno Barilli, and Lorenzo Montano.

If the journal had originally been conceived as a publication which shared some of the most essential cultural premises of *La Voce* it had, by the time it came to be printed, been transformed into a publication which bore all the signs of Cardarelli's sense of shame at his own pre-war past. More importantly, the journal did not set out to change an existing state of affairs but actively militated for a return to order. Its purpose was not to fulfil an avant-garde strategy but to advocate reaction at a time when the forces of the right were increasingly prepared to use violence in order to combat what they regarded as the threat of a Socialist revolution. The full extent of the reactionary nature of *La Ronda* did not become clear until the journal was in its second year of publication, but already in the preface to the first issue Cardarelli stated that it was his desire to distance himself from his more radical past. Rather than beginning with a direct statement of objectives, the preface he wrote opened with an elaborate valediction to youth. The editor made it clear that he and his colleagues were determined not to repeat the errors which they committed when they were younger. He wrote:

Noi non siamo più giovani. Ciò deve esser confessato prima di tutto umilmente. O animosa e benedetta gioventù, addio! . . . Essere giovani significa costituire una promessa, una simpatica e audace promessa, verso la quale il mondo poteva anche mostrarsi prodigo di fiducia. Da qui nasceva che a noi era dato illuderci e credere chissà che cosa. ('Prologo in tre parti', *La Ronda* (Apr. 1919), 3)

[We are no longer young. We have to confess humbly to this before anything. O sweet and blessed youth farewell! . . . To be young signifies bearing a promise, a sympathetic and daring promise, to which the world can show itself to be full of faith. [Armed with our sense of mission] we were able to deceive ourselves and believe who knows what.]

Pronouncing an elegant funeral oration on the passing of youth may at first sight seem odd. When we consider that nearly all journals of the first two decades of the twentieth century, from Corradino's *Il Regno* to Papini's *Lacerba*, contained an introductory article in which the editor, speaking on behalf of the periodical's contributors, hastily justified to the public the *raison d'être* of the new publication, then the above writing seems still more eccentric. Yet, on closer examination, the opening page of the first issue of *La Ronda* reveals itself to be more subtle than it may initially seem. Throughout its existence *La Voce* had boldly proclaimed itself to be the mouthpiece of 'intelligent young people'; thus, by declaring that he and his fellow contributors were no longer young, Cardarelli indicated, obliquely but forcefully, that they no longer espoused many of the ideals which had earlier inspired the youthful writers of *La Voce*. If, in the opening section of his preface to *La Ronda*, he set out to show the divide that separated his review from *La Voce*, he simultaneously implied that the ethical and philosophical notions which once fired his generation had, on being put to the test, revealed themselves to be no more than a set of distracting illusions, powerless to alter reality. He continued:

Ora siamo fatti grandi. La realtà è tutt'altra. . . . E ciò vuol dire proprio che noi non siamo più giovani. Che importa che i nostri anni siano sempre pochi? Non è il tempo, è il metodo, la fedeltà temeraria a un proposito, la silenziosità delle intenzioni che rendono adulta la vita e quasi la fanno apparire come una colpa.

[Now we have grown older. Reality is quite different. . . . And this means simply that we are no longer young. What does it matter if our years are still few? It is not time, but method, the audacious fidelity to a proposition, the silence of one's intentions which make life seem mature and which make it seem almost as if it were something to be atoned for.]

Instead of aiming to unite young intellectuals with a desire for change as *La Voce* had aspired to do, it was the intention of *La Ronda* to provide a forum for writers who had been disabused of their beliefs and who were largely resigned to the harsh immutability of reality. The journal did not open with 'an audacious promise' (Prezzolini's introductory article to *La Voce* had borne the title 'La nostra promessa') but with an admission of defeat and a humble confession of its limitations. The very style of the introduction contrasted markedly, if not to say polemically, with that most often employed by the editorial staff of *La Voce*. Whereas Prezzolini and, in particular, Papini made a point of using a simple, concise, and direct style which frequently erred on the side of terseness and which accommodated numerous injunctions and admonishments to the reader, Cardarelli employed a self-consciously refined mode of expression. The tone he adopted in the first paragraph of his preface was sober and restrained, while his style, heavily reliant on metaphor, classical allusion, and apostrophe, at times deliberately cultivated an aura of ambiguity.

The first section of Cardarelli's 'Prologo in tre parti' usefully pointed to the essential characteristic of *La Ronda*, namely that the journal, although run by a group of former *vociani*, was above all else a reaction against *La Voce*. On most important issues, *La Ronda* liked to assume a position that was diametrically opposed to that once taken by *La Voce*. For instance, both periodicals proposed fundamentally divergent solutions to the question as to what role the intellectual should play within society. Part of the very purpose of Prezzolini and Papini in setting up *La Voce* had been to encourage young Italian writers to become actively engaged in the politics of the nation; it was one of the most original features of Prezzolini's *Voce* that in its pages literary criticism appeared alongside essays and leader articles which, more often than not, were intensely critical of political figures and institutions. Moreover, the kind of literary criticism and creative writing which the *vociani* wrote owed much to the journal's desire to provoke a spiritual and moral regeneration of the country. But Cardarelli and his fellow *rondisti*, far from claiming that the writer should seek to play an active role in matters affecting the moral and political destiny of the nation, affirmed the opposite. In their view the writer should be a pure *letterato* who should, so far as was possible, abstain from contributing to debates of a political nature. At no stage in the life of the journal did its editors offer a statement of their collective political ideas, preferring to assume a detached and ironic stance with regard to politics, and frequently satirizing those writers who continued to believe, after the demise of *La Voce*, that the *letterato* had a political role to play. Lorenzo Montano, writing in the editorial section, expressed the collective opinion of the *Ronda*'s editors. He deprecated the concern for politics of many writers, objecting that they 'wrote about politics, shouted about politics and dreamed about politics'. He claimed that 'Parnassus was deserted and Helicon abandoned' and that 'the Muses in Italy presided over factory councils, while speculating over events'.[25]

The apparent abdication from political engagement which *La Ronda* appeared to advocate won the censure of a number of Cardarelli's contemporaries, including Gobetti, and has attracted a huge amount of adverse criticism from those critics who have written about the period in the years since 1945. The journal's stance of political detachment becomes all the more remarkable when the period in which it was printed is considered. The ex-*vociani* who made up the editorial staff of *La Ronda* appeared to have lost any enthusiasm for radical political change, but that waning of enthusiasm was by no means shared by other groups within Italian society at the time. A great many ex-combatants had been won over to the cause of Nationalism. Both the reality of war and 'the mutilated peace' had legitimized opposition in whole sections of the working classes to the institutions of parliamentary government. Radical Socialist activity had been lent considerable impetus by the success of the Russian Revolution. Socialists clashed violently with forces on the right, including Futurists and Arditi, who considered it the purpose of the Fascist movement to continue the revolution which had begun with Italian intervention in the war. In September 1919 Gabriele D'Annunzio effectively extended the problem of war by leading his famous expedition to Fiume. Curzio Malaparte, with his hugely polemical texts such as *Viva Caporetto! La rivolta dei santi maledetti* (1921), became the voice of the new revolutionary climate.

If *La Ronda* had stood simply for political disengagement then it is likely that it would not have been the object of the same degree of adverse critical comment. However, the essential point is that while the journal seemed on the one hand to discourage the involvement of writers in politics, the literary aesthetics which it propounded had an unmistakable political dimension. It is through an examination of those

[25] Lorenzo Montano, 'Commento alla cronaca', *La Ronda*, (Aug.–Sept. 1920,) 618.

aesthetics that it becomes possible to see the reactionary nature of *La Ronda* and the role which the journal performed in providing the theoretical basis for an important strain in pro-Fascist literature. From the outset Cardarelli and his associates claimed that the purpose of their journal was to promote a serious approach to the exercise of writing. Years after *La Ronda* had ceased publication, Emilio Cecchi wrote in its defence that the periodical was intended to be 'An example of serious artistic commitment.'[26] The very title *La Ronda*, with its obvious military connotations, alludes to the journal's self-imposed role of protecting the 'republic of letters' at a time when Italy was, again according to Cecchi, being invaded by cheap literature from abroad and when the tradition of Italian literature needed most to be protected.

If the *rondisti* set themselves the task of safeguarding Italian literary standards, then they sought to accomplish this in a variety of ways. During the first year of its publication, each issue of *La Ronda* contained an editorial section entitled 'Incontri e scontri' to which the founder members of the periodical at various times contributed, although the signatures of Cardarelli and Bacchelli appeared more frequently than those of their colleagues. The short articles which made up this section of the journal were almost without exception of a polemical nature. The writers of *La Ronda* aimed their polemics at an extensive range of targets, but the avant-garde movements of the early part of the twentieth century bore the brunt of the journal's attacks. For example, Bacchelli satirized the Dada movement,[27] and Cecchi ridiculed Futurist experiments with language.[28] But not only did the *rondisti* poke fun at certain types of avant-

---

[26] See Cecchi's preface to G. Cassieri (ed.), anthology of *La Ronda* (Florence: Landi, 1955), p. x. On the same page he went on to write: 'Quanto al reazionarismo letterario: il primo dopoguerra fu caratterizzato, come tutti ricordano, da una produzione scollacciata, che spesso rasentava la pornografia, e che in compenso era malissimo scritta. Fu uno scatenamento di volgarità che durò alcuni anni: una vera danza delle scimmie. In mezzo a tale scatenamento, *La Ronda* esercitò la funzione d'un richiamo all'ordine, per un ritorno alle nostre più nobili tradizioni letterarie.'

[27] R. Bacchelli, 'Notizie oltramontane (La Nouvelle Revue Française)', *La Ronda*, (June 1920), 377.

[28] E. Cecchi, 'Comunicazione accademica', *La Ronda*, (May 1919), 4.

garde writing, showing the degree to which they wished to distance themselves from their past associations, they also directed their satire against various types of writer. A frequent object of ridicule in the editorials of La Ronda was the figure of the enthusiastic young writer who believed that the world could be modified by 'the exercise of the pen'. Within such a characterization it is again not difficult to trace an image of the avant-gardist, and one issue of La Ronda even contained an ironic 'Vademecum del giovane scrittore'.[29] The language used under the rubric 'Incontri e scontri' was often so sarcastic that the criticisms which were levelled against other movements or opposing groups in that section of the journal degenerated all too quickly into a series of defamatory personal tirades.[30] Indeed, largely because of its cultivation of a sour moral tone, the section soon proved to be repetitious in character. After scarcely more than a year it ran out of energy and was replaced, in 1921, by Lorenzo Montano's column, 'Commento alla cronaca'.

The hostility towards the sort of subversive experimentation that avant-garde groupings such as the *vociani* had earlier championed represented the first basic tenet of the literary ideology of La Ronda. But as well as openly promoting reaction, the *rondisti* set out to establish a new version of classicism. Cardarelli later claimed that his journal was motivated by 'the search for a mode of writing and a formal certainty during times of extreme confusion'.[31] It is worth noting that such a search showed a number of similarities with that undertaken by those artists who had been attracted to 'valori plastici'. Indeed, De Chirico and Carrà both wrote a number of pieces for La Ronda, as did De Chirico's brother, the writer and painter Alberto Savinio. In the third section of the 'Prologo in tre parti' Cardarelli indicated broadly the aspirations the writers of La Ronda shared for a new kind of classicism. Reiterating his disdain for the avant-garde

[29] *La Ronda* (Feb. 1920), 71.

[30] For an example of the vituperative tone of the column see Cardarelli's attack on Gobetti, whom he describes as, among other things, an 'imberbe e prodigioso personaggio' and 'un cervello scombicccherato', in 'Incontri e scontri', (*La Ronda*, Aug.–Sept. 1920), 589.

[31] Cardarelli's reflection was contained in an open letter addressed to Bacchelli and published in *Il resto del Carlino* on 15 June 1932.

movements of the early part of the twentieth century, he deliberately emphasized the validity of the old. He spoke of his and his fellow contributors' 'cult of the past' and of their desire to resurrect 'that which may seem dead' by cultivating a 'defunct style'. He went on to conclude that the classicism of *La Ronda* was 'double-edged and metaphorical', that it meant using an antiquated style to perpetuate 'new elegancies' and by so doing 'perpetuating the tradition of one's art'. Such a form of classicism represented a means by which the writer could be 'modern in the Italian manner'.

As well as providing a series of broad neoclassical notions, Cardarelli insisted that any aspiring writer must first and foremost develop an awareness of his country's literary past. Cecchi later affirmed that the *rondisti* were united by 'an illuminated sense of 'our tradition, personified by the genius of Manzoni and Leopardi'.[32] Every issue of *La Ronda* opened with a section entitled 'The Guests of Stone' (Convitati di Pietra), in which a didactic excerpt from the work of an illustrious writer was printed, and most of the *rondisti* wrote a piece on one of the classics of modern Italian literature. In the tendency to look nostalgically upon the great writers of the nineteenth century, there is an echo of the views which Serra had expressed shortly before his death. In particular, the writers of *La Ronda* evidently shared his dismay for what he had seen as the earlier 'liquidation of the past'. Perhaps more surprising is the extent to which the opinions Cardarelli and his colleagues expressed coincided with those which Eliot articulated in his essay 'Tradition and the Individual Talent', published, like *La Ronda,* in 1919. There is no evidence to suggest that the *rondisti* were aware of Eliot's theories, yet they conceived of writing not as a vocation but as a 'métier', they insisted that a knowledge of the writers of the past represented the sole means by which a modern author could attain a measure of originality, and they would certainly have endorsed Eliot's proposition that: 'Poetry is not a turning loose of emotion, but an escape from emotion; it is not the expression of personality, but an escape from personality.'

---

[32] Preface to Cassieri (ed.), anthology of *La Ronda.*

Indeed, what emerges strongly from the 'Prologo in tre parti' is the emphasis Cardarelli, when referring to style, places upon the value of order and constraint. Unlike the poetic of *La Voce*, which was principally one of liberation, the aesthetic proposed by the *rondisti* was one which encouraged the vigilant exercise of control. Whereas the writers of *La Voce* had sought consciously to forge a new literary language, one which incorporated the rhythms of everyday speech and which could reflect the chaotic and fragmentary nature of individual existence, the *rondisti* made it their purpose to restore a more traditional and inherently more ordered manner of composition, in accordance with their 'cult of the past'. In the preface to the first issue of the journal, Cardarelli asserted that the Italian language was governed by a set of inflexible laws: 'We are aware that our language must obey strict laws.' A natural corollary of such reverence for linguistic order was that the *rondisti* generally and Cardarelli in particular conceived of style as consciously restrictive. One editorial section of the journal contained the illuminating phrase: 'Style, above everything else is a means of defence. The artist must be formally superior to his humanity.'[33] Although the precise significance of this curious proposition is unclear, it seems to imply that the function of style is to restrain and control the raw material of content.

The belief that style represented a means of defence was elucidated further by Cardarelli in a later essay, 'Le opere e i giorni', which looked back at the literary programme of *La Ronda*.[34] In this essay, he went so far as to attribute an ethical role to style by comparing it implicitly with conscience:

Lo stile è un fatto naturale e ereditario come il carattere. Non è possibile modificarlo e neppure sfuggirgli. Esso ci dà la misura di quello che siamo, delle nostre qualità, dei nostri limiti e dei nostri difetti. È qualche cosa d'obbligatorio, ci si presenta come un'imposizione. Affidarglisi, arrenderglisi, non c'è altro da fare.

[Style is something that is natural and inherited like character. It is not

[33] 'Lo stile, oltre il resto, è una difesa. L'artista deve esser superiore formalmente alla sua umanità', 'Incontri e scontri', *La Ronda* (Oct. 1919), 55.
[34] The essay was included in Cardarelli's collection of essays, *Solitario in Arcadia* (Milan: Mondadori, 1947) and is reprinted in Martignoni's edition of Cardarelli's works, pp. 311–17.

possible to modify it or escape from it. Style indicates to us what we are, it
shows us our qualities, our limits and our defects. It is something which is
obligatory, it presents itself as an imposition. There is nothing one can do
except entrust oneself to it, surrender to it.]

Here style is presented as an agency which, like conscience,
projects its prohibitive, even repressive, laws upon the self,
while paradoxically being a part of the self. Style, as the
'Prologo in tre parti' maintained, is governed by 'inflexible
laws', it is the site where the conquests of the Italian literary
canon are enshrined,[35] and it is the means through which
order may be imposed, 'it presents itself as an imposition'. If
style is immutable and eternal then the self is contingent
and ephemeral, the self is the subject upon which the action
of style is exerted, and yet it may assent to confine its fluidity
within the fixity of the rules dictated by style.

Although in many of his writings on style Cardarelli referred collectively to the masters of the Italian literary tradition, he singled out one writer and poet in particular as his
model of style, Giacomo Leopardi. His reading of Leopardi
was remarkable neither for its objectivity nor for its erudi-
tion, and many Italian critics have pointed to its flaws and
inconsistencies.[36] Indeed, the canonization of Leopardi was
the result of an intuitive reading of his theoretical pronouncements in *Lo zibaldone* and *Le operette morali*. The point
can be made clearly by looking at the section from his essay
'Le opere ed i giorni', where he retrospectively evokes his
first encounter with Leopardi. He speaks of an encounter
of 'extreme importance' which immediately 'put his head
straight':

Non soltanto era una voce antica e famigliarissima a cui sarebbe stato
impossibile disubbidire, ma un santo della tradizione che si staccava dalla
sua polverosa nicchia per rivelarci un autore modernissimo. . . . Da
quando abbiamo capito questo siamo rientrati nell'ordine.

[35] In the 'Prologo in tre parti', Cardarelli had also written: 'Il nostro alfabeto
esisteva appena da qualche secolo che già il genio preistorico dei nostri antichi ne
aveva sfiorato e immortalato tutte le lettere.'
[36] Luigi Russo wrote of 'an acritical reading of a hypothetical Leopardi', while
Pier Vincenzo Mengaldo criticized the purely stylistic nature of Cardarelli's reading
of the nineteenth-century poet, defining it as qualitively inferior to the readings of
Leopardi of Ungaretti and Montale. L. Russo, *I narratori* (Milan: Mondadori,
1951), 308–10; P. V. Mengaldo, *Poeti italiani del Novecento* (Milan: Mondadori,
1990), 368.

[This was not only an antique and yet entirely familiar voice which it would have been impossible to disobey, but a saint of tradition who had come down from its dusty alcove to reveal himself an extremely modern author. . . . As soon as we had understood this we had re-entered the realm of order.]

The tone of the extract is solemn and the vocabulary has obvious religious overtones: Leopardi appears as a saintly, even Christlike, figure who returns from the dead to admonish the living with a voice that compels submission to his law. Cardarelli presents himself as a convert who fervently embraces a new faith. In the representation of his literary conversion he alludes to his ideological shift from *vociano* to *rondista*, and indeed it was *La Ronda* which provided him with the platform from which to expound the tenets of his new-found faith.

In another, largely biographical, essay on Leopardi[37] he wrote that the poet was not the messiah of a new religion so much as the restorer of an ancient faith, or, in his words, 'the Saint Paul of Italian classicism'. While such an epithet when used to define Leopardi is perhaps of dubious validity, it perfectly characterizes the role Cardarelli assumed in the years of *La Ronda*, that of the self-appointed apostle of the earlier writer's stylistic canon. In the March–May edition of *La Ronda* in 1921 he published, under the heading 'Testamento letterario di Giacomo Leopardi', selections from *Lo zibaldone*. The extracts from Leopardi's notebooks which appeared in this issue were divided into six sections and stretched to no fewer than 220 pages in all. The very length of the selection is testimony to the importance with which it was endowed by the *rondisti*, but it was the parts in which Leopardi spoke on language and style, adumbrating his theory of elegant writing, which were italicized by Cardarelli.[38] According to the view initially advanced by Leopardi but publicized by his later admirer, the writer's aspiration

[37] 'Lo zibaldone', again contained in *Solitario in Arcadia* is reprinted in *Opere*, ed. Martignoni, pp. 347–60.

[38] The section 'Sistema di restaurazione della lingua antica italiana fondato sul concetto dell'eleganza' runs from p. 17 to p. 54 of the edition of *La Ronda* dedicated to selections from the *Lo zibaldone*. Indicated in brackets are the pages of *La Ronda*'s 'Testamento letterario di Giacomo Leopardi' from which the elements of my summary are taken.

towards an elegant style could be facilitated by adhering broadly to the following guidelines. The writer should use words, combinations of words and clusters of metaphors distant from those employed in ordinary speech (p. 37); he should mingle modern, everyday locutions and speech rhythms with unusual and self-consciously literary words and phrases (p. 32); he should show a predilection for old-fashioned words and an attentiveness to the noble and poetic elements present in the language of 'il popolo' (p. 54); his style should tend more towards the lyrical and evocative than the narrative, indeed, his prose should be close to poetry, or rather his style should be coloured by 'una mezza tinta generale di poesia' (p. 50). As can be deduced from the character of such maxims, the style advocated by Cardarelli through Leopardi, while peculiarly inappropriate for the novel, would be perfectly suited to the short prose piece or 'elzeviro'.

From the observations in the 'Prologo in tre parti' and in the selection of the linguistic theories from *Lo zibaldone* it is possible to extract a fairly coherent, if largely derivative, set of ideas on style. On the subject of content, however, the *rondisti* were less forthcoming. Neither Cardarelli nor any of his colleagues ever succeeded in enunciating what they regarded to be the suitable thematics of a literary work, and their apparent inability to do so has prompted two kinds of criticism. First, various critics have considered the journal to be the product of a reactionary inclination too intent upon castigating the avant-garde movements of the early years of the twentieth century to be able to construct and propose a viable poetic manifesto for future application. Even contemporaries of Cardarelli who were hostile to *La Ronda* complained of the 'confused' nature of many of the statements which the journal made.[39] The second and more damaging accusation that has been levelled against the writers of *La Ronda* is that the intellectual and sentimental content of their work was limited or even sterilized by the importance they attached to obeying the finer points of

---

[39] For a discussion of the reaction of some of Cardarelli's contemporaries to the literary project of *La Ronda*, see L. Guzzetta Fava, '*La Ronda* cinquant'anni dopo: Ideologia e letteratura', *Lettere italiane* (Jan.–Mar. 1971), 69–84.

grammar and by their insistence upon working within a stylistic framework dictated by canonical authors of the Italian literary tradition. When Cardarelli had already published in *La Ronda* the first of his *Favole della Genesi* and Cecchi some of the articles that were later to be included in *Pesci rossi* (1920), Maria Marchesini wrote a perceptive attack on the writers of *La Ronda* in Gobetti's journal, *Energie nove*. In her opinion, the desire of the *rondisti* to control expression meant that their prose was curiously limited. The pages of their work, while as elegantly polished as precious stones, were as cold and as lifeless as such stones. Their prose seemed 'isolated, cut off from the flux of life'.[40]

It is certainly true that the *rondisti*, in contrast to the writers of *La Voce,* did show a deep-seated distrust of works with a strong emotional content. Most of the *vociani* had fervently believed that creative and critical writing provided the writer with a means to explore the self; they had valued the expression of intense emotion and had often gone to the extent of using such vague and indefinable notions as sincerity or authenticity as criteria with which to assess the worth of a literary text. The *rondisti*, however, scorned the idea that a work's authenticity was any guarantee of its success or validity, and their aesthetic was not one which encouraged the expression of raw sentiment. In his preface to the first issue of the journal, Cardarelli spoke of the need to find what he cryptically called 'a simulacrum of formal chastity', and a notorious passage in one editorial of *La Ronda* contains the following observations:

All'arte non deve essere assegnato un dominio illimitato ed imprescritto. Le ragioni sono morali, d'ordine e di salute, non meno che formali. Lo diciamo quali artisti, che è la parte nostra; e arriveremmo a sostenere senza difficoltà che non ci disturberebbero per nulla delle buone leggi restrittive.[41]

[Art should not enjoy unlimited and unmanaged freedom. There are moral reasons (concerning order and healthiness) as well as formal reasons for this. We declare this as artists and we would have no difficulty

---

[40] 'La loro opera ci dà l'impressione di una serie di frammenti perfetti in se stessi, ma isolati, scissi dal fluire universale della vita.' *Energie nove,* 5 July 1919.

[41] 'Incontri e scontri', *La Ronda,* (Oct. 1919), 55.

in saying that we would be in no way disturbed if some good restrictive
laws were to be introduced.]

A statement such as this, with its emphasis on conformism
and its advancement of a notion of propriety, would seem to
make the divide between the reactionary *Ronda* and the
modernist *Voce* all too clear. Yet a paradoxical feature of *La
Ronda* was that, while the periodical was expressly intended
to be a reaction against the spirit and the aesthetic of *La
Voce*, that reaction was both partial and contradictory.

The *rondisti* may have made a show of satirizing the *moralismo* of the *Voce* and its adherents, and yet scarcely beneath
the surface of Cardarelli's pronouncements on aesthetics we
find residues of the harsh moral code of the *vociani*. In the
ethical role which Cardarelli attributes to style, there is a
yearning for discipline and a declaration of the need to
impose order on the chaos of lived experience. In the
elevation of Leopardi to the status of a moral giant one can
detect the deliberate mingling of ethical and aesthetic concerns which had been such a characteristic feature of the
way in which the *vociani* had spoken on cultural subjects. All
Cardarelli's views on writing were advanced in a combative,
self-assertive voice. Moreover, while the *rondisti* attempted to
cast aside such notions as the sincerity of the artist or the
spontaneity of the creative act, they nevertheless shared the
uncompromising dislike of the *vociani* for the novel. The
notions which they set forth concerning an ideal form of
prose worked to shore up rather than challenge the hege-
mony of the fragment which *La Voce* had earlier established.
They tacitly accepted that the problems of perception and
representation could not be resolved by narrative, and they
did not cast serious doubt on the autobiographical assumptions which had underpinned the aesthetic proposed by *La
Voce*. The *vociani* experimented with language in an attempt
to discover a form that would allow its creator the immediate
and unalloyed expression of his self. Their works cultivated a
spare, essential, and assertive style which tended naturally
towards the enunciation of an overbearing temperament.
The *rondisti*, by contrast, prized a classically restrained and in
some ways lyrical prose style designed not so much to enable

the undiluted expression of emotion, but rather its sophisticated concealment. Indeed, the dynamics of self-elevation, which had been central to the autobiographical aesthetics of the *vociani*, remained an important element in the kind of writing which *La Ronda* sought to propose. Cardarelli and his fellow *rondisti* may have shown a reactionary aversion to experimentation, but the model of a classical high style that they put forward was designed as a means of elevating the figure of the author.

Parallels with Fascism

It is clear that, in the years which led up to the First World War, some of the most important writers of *La Voce* had helped to disseminate ideas which it is now possible to equate with Fascist ideology. Most *vociani* had been keen to propagate the myth of Italian Nationalism. In the course of militating for wide-ranging cultural and political renewal they had shown an implacable hostility towards a number of the institutions of parliamentary democracy and towards the concept and practice of reformist Socialism. The *vociani* had successfully struggled for Italian intervention in the First World War as a means of rapidly advancing their 'moral revolution'. As well as battling for change on a national scale many *vociani* had, through their experimental autobiographies, presented a type of individual who succeeded in altering things through self-assertion and through violence. It is interesting that in the aftermath of war writers like Papini assumed a rather disengaged stance with regard to mass agitation and the rise of Fascism. The role of participating in violent attacks on Socialist targets fell, initially at least, to the Futurists.

The band of ex-*vociani* who gathered together to publish *La Ronda* did not participate actively in the Fascist rise to power which occurred in precisely the same period in which their journal appeared. Indeed, the *rondisti* attempted to remain aloof from politics. The polemic which the journal directed against Futurism and against avant-garde movements in general served to distance the editors from their former associations. But however much the *rondisti* attempted to adopt an apolitical position, they were nevertheless engaged in an attempt to mould the opinion of intellectuals, and on a number of counts they found themselves supporting Fascist initiatives. Although the core of Mussolini's movement had initially been made up of a heterogeneous group including veterans and Futurists, the Fasci di Combattimento began to achieve an impressive degree of support when large sections of the middle classes began to see the Fascists as an effective bulwark against the threat of a Bolshevik-style revolution. Indeed, between the end of 1920 and the beginning of 1921 Mussolini began to assume a marked distance from the more revolutionary elements within his association and to move his party towards the defence of long-standing privileges and rights of property. It was in 1920 that the Futurists were effectively marginalized. When reflecting on the reasons behind the rapid growth in support for Fascism in Italy from 1921 onwards, the historian Gioacchino Volpe pointed to the faith which many sections of society were prepared to invest in a movement which seemed not to threaten existing power structures. He spoke also of people's 'obsessive need for order', for 'hierarchies to be respected' and for people 'to stay in their rightful place'.[42]

It is not difficult to draw an analogy between Mussolini's attempt to restore a kind of political and social order and the endeavour of Cardarelli and the *rondisti* to promote a return to order in the world of Italian letters. If Fascist activists gained a large measure of popular support through their promise to restore the authority of the state, then similarly the *rondisti* tried to secure support in the literary community by lambasting any example of radical innovation. *La Ronda*, with its military title and the figure of the soldier who appeared on the cover of every issue, aimed to call attention to Italy's classical heritage and unite a growing band of writers in defence of the country's traditions. The journal defined possible future directions for creative writing by sublimating the literary past of the nation. After

---

[42] Volpe's views first appeared in *Gerarchia* in January 1923. They are quoted in Emilio Gentile's *Le origini dell'ideologia fascista*, 258.

having conducted a successful campaign of terror against the perceived threat of a Socialist revolution, Mussolini sought to broaden the appeal of Fascism by stressing its conservative credentials. Indeed, in late 1921 the movement was attempting to win the explicit support of the Nationalists who, situated on the extreme right of the political spectrum, took a poor view of the residues of revolutionary syndicalism which had appeared in the immediate post-war activities of the Fasci di Combattimento. Writing in the paper *Idea nazionale* in November 1921, the Nationalist Ugo D'Andrea drew a parallel between tendencies apparent within the literary and artistic community and the conservative direction which Fascism had decided to take:

La tendenza all'ordine, alla quadratura, al classicismo è ormai decisa in tutte le manifestazioni del pensiero: è un bisogno prepotente dello spirito moderno, stanco dell'instabilità, dell'irrequietezza, dell'imprecisione. Dopo l'impressionismo e il futurismo si cerca ora la massa, la solidità, il valore plastico: dopo il verso libero si torna alla forma chiusa perfetta del sonetto, così in politica. . . . Il fascismo da romantico deve divenire classico, come vuole essere romano e imperiale.[43]

[The tendency towards order, stability and classicism is now decisive in all intellectual manifestations: it is a fundamental desire of the modern spirit, which is tired of instability, preoccupation and imprecision. After Impressionism and Futurism what we look for now is certainty, solidity, 'plastic values': after free verse we have returned to the perfect closure of the sonnet and the same must be true in politics. . . . Fascism, after having been romantic must become classical, if it wishes to become Roman and imperial.]

Although D'Andrea does not refer explicitly to *La Ronda*, in the observations he makes upon the need for order and the return to classicism he posits a clear similarity between the literary reaction promoted by groups such as the *rondisti* and the conservative political action which Mussolini's Fascists were increasingly seen as being able to carry out.

There are more than generic similarities to link the literary project of *La Ronda* to a wider and more sinister pattern of reaction. The journal was published during the period in which Fascist squads attacked trade unions and Socialist

[43] Quoted in ibid. 287.

organizations, and yet its editors offered no comment upon or condemnation of the violence of such actions. Indeed, they regarded abstention from comment and the express desire not to become involved in matters which extended beyond the confines of the specifically literary as enough of a political statement in itself. But in January 1922 the sympathy of the *rondisti* for the Fascist reaction did become explicit, with the publication of an essay by no less a figure than Vilfredo Pareto. In his piece, entitled 'Il Fascismo', Pareto argued in favour of the respectability of Mussolini's movement. He contended that it represented a force that had the power to protect the institutions of the state and, in a longer time-scale, promote an important renewal of the whole of Italian society.

An interesting insight into the life of members of Rome's intellectual community during the period between the end of the First World War and the march on Rome was provided in an article written by Curzio Malaparte, 'Il muro di Baudelaire'.[44] By the time the article was published, Malaparte had risen to various positions of power within the regime and had occupied, among other posts, the editorship of *La Stampa*. In his retrospective piece, he spoke of Cardarelli with reverence and affection. He characterized the older man as a stern and noble figure, suggesting that his physical appearance alternately resembled that of Goethe, a Roman Caesar, and an Etruscan god. While Cardarelli was defined as the 'imposing prophet of a new-found classicism', the group of writers and painters who frequented the offices of *La Ronda* in the square of the Trinità dei Monti included such figures as Soffici, De Chirico, Arturo Martini, and Mario Broglio. In his article Malaparte referred to the atmosphere of friendship which prevailed within the group and spoke of the frequent excursions that they made in his company to the countryside outside Rome. The latter part of the article evokes, through a series of mythological tableaux, the atmosphere in Rome in the months immediately before Mussolini's successful coup: Malaparte wrote of squads of young men dressed in black appearing in the

---

[44] *Corriere della sera*, 10 Aug. 1931.

streets of the city; of ancient monuments being seen to move or utter syllables; of symbols of Roman imperialism, hidden for centuries, suddenly being unearthed. He described Cardarelli as being particularly attentive to the signs of the storm that was gathering force, and as participating in whatever activities appealed to his neoclassical sensibilities; one such activity included the attempt to free two eagles kept in cages in the Campidoglio. At the end of the piece, as the Fascists are about to seize power, Malaparte in the company of his friend watches the latter as he writes 'Viva la rivoluzione!' on the exterior wall of his lodgings.

At various points in the 1920s there was a remarkably high level of coincidence between both the opinions which Cardarelli and Malaparte expressed and the formal properties of their writing. When the historical circumstances which lay behind the genesis of *La Ronda* are considered, together with the journal's ambiguous links with avant-garde nationalism and its overtones of political authoritarianism, it is not surprising to discover the extent to which the neoclassical revival promoted by *La Ronda* helped to spawn a form of literature which was overtly pro-Fascist.

4

FASCIST IDEOLOGY AND THE 'PROSA D'ARTE'

Italy in the 1920s: The Consolidation of Fascist Power

The march on Rome did not mark the unequivocal establishment of a new form of political power. Mussolini and the Fascist movement had successfully taken over government but they still lacked a clear idea of how to organize the power which they had seized. The problem of setting a precise course of action to follow was compounded by the varied nature of the interest groups which were either present within the Fascist movement itself or were sympathetic to it. Mussolini faced the task of laying the foundations for an authoritarian system of government, while managing the tensions which existed between an extremely wide coalition of forces. Within the PNF there were those who saw the priority as being the normalization of the party as part of the wider process of reforming the state and those, the former *squadristi* or intransigents, who wanted to continue the Fascist revolution with the same means that had secured initial success. Mussolini's attempts to widen Fascism's appeal to figures within the Liberal establishment and to secure the support of a number of important institutions were constantly opposed by the more unruly elements within his party. The intransigents were hostile to the merger with the Nationalists which took place in 1923 and which openly signalled the growing alliance of conservative forces. The creation of the Fascist Militia, again in 1923, was intended not solely as an additional means of controlling public order, but, was also seen as a measure for gaining greater control over the squads. However, the effective management of agitation served to enhance Mussolini's personal standing. In the mid-1920s he was to show himself adept at exploiting the existing structures of power, at changing his alliances when necessary, and at tailoring the ideology of his party to suit his own purposes.

His method of consolidating power involved both coercion and the securing of consent. On the one hand, the threat of *squadrista* violence was employed to encourage co-operation. On the other, the Fascists did not waste time in drafting legislation which would give them the means of legalizing their present hold on power. When the electoral reform bill, drafted by Giacomo Acerbo, was passed in 1923, the parliamentary chamber was ringed with militiamen as a device to ensure its safe passage. The law entitled the party list which received the greatest number of votes in a general election to two-thirds of the seats in the lower house of parliament. It thus provided the PNF with a potentially massive advantage. In order to ensure victory in the general election, which was set for April 1924, huge numbers of former Liberals, conservative members of the Partito Popolare Italiano (PPI), and independents were persuaded to form part of the Fascist *listone*, or big list. Philip Morgan has compared the extension of enforced co-operation to the relationship between a blackmailer and his victims.[1] The widening of support for the *listone* had the effect of weakening the popular basis of opposition groups, while sporadic acts of violence both before and during the elections made it clear that coercion was not always masked as co-operation.

Unsurprisingly, the parties gathered together in the *listone* were to prove successful in the elections. The Fascists' acquisition of constitutional legitimacy did not, however, go unchallenged. The Socialist deputy Giacomo Matteotti, in a speech delivered in May 1924, denounced the tactics of the *listone* and contested the right of the new government to hold office. As is well known, he was abducted by a band of *squadristi* on 10 June and his body was eventually recovered on 16 August. The response of the representatives of the PPI, the Socialists, and the Communists was to withdraw from parliament in a gesture known as the Aventine Secession. The action of the Aventine leaders was a clear moral statement, but one which did not prove politically effective.

[1] P. Morgan, *Italian Fascism* (London: Macmillan, 1995), 69.

Fearing a second wave of Fascist violence, the king failed to dissolve parliament. Liberal politicians who remembered the disorder of the *biennio rosso* were unwilling to see the government fall and their reluctance was shared by powerful interest groups within the business community. Mussolini not only weathered the storm but turned it to his advantage. In October 1924 Turati's reformed PSI, the Partito Socialista Unitano (PSU), was officially banned, and in 1926 Turati went into exile in France. In the same year the leader of the constitutional Liberals and former contributor to *La Voce*, Giovanni Amendola, died in Cannes from injuries sustained at the hands of a Fascist squad.[2] In October 1926, after a second attempt was made on Mussolini's life, all opposition parties were outlawed. Italy had become a one-party state.

The Matteotti crisis served to make it clear to Fascist leaders that, if they were to remain in power, they could not hesitate in carrying out a radical reorganization of Italian society. From 1924 onwards the coercive role which the squads had exercised was transferred to the state. Between November 1925 and April 1926 a series of repressive laws was passed. The police, reorganized and strengthened under the management of Arturo Bocchini, was able successfully to implement the new legislation. By 1926 the local prefect had the power to arrest anyone suspected of inciting opposition to the regime and, since the citizen was deprived of rights of redress, the law effectively sanctioned police harassment. The restrictions on personal freedoms, designed as part of the consolidation of power, were accompanied by the restructuring of all areas in which the individual interacted with the state. In July 1926 the Ministry for Corporations was set up to promote the organization of both unions and production in such a way as to avoid divisions and, by extension, agitation. The new organization favoured employers, but the theoretically united and disciplined industrial base of the country was directly under the supervision

---

[2] For a description of the development of Amendola's political thought and actions see Giuseppe Carocci, *Giovanni Amendola nella crisi dello stato italiano*, (Milan: Feltrinelli, 1956). Prezzolini's own reflections on Amendola's progress from *vociano* to martyr of Fascist violence is contained in his *Amendola e La Voce* (Florence: Sansoni, 1974).

of the state. With industry following a corporate logic, the state was in a position to deal with the economic crises that the country faced. Indeed, the 1920s saw the state openly involved in a number of 'battles', ranging from the struggle to maintain the value of the lira (1925–7) to the battle for grain (1926–30).

Not only did Mussolini's government attempt to regulate the working lives of Italians according to its set of corporativist principles, it also sought to exercise control over their leisure time. In 1926 the Opera Nazionale Balilla was established, with the purpose of guiding the energies of young people, while the setting up of the Opera Nazionale Dopolavoro served to encourage collective activities from sport to cinemagoing. The drive to regiment every aspect of the citizen's life was accompanied by the promotion of popular rituals and celebrations, considered to be innately Italian and therefore at one with the aims of Fascist culture. The elevation of aspects of popular culture served, in the words of Roger Griffin, to 'reinforce the *strapaese* emphasis on the purity of rural life'.[3] In the course of the development of Mussolini's power, the Church had remained largely distant from direct political engagement. However, the Fascist attempt to subordinate all elements of society to the will of the state was to extend towards the Church when the government found common ground with the Vatican in the Lateran accords of 1929.

Active participation in the organizations of the Fascist state was fostered by the regime's insistence that the march on Rome had marked the beginning of a period of national renewal. The 'fascistization' of society was designed not only to strengthen Italy's position within Europe and the world but to renew the country's association with its Roman past and thus enhance its sense of national identity. For Mussolini the power which Italy could eventually exercise on a world stage was directly related to the population levels. Strength lay in numbers. In an important speech, delivered on 26 May 1927, he expressed his belief that falling birth rates were associated with growing urbanization and that, if Italy's

---

[3] R. Griffin, *The Nature of Fascism* (London: Routledge, 1991), 72.

population was to rise, its rural communities should not only be protected but developed. The emphasis on rurality naturally entailed the exaltation of the lifestyle and mentality of the agrarian classes. Such exaltation reflected both the *squadrista* phase of the development of Fascism and the importance to the regime of the rural petty bourgeoisie. Between 1927 and 1928 a series of measures were introduced to increase the birth rate nationally. By the autumn of 1928 the campaign to halt the growth of cities had resulted in the police being given extra powers to curb migration from rural areas.[4] The campaign was ideologically driven and, while it saw massive state expenditure on initiatives to keep an active workforce in the countryside, such as the famous programme of land reclamation, it failed to recognize the economic advantages which could be derived from a flexible labour force. Whether or not the policy of rurality helped advance the demographic campaign, it is undeniable that it played an important part in defining what the cultural values of Fascism were, and that it attracted the support of a number of the intellectuals who had previously been active contributors to *La Voce*.

Cardarelli's Autobiographical Fables

The history of Italian Fascism in the 1920s is the history of a movement which consolidated power by gathering support from the conservative elements of society. It is not possible to identify Fascism with a rigid set of ideological beliefs, since every inclusion of flankers or previously autonomous institutions entailed an alteration in the original theoretical conceptions of the movement. What is interesting, however, is the degree to which both individuals and larger groupings were willing to reinvent or repackage their views in order to conform to officially sanctioned doctrines. Nowhere was such a tendency more evident than in the behaviour of figures belonging to the literary community. Cardarelli is a case in point. The reactionary views which he and his col-

---

[4] For analysis of the policy of rurality see Morgan, *Italian Fascism*, 101–5, and Lyttelton, *The Seizure of Power*, 349–54.

leagues had expressed in *La Ronda* had to some extent coincided with the return to order violently promoted by the PNF. In the years in which Mussolini's government extended its rule, Cardarelli purported to follow a literary aesthetic that insisted on the autonomy of the written word, and yet such a written word echoed and reinforced elements of orthodox Fascist thinking as it developed. Not only did his critical pronouncements accord with those of the regime, but his creative texts were also involved in a symbiotic relationship with the political realities of his time: he showed a remarkable willingness to fuse the elegant narration of personal story with the legitimating myths of Fascism. The texts which he wrote in the 1920s offer pages of intensely imaginative introspection, but at the same time they prove disturbing (and at times even repellent) in the way in which they merge political ideology with literary fantasy.

The prose writings which were to spring directly from the experience of *La Ronda*, and which were to exemplify its teaching most closely, were *Viaggi nei tempi*, *Favole della Genesi*, and *Memorie della mia infanzia*. The first edition of *Viaggi nel tempo* was printed in 1920 and was made up of two sections: the first, 'Poesia', contained lyrics and short prose pieces;[5] the second, 'Retorica', contained a series of critical and anecdotal reflections. *Favole della Genesi* comprised twelve prose pieces, most of which were first published in *La Ronda* between 1919 and 1922. The compositions took the form of biblical stories reworked into elegant stylistic exercises. They were published for the first time in book form together with *Memorie della mia infanzia* in the volume *Favole e memorie* (1925). The prose writings of *Memorie della mia infanzia* also first appeared in *La Ronda*. They represented essentially a series of nostalgic rememberings. The idea of writing about the people, the customs, and the history of his birthplace was one which Cardarelli had nurtured from the days when he had been employed as a columnist for *Avanti!* In many of the articles he wrote for that paper, he had expressed his distrust of urbanization and his abiding nostalgia for the

[5] Several of these prose pieces first saw publication in the pages of *La Voce* of De Robertis, in the summer months of 1916.

Italy of small, self-contained, and essentially rural communities. More significantly, his admiration for Charles Péguy,
while to some extent eclipsed by the discovery of Leopardi,
was never disavowed. Indeed, there is everything to suggest
that in writing *Memorie* he had the model of Péguy's autobiographical works firmly at the back of his mind. In the
course of the article he had written for *La Voce*, he had made
a number of assertions that indicate an awareness of an area
that he intended to explore in his own creative writing. He
had, for example, affirmed that the return to one's origins,
the attempt to become 'a countryman, a national citizen in
the way of one's forefathers, using their language and their
customs' was 'not only an interpretation of oneself, but of
one's ancestors and of one's race'.[6] Yet, although he may
well have toyed with the idea of writing on Tarquinia from as
early as 1911, *Memorie della mia infanzia* was first published in
the pages of *La Ronda* between July and August 1922 and the
style in which the text is written demonstrates important
elements of the literary ideology of the journal.

An important element of the aesthetic doctrine proposed
collectively by the *rondisti* was that literary works should aim
not to depict but to conceal the rawness of reality, and that,
instead of representing the personality of the writer in its
totality, they should work to shroud the identity of the
author. If the content of *Favole della Genesi* had been intrinsically fabulous and therefore evasive, the same cannot
be said without qualification of *Memorie della mia infanzia*
where Cardarelli worked upon potentially disturbing autobiographical material. *Memorie* is a short collection (barely
twenty pages long) of prose fragments divided into two
chapters: the first chapter evokes the town of Corneto Tarquinia, while the second describes recollections from childhood and portrays the character of the narrator's father.
Throughout *Memorie*, however, the happenings and places of
the narrator's past are transferred from the plane of reality
to that of fantasy; the speaking voice strives to create a
personal mythology, investing his childhood with an aura of
the unreal, and portraying Tarquinia in such a manner as to

---

[6] 'Charles Péguy', *La Voce*, 7 Sept. 1911, p. 713. For a discussion of this area of
Cardarelli's thought see Carpi, 'Cardarelli e Péguy'.

bring to life a mythological location. The town that is signified does not exist in the world of objective reality; it is a
place which has been idealized through memory. Cardarelli
insists on the walled quality of his home town to enforce the
notion that Tarquinia is set apart from the rest of the world
and, as is fitting for a place that is remembered, aloof from
time. In the opening paragraph he wrote:

Sono nato e cresciuto in Maremma, a poca distanza dal mare, in un paese
urbano e campagnolo, rustico e civile, che ha serbato intatto il secolare
orgoglio della sua piccola cerchia antica, torreggiante e murata, e tiene la
qualità di forestiere per indice di villania. . . . È esposto a mare e monte e
ne sorveglia le strade, rifiata lo scirocco e la tramontana, ma i venti
variano e passano su di esso come le eterne stagioni, ne dal tempo dei
tempi sono buoni da raccontargli più nulla. Il suo costume non cambia.
(*Opere*, 247)

[I was born and I grew up in Maremma, near to the sea, in a town that is
both urban and rural, rustic and civilized, and which has for centuries
retained the pride of its ancient walled circle. The town remains deeply
suspicious of outsiders. . . . It is exposed to both the sea and to the
mountains, it breathes winds from different directions, but the winds
change and pass and can tell the town nothing. Its habits do not change.]

Among the set of theories on language and on style which
Cardarelli had extracted from *Lo zibaldone* and published in
La Ronda was Leopardi's reflection that the poetic register of
prose could be raised by the use of words and concepts
which brought to mind the infinite extension of the past. It
is easy to see that the writing of *Memorie della mia infanzia*
follows such an injunction. On each occasion that the narrator evokes the town of his childhood, he represents different
strata of its history. Sometimes, as in the opening paragraph
to the collection, Tarquinia is presented as apparently beyond the notion of temporal duration, at others the town,
with its towers, its encircling walls, and its manifold proces-
sions, seems to belong to the Middle Ages, while throughout
the collection allusions to its ancient history abound. References to the original inhabitants of Tarquinia, the Etruscans,
run like a refrain through *Memorie della mia infanzia*. Those
passages which portray the Etruscans are, according to the
canon of the *rondisti*, intrinsically poetic precisely because
they conjure up a world that is irretrievably lost and which

therefore can be apprehended, as Leopardi argued, only by the imagination. The poetic quality of this vision of Tarquinia is compounded by the manner in which, in one paragraph, the parable of Etruscan civilization is related:

Qui rise l'Etrusco un giorno, coricato, cogli occhi a fior di terra, guardando la marina. E accoglieva nelle sue pupille il multiforme e silenzioso splendore della terra fiorente e giovane, di cui aveva succhiato il mistero gaiamente, senza ribrezzo e senza paura, affondandoci le mani e il viso. Ma rimase come seppellito, il solitario orgiasta, nella propria favola luminosa. Benché la gran madre ne custodisca un ricordo così soave che, dove l'Etruria dorme, la terra non fiorisce più che asfodeli. (*Opere,* 250)

[Here the Etruscan once laughed, lying down and looking towards the sea. In his eyes he welcomed the various and silent splendour of the young and flourishing earth, from which he had joyfully drawn out the mystery; sinking his hands and his face into earth without or fear or hesitation. But the lone reveller was to be buried in the brightness of his own fable. Although the great mother retains such a sweet memory of his passing that where Etruria sleeps only asphodels will flower.]

The style of this paragraph is deliberately reminiscent of the linguistic modalities of myth: instead of referring to the ancient civilization as a whole, a figure who is symbolic of the Etruscan culture is suddenly brought to life. The pre-rational character of the Etruscans is not stated but implied by the way in which the relationship between the earth and the solitary Etruscan is evoked. The earth itself, like the Etruscan, is granted a symbolic status: it assumes first the guise of a lover who lies together with the Etruscan, then that of a maternal figure, then that of an eternal resting-place. The piece begins with a verbal picture of the Etruscan's adoration for the earth and it ends with the earth paying homage to Etruria. Etruscan civilization has been absorbed within the earth and is forever associated with it.

Following the initial evocation of Tarquinia and the various moments of its history, there is a shift in the mode of narration; each of the paragraphs of the concluding section of the first chapter of *Memorie* take the form of a vignette, depicting either the festivities that mark the succession of the seasons or the effects wrought by the seasons upon the appearance and the activity of the town. Thus the notion of time which obtains within the text is fluid; in the first part of the chapter the temporal plane is that of memory and of myth, while in the second section time progresses, but in a way that is cyclical. But if a striking feature of *Memorie della mia infanzia* is the way in which various contrasting time-schemes are interwoven, a no less interesting aspect of the text is the flexibility of its narrative voice. Frequently the stylistic register alters; on occasions, as in the opening sections of the collection, the narrator adopts the learned and nostalgic discourse of a figure distanced spatially and temporally from the world he depicts, but at other times he speaks with the voice of a character who apparently belongs to the scene that is evoked. When describing moments in the yearly cycle of Tarquinia, for instance, he writes:

O le piogge invernali del mio paese! Piove, talvolta, per lunghe settimane, senza che ne ristia un minuto, neppure la mattina. Pozzi e disotti vengono allagati e corrono le pienare. Di notte si ode il fabbro ferraio, cui prende il male, che ulula e si ruzzola nell'acqua per la via. Sono tornate le streghe in massa, i diavolacci e il lupo mannaro. Tutta quest'allegra e nottambula compagnia schiamazza sui tetti e lungo le grondaie, bofonchia per il cammino. È quello il tempo che la cornacchia e il colombo torrigiano e non escono dal loro buco. (*Opere*, 253)

[Oh the winter rains of my home town! Sometimes it rains for week after week, without stopping for an instant even in the mornings. Wells and cellars become flooded and canals and rivers are in spate. At night you can hear the blacksmith who, having gone slightly mad, howls and rolls around in the water of the streets. Witches return, as do devils and werewolves. And this joyous, nocturnal company becomes rowdy on the roofs and down the gutters, and it growls down the chimney. This is the time when crows and doves stay in their towers and do not venture out.]

Although in *Memorie* the use of reported speech or dialogue is avoided, words and phrases drawn from a popular lexicon are frequently deployed. The use of such expressions reinforces the archaic character of the style. In the edition of *La Ronda* dedicated to the exposition of Leopardi's linguistic theories, Cardarelli had taken care to underline Leopardi's proposition that the everyday language of 'il popolo', the people, was inherently poetic because, being neither abstract nor logical, it tended naturally towards the metaphorical. In a passage such as the one above, each phrase serves a figurative function. In this type of writing, Cardarelli adopts not only the idiom but also the world-view of one of the rural inhabitants of Tarquinia, strengthening the temporary illusion that the events described are not recounted by a narrator who remembers, but by a character who takes part in the activities of the community. It is immediately noticeable, for instance, that the paragraph is written in the present not the past tense, a linguistic feature which suggests a simultaneity of action and narration. Further, the character who speaks is aware of the effect that the rains produce on the countryside and the implications they have for the various kinds of livestock. He refers to the town as a closely knit whole whose collective life is governed by seasonal changes.

The writing in the second chapter of *Memorie* is in one sense more straightforward than in the first. Writing in the past tense, the narrator recalls some of his earliest memories and depicts the appearance of his father, whose life story he recounts. The relationship between father and son as it is conveyed in *Memorie* becomes progressively more subtle. The narrator often implies that the existence of his father has foreshadowed the course that his own life has taken. He draws a number of analogies between his father's tormented life and the struggles which he, as a poverty-stricken writer, has had to face. But if he sees in his father's life the mirror of his own destiny, his father in his lifetime was, we are encouraged to believe, wholly unaware of the affinity between himself and his son. The relationship between father and son that forms the thematic substance of the second part of *Memorie* goes far beyond a simple process of identification. It reveals itself to be riddled with ambiguities and bizarre emotional entanglements. The father is initially evoked in the following passage:

Di complessione adusta e sanguigna, benché piccolo di statura, tutto muscoli ed ossa, aveva le spalle ampie e ben rilevate come in un torso di Michelangelo. Privazioni e fatiche pareva si fossero conteso [*sic*] a loro piacimento il privilegio di plasmare quel suo corpo di ferro, ponendo in eccessivo risalto alcune parti comprimendone altre, e lasciando nel suo respiro qualche cosa di lievemete affannoso e non soddisfatto. . . . Autoritario, di poche parole, pateticamente chiuso, ad ogni menomo accenno di familiarità si adombrava. . . . Su quella faccia rudemente scolpita e

disadorna, piena tuttavia di delicati caratteri di razza, soltanto due piccoli
mustacchi portati senza nessuna baldanza avrebbero potuto richiamare
per un istante uno sguardo di compiacenza, mentre le mascelle assai
sviluppate e la testa rasa finivano per darle un aspetto barbarico e un
poco incutente. (*Opere*, 265)

[His complexion was dry and sanguine. Though short, he was thin and fit.
His shoulders were wide and heavy like those of one of Michelangelo's
statues. It seemed as though the deprivations and labours that he had
suffered had contended with each other for the privilege of moulding his
iron body, excessively developing some parts while weakening others and
leaving something pained and unsatisfied in his breathing. . . . He was
authoritarian, of few words, pathetically inward-looking and at the slightest hint of familiarity he would become frosty. . . . On that harshly
sculptured and unadorned face, a face that was nevertheless full of fine
racial features, only the moustache might have displayed any notion of
vanity, while the developed jawline and the shaved head conveyed a
barbarous and somewhat awesome impression.]

For a variety of reasons, this description is both striking and
significant. It is striking largely because the figure is invested
with a strong element of the fantastic: many of the adjectives
which are used to define the father are indicative of extraordinary physical qualities. More interestingly perhaps,
Cardarelli implicitly works upon an analogy between the
appearance of his father and that of a statue. Not only does
the father's physical frame seem imposing, but those aspects
of his character that are adumbrated are also made to appear
awe-inspiring: the father is taciturn, authoritarian, quickly
angered, and closed to any expression of affection. The
inner torment of his life is engraved on his physical features.
The insistence on his father's statuesque appearance, as well
as the selective mention of aspects of his temperament,
serves to create the impression that Cardarelli invokes not so
much a plausible human character as the figure of a saint or
godlike being who belongs to the mythical universe which
has been fashioned from the subjective process of remembering Tarquinia.

   The imaginative description is significant in that it points
to Cardarelli's iconic mode of depicting human characters.
The figure who emerges from this passage is, like Tarquinia,
possessed of a certain grandeur, he has a mythical dimension, and the story of his life reads like a fable. The father is

not portrayed as psychologically complex. Not afforded the
status of an objective and independent entity, he is remembered rather than brought to life. Yet if Cardarelli shows a
reluctance to penetrate the mind and the motivation of his
father, that failing is compensated for by the acuity with
which he examines the effect produced upon his own psyche
by his father's enduring memory. *Memorie della mia infanzia*
ends with the following passage:

Io non so come i figli, in genere, amino il loro padre. Io so di averne
respirato il fiato. In me egli non è morto. Lo sento durare e parlarmi
ancora attraverso la mia povera voce, ridestarsi di schianto in fondo al
mio petto, gemere, patire in me. E ho paura ch'egli m'abbia lasciato
anche il suo sguardo! Noi soffriamo gli stessi mali, sebbene con ineguale
pazienza. Nei giorni in cui sono più serio e triste io mi riconosco la sua
faccia. Tutto ciò è ben sepolto nella carne! . . . Ma io non sono che una
piccolissima parte indegna della sua lunga, leggendaria esistenza. Il suo
cruccio è implacabile. (*Opere*, 269)

[I do not know in general what kind of love sons have for their fathers. I
know that I have breathed the same breath as my father. I can feel him
continuing to exist and to speak to me through my own poor voice. I can
feel him awaking suddenly in the depth of my own self and groaning and
suffering within me. And I fear that he has left me his stare! We suffer the
same afflictions, although I with less patience. In the days in which I am
most serious and most sad I recognize his face. All has been buried in
flesh! . . . But I am no more than a tiny and unworthy part of his long,
legendary existence. His anxiety is implacable.]

The father visits the son, not as a ghostlike figure who
appears from without, but as a presence existing within the
son's consciousness: his memory has assumed corporeal
form in the physical features of the son, who sees in himself
the image of his father. Paradoxically, therefore, the figure
of the father is at once distinct and yet inseparable from that
of the son. But, even within the brief space of the paragraph,
the internal portrait of the father alters, thus encouraging
different responses from the son: at one level he identifies
with the father, at another he experiences pity for him. Yet
embedded within these responses is another kind of narrative statement. In precisely the same way that Cardarelli,
when speaking of the creative act of writing, had stressed the
necessity of submitting to the exigencies of an illustrious but

at the same time internal model of style, when speaking of
the father he again invokes the spectre of a repressive agent
who dictates a series of ineluctable but at the same time
prohibitive laws. The father bears down upon the son with
supernatural force. While acknowledging his tremendous
probity, the son is overshadowed, intimidated by his example: the father stands as the higher, moral, suprapersonal
side of the son's character, yet the obedience he demands is
too exacting to be sustained. Thus, consciously or unconsciously inscribed within the piece, is the message that the
dictatorial moral example is stifling, just as in the aesthetic
pronouncements one finds the inscription that the classical
style, so overtly venerated, may be simply a straitjacket that
throttles expression. Finally, the memory of the father has
become so entrenched within the consciousness of the son
as to become an intrinsic part of it, just as the son is only a
moment in the being of the father. The son is haunted and
seemingly smothered by a facet of his own character.

   Despite its varying time-schemes, its flexible narrative
style, and its occasional moments of intense introspection,
Memorie della mia infanzia is nevertheless a relatively slim text.
In it, however, Cardarelli had adumbrated a number of
autobiographical themes to which he would later return. In
the years following from the closure of *La Ronda* he continued to write intricately constructed prose pieces which
adhered to *La Ronda*'s doctrines, while developing an ideological slant which marked them out as clearly pro-Fascist.
By the mid-1920s he was publishing a new series of prose
writings in the pages of different journals and magazines; all
of these pieces would be included in the later volume *Il sole a
picco*.[7] The longest and best known of such writings was first
published in *Il Tevere* on 15 October 1927. The piece, 'Il mio
paese', was later to be the opening chapter of *Il sole a picco*
and more than any other it demonstrates how a neoclassical
aesthetic could produce pages of prose poetry. The piece
focuses on the landscape which surrounds Tarquinia, insist-
ing on its grandiose, melancholy appearance and comparing
the appearance of his home town with the image created by

----

[7] For a thorough account of the editorial history of *Il sole a picco*, see Martignoni's
edition of the collected works of Cardarelli, pp. 1060–86.

Böcklin in his painting *The Isle of the Dead*. The re-creation of Tarquinia relies upon an intricately constructed, phonetically complex verbal medium, one which implies control, distance from the material, and the supremacy of the artist. Yet, a brief analysis of an extract from the prose piece (*Opere*, 374–84) reveals some of the complexities that are concealed by the Leopardian façade of its style:

Ma dalla vista consueta della marina, con le sue saline e il suo Bagno Penale, dalla Maremma fortunosa, l'occhio si torceva e riposava contemplando, più sotto, il pensoso raccoglimento delle valli che circondano la morta Tarquinia: così immensamente remota, con quell'ombra di vetustà che la intristisce ad ogni ora, in ogni stagione; acquattata dietro altissime rupi da cui . . . si sporgono chiesuole dell'anno mille e dove il silenzio e la solitudine hanno del sovrumano. Stavo sul ciglio di un abisso. E di lì vedevo la pericolante positura del mio protervo paese. . . . Stavo direi quasi, ascoltando tutte queste cose che apparivano sotto i miei occhi, allorché uno stormo di cornacchie che mi passò sopra il capo venne a darmi l'annunzio più certo che ero nel cuore della mia terra. (*Opere*, 377)

[From the familiar sight of the marina with its salt-pans and its prison house and from the stormy land of Maremma, my glance turned and rested in contemplation of the valleys which surround the dead Tarquinia: so immensely remote, with that shadow of antiquity which makes it appear melancholy at every hour and in every season; crouched behind towering rocks, tiny churches from the year 1000 rise up. There silence and solitude have something which transcends the human. I was standing on the edge of an abyss. And from there I could see the precarious position of my proud town. . . . I was, you might say, listening to all these things which appeared before my eyes when a flock of crows flying above me came to announce that I was in the heart of my homeland.]

From a formal point of view, a passage such as this clearly conforms to the major stylistic theories expounded by the *rondisti*. Syntactically it is tightly structured. Each sentence contains a relatively large number of sub-clauses, and each of these tends to be of similar syllabic length and rhythmical arrangement. The impression that this creates is that the prose obeys a metrical arrangement, and this impression is strengthened by other techniques which, borrowed from verse, enrich the phonetic texture of the passage. Cardarelli tends to employ abstract, non-visual adjectives and nouns often suggestive of the infinitely old, and he likes to use such words not singly but in groups of semi-rhyming pairs. The elementary sound structure that this stylistic choice encourages is supported by other patterns of alliteration and conspicuous repetition of the same parts of speech. The divide that separates such an elaborately contrived form of utterance from ordinary speech is obviously great, and yet it is further emphasized by the intertextual reformulation of concepts and phrases taken from Leopardi's 'L'Infinito': if the persona of Leopardi's famous poem becomes submerged in the process of attempting to circumscribe the inconceivable distances travelled by the imagination, then similarly the speaking voice of Cardarelli's lyrical prose explores 'sovrumani silenzi' and a 'profondissima quiete'.

The Literature of Strapaese

In an appraisal of the work of Cardarelli, written on his death in 1959, Emilio Cecchi expressed his opinion that his former friend had been 'a true and great poet in prose'.[8] A formal analysis of a piece of writing such as 'Il mio paese' does reveal the linguistic complexity of the form of expression which Cardarelli cultivated. But such an analysis also implies that this type of prose bears little relation to the social and political realities of the time. The *rondisti*, believing that the role of the writer was not to interfere with matters concerning the political destiny of the country, had advocated the separation of literature from politics, and their works have frequently been castigated by more modern critics for their apparent lack of commitment. Asor Rosa, for example, has judged the texts of the writers of *La Ronda* to be the type of literature that was best adapted to survive in 'the asphyxiating reality of Fascism'.[9] It would, however, be wrong to suggest that Cardarelli's prose writings are anything as innocent as elegantly written exercises in nostalgia.

During the years that he was engaged in the writing of the prose pieces that were ultimately to make up the collection *Il*

[8] E. Cecchi, 'Ricordo di Vincenzo Cardarelli', *L'Approdo letterario*, 7 July–Sept. 1959, 11.

[9] Asor Rosa, *Storia d'Italia dall'Unità a oggi*, ii. 1416–22.

sole a picco he was also an active contributor to a number of overtly nationalistic, pro-Fascist newspapers and periodicals. The position which he had occupied as editor of *La Ronda* had secured for him a fair amount of prestige in cultural circles and meant that publishers were willing to pay for his copy. In 1925 *Il Tevere* was set up as a daily newspaper based in Rome and under the editorship of Telesio Interlandi. The newspaper provided an unofficial mouthpiece for Mussolini to air his views on controversial subjects and prepare the ground for future legislation. Adrian Lyttelton has pointed to the 'extremist, unrestrained and speculative' character of the articles Mussolini published in *Il Tevere* and to the role which the publication served in creating a climate of anxiety among those individuals and groups who were not explicitly allied to Fascism.[10] From 1925 onwards Cardarelli was in contact with the literary editor of *Il Tevere*, Corrado Pavolini,[11] and began to publish a series of reviews, commentaries and prose pieces in its pages.

His contibution to the Fascist press was not limited to his active participation in the enterprise of *Il Tevere*. In July 1924 the writer and painter Mino Maccari set up the journal *Il Selvaggio* in the small Tuscan town of Colle Val d'Elsa. The purpose of the journal was initially to defend the Fascist revolution which the *squadristi* believed they had been instrumental in bringing about. By 1925 the journal had shifted its interest from politics to culture, but it remained intimately associated with provincial Tuscan Fascism. In the words of one of its leading articles, the journal sought to be 'the resolute affirmation of the essential and indispensable values of characteristically Italian traditions and customs' ('Gazzettino ufficiale di Strapaese', 27 November 1927, p. 85). The *strapaese*[12] movement, which the journal spearheaded, was intended to 'defend the rural character of the Italian people against the invasion of modern fashions, foreign civilizations

[10] Lyttelton, *The Seizure of Power*, 400.

[11] Cardarelli's letters to Pavolini are reprinted in *Cardarelli e Ungaretti: Lettere a Corrado Pavolini (1926–1930)*, ed. with an introduction by Marinella Mascia Galateria and F. Bernardini Napoletano (Rome: Bulzoni, 1989).

[12] The term *strapaese*, which literally translated means 'superprovince', was coined by Malaparte and pointed proudly to the chauvinistic character of the movement.

and ways of thinking' ('Programma di Strapaese', 16 September 1927, p. 65). The way in which Maccari identified Fascism with 'the healthy traditions of popular sobriety and wisdom'[13] won the support of a number of leading pro-Fascist intellectuals: Soffici, Malaparte, and Papini all wrote for *Il Selvaggio*, while painters such as Ottone Rosai, Carlo Carrà, and Giorgio Morandi contributed sketches and illustrations. From the early months of 1926 the chauvinistic message which *Il Selvaggio* had set out to propagate was supported by the appearance of a new periodical. Together with a number of close friends in Bologna, the 21-year-old Leo Longanesi began to publish *L'Italiano*. The journal was explicitly committed to upholding the principles of the Fascist revolution, which it regarded as the concrete expression of the will of the Italian people.

L'Italiano attracted many of the same contributors as *Il Selvaggio*, and from 1933 the two journals shared the same offices in Rome. It comes as little surprise that Cardarelli was an important voice in both periodicals. In the aftermath of the First World War he had set himself up as the defender of the traditions of Italian national culture. The insularity of the cultural programme of *La Ronda* had been accompanied by an eagerness for a measure of censorship. With the Fascist accession to power, this had not been long in coming. By 1923 the prefect of every region could punish the proprietors of publications which printed material which could be seen in any way as false or harmful to the country. Immediately after the assassination of Matteotti the authorities gained the right to sequester material that was deemed to be seditious. If the actions of the authorities served to curb experimentation and encourage conformity, then publications like *Il Selvaggio* and *L'Italiano* lent support through their attacks on foreign ideas and on innovative ways of writing. *L'Italiano* explicitly saw its role as akin to that which *La Ronda* had earlier fulfilled. In one article, significantly entitled 'La difesa della *Ronda*' (December 1926), Giuseppe Raimondi characterized the defunct journal as having

---

[13] Maccari's observation is quoted in the introduction to Carlo Ludovico Ragghianti (ed.), anthology of *Il Selvaggio* (Vincenza: Neri Pozza Editore, 1959), 10.

served the purpose of defending Italian culture from harmful innovative currents.

In its drive to promote a form of literary classicism, *La
Ronda* had lambasted a series of modernist groupings. In a
precisely analogous fashion, the two Fascist periodicals set
out to attack any movement which seemed to undermine
what was arbitrarily defined as belonging to the Italian
tradition. The most famous polemic which developed as a
result of the policy towards culture assumed by journals such
as *L'Italiano* was that between *strapaese* and *stracittà*. The latter
term was used to define the group of writers who had been
drawn to Massimo Bontempelli's periodical *900*, the first
issue of which appeared in the autumn of 1926. Bontempelli
was a supporter of Fascism, yet he did not see the movement as synonymous with cultural provincialism. His journal,
which appeared every three months, was (to begin with at
least) published entirely in French. The editorial board
contained a number of European writers and in the course
of its existence *900* published the writings of figures such as
James Joyce, Virginia Woolf, and D. H. Lawrence. Bontempelli, refuting attacks made against both him and his journal,
defended the role of creative imagination in producing
works capable of withstanding the test of translation. He
implicitly criticized the provincialism of *La Ronda* and maintained that the secret of 'linking oneself with tradition' was
not to emulate earlier models, but to forget about tradition
('infischiarsene').[14]

The attacks on the proposals of *900* which the *strapaesani*
made were more frequent, more vulgar, and more extreme.
Although he had initially collaborated with Bontempelli in
setting up *900*, Curzio Malaparte soon switched sides and, in
the issue of *Il Selvaggio* of November 1927, he attacked the
grouping as a collection of 'fashionable, petty bourgeois
letterati' always aware of 'the latest novelties to emerge from
Paris, London and New York'.[15] His mocking observations

[14] The quotation is taken from a selection of Bontempelli's writings for *900*
which appeared between 1926 and 1927, compiled by Giuliano Manacorda in his
volume *Letteratura e cultura del periodo fascista*, 101.

[15] Malaparte's views are quoted in G. Manacorda's volume, *Storia della letteratura
italiana tra le due guerre 1919–1943* (Rome: Riuniti, 1980), 119.

were supported by Soffici's acerbic comments on any form of Europeanizing innovation.[16] At the same time that such caustic accusations were being made against 900, Cardarelli was establishing himself as a Fascist intellectual and as one of the principle architects of a notion of 'italianità'. In the columns of *Il Tevere* he poured scorn on Bontempelli's initiative ('A proposito di 900', 20 September 1926), defining it as both 'anti-Fascist' and 'anti-Italian' in its attempt to foster a European literary community. Bontempelli's interest in the work of contemporary modernist writers from a variety of national backgrounds was certainly at odds with the Italo-centric and retrogressive views which Cardarelli entertained. Indeed, the immediate and total hostility towards 900 that Cardarelli expressed served to clarify the xenophobia inherent within his notion of classicism.

If participation in the *strapaese* movement meant engaging polemically with cultural manifestations such as 900, it also entailed establishing the theoretical principles of a committed Fascist literature and producing writings in conformity with those principles. Of all the *strapaesani*, Malaparte offered the most sustained articulation of the principles of the movement. The main document in which he set forth his vision of the Italian nation was entitled *Italia barbara* and published in 1925.[17] Surprisingly enough, the first edition of the work was published by Piero Gobetti, who had defined Malaparte's style as moving between that of Leopardi, Cardarelli, and the English essayists of the eighteenth century.[18] In his prefatory statement to *Italia barbara*, Gobetti described its author as 'Fascism's strongest pen'. The argument presented by Malaparte's text is premised on an antipathy towards modernity, coupled with a vision of the future as bringing only the menace of foreign influence. The concept of modernity against which Malaparte railed included the value system established by the Enlightenment. In *Italia*

---

[16] Soffici's stance is reported in M. Galateria's introduction to *Cardarelli e Ungaretti: Lettere a Corrado Pavolini*, 32.

[17] In December 1924 Gobetti, in a serious attempt to combat some of the more extreme simplifications of Fascist culture, had started publication of his journal *Il Baretti*. The journal was to survive until 1928.

[18] P. Gobetti, 'Profili di contemporanei: L'eroe di corte', *Il Lavoro*, 17 Jan. 1924.

barbara the writer provocatively attacks Enlightenment principles (considered to be imports from abroad) and criticizes
the Risorgimento and D'Azeglio's attempt to remake the
Italians. He simultaneously constructs a model of the Italian
people which predates the modern developments which he
so laments. Positing himself as the interpreter of the 'Italian
spirit', the writer gives life to a vision of a rural Italy made up
of small communities each of which serves as a repository of
the most authentic values of the Italians, or, as the text
claims, 'the ancient customs of our civilization'.[19] Malaparte
endows what he calls the 'ignorance, superstition and dis-
trustfulness' of the people with positive connotations. The
stereotype of the 'good Italian' or 'barbarous Italian' that
the text creates is that of a person hating anything foreign,
disposed towards violent action but ready to trust existing
hierarchies. National identity resides in regional identity, the
people are the custodians of tradition, and it is the duty of
Fascism to uphold such traditions and thereby perform a
function akin to that of the Counter-Reformation. It is the
duty of a committed Fascist literature to 'sing the praises of
the Italian barbarians, with their free and ingenuous spirits
and their attachment to tradition'.

In Malaparte's construction of the stereotype of the Italian
there are clear echoes of Soffici's *Lemmonio Boreo*. In turn,
the views on Fascism and Italian national identity which
Cardarelli was expounding in the pages of *Il Tevere* and other
journals in the mid-1920s coincided to a remarkable extent
with those put forward by Malaparte.[20] In one article,
'Stato popolare. Riflessioni intorno al Fascismo' (*Il Tevere*,
31 December 1925), Cardarelli contended that attempts to
unify Italy according to the principles of liberal democracy
were alien to the 'spirit' of the nation. Such a spirit,
long predating the Risorgimento, was not the preserve of

[19] The edition from which the quotation is taken is *Opere complete di Curzio Malaparte*, 4 vols., vol. ii: *L'Europa Vivente*, ed. Enrico Falqui (Florence: Vallecchi, 1963), 500.
[20] The coincidence between the two positions was not accidental. Malaparte not only knew Cardarelli reasonably well, he imitated aspects of his style and referred in his prose to figures who appear in the latter's writings. An instance of this kind of reference is to be found in the prose piece 'Cardarelli, Papini e il barocco', *L'Europa vivente*, 347.

an aristocratic élite, but resided firmly in the customs and beliefs of the people. In his article, he transformed 'il popolo' into a vehicle for the expression of anti-modern and anti-European sentiment. He argued that the people were faithful to a notion of tradition which ran deeper than changes of political organization. In his view the native Italian tradition had its origin in Greek and Roman civilization, as well as in Catholicism, and it was clearly separate from 'anything which reeks of Europe or protestantism'. As well as presenting himself as the medium for the expression of the spirit of the Italian people, he arrogated to himself the role of the interpreter of the will of the Duce. He set out to establish a series of historical antecedents to Fascism and attempted to show how Mussolini's system of government was not only consonant with the soul of Italy's people but was likely to preserve, as he put it, 'the entire patrimony of popular values'.

In *Italia barbara* Malaparte had claimed that it was time to 'praise the honest men of order and disorder who populate the squares of Italian towns and villages' (p. 521). While endorsing such a thesis, Cardarelli nevertheless placed a strong accent on the nobility of 'il popolo' and contended that the classically inspired, high style of prose writing that he and other *rondisti* had cultivated was the kind of writing which was most suited to the expression of the values and beliefs of the Italian people. In an article, fittingly entitled 'A proposito di arte fascista', and published in *L'Italiano* (15 February 1927) he articulated his desire for a kind of writing that would be the expression 'of the new Catholic and popular Italy', a kind of writing that would be both classical and, in the sense in which Malaparte had employed the term, 'barbarous'; a kind of writing, finally, in which it would be possible to hear the 'song of our race'. The ease with which Cardarelli managed to advance a highly subjective, mythical, and ahistorical conception of 'the people' as a self-evident truth is striking. The extreme chauvinism of his argument is made clear when in his article 'Stato popolare' he refers to nations with a less pronounced sense of tradition as 'inferior'.

The ideological position adopted in articles such as 'Stato

popolare' had a number of obvious resonances. Looking
back at the events of the 1920s, Mario Missiroli, the editor of
the *Corriere della sera*, suggested that the most important
influence on Leo Longanesi's idea of an Italian nation, both
noble and popular, was that exerted by Cardarelli.[21] When in
the preface to the first issue of *L'Italiano* in 1926 Longanesi
enumerated the essential features of his perception of Italy,
he implied a knowledge of Cardarelli's thinking. He wrote:
'Italy is bathed by the sun and along with the sun one can
only conceive of the Church, classicism, Dante, enthusiasm,
harmony, philosophical healthiness, Fascism, antidemocracy
and Mussolini'. The literary editor of *Il Tevere*, Corrado
Pavolini, defined Cardarelli as the 'most significant writer of
the new Italy' ('Voyages dans le temps', *Il Tevere*, 17 March
1928) and Mino Maccari characterized him as 'the master
poet of *strapaese*' ('Adagio Biagi', *Il Selvaggio*, 24 November
1927, p. 82).

Cardarelli's Strapaese *Writing*

Cardarelli's main contribution to the creative writing of the
strapaese movement was to be found in his collection of
twelve prose pieces, *Il sole a picco*. The collection was printed
in 1929 by the presses of *L'Italiano*, Longanesi being keen
to publish writing which presented a vision of Italy that
coincided with that promoted by the journal. *Il sole a picco*
oscillates between prose poetry and writing which makes
coded ideological statements. The collection opens with the
piece 'Il mio paese' (discussed above), and it concludes with
a select number of carefully crafted autobiographical inves-
tigations. In between these two poles, however, the writing
can best be defined as the creative analogue of the pro-
Fascist articles Cardarelli had published in such journals as *Il
Tevere* and which were published in book form under the

---

[21] Missiroli wrote: 'Io persisto a ritenere che la maggiore influenza su di lui fu
quella del Cardarelli, che dava dignità storica e filosofica alle sue intuizioni e
anticipava la sua concezione di un'Italia popolare e comunale.' His view was
initially printed in *Il Borghese*, 10 Oct. 1957. It is quoted in A. Andreoli's biography,
Leo Longanesi (Florence: La Nuova Italia, 1980), 43.

title of *Parliamo dell'Italia* (1931). The prose pieces of the central section of *Il sole a picco* recount legends of Tarquinia and present a series of narrative portraits of characters who are emblematic of the small rural community. One piece, 'Il contadino', is dedicated to the celebration of the values of those inhabitants of Le Marche who, initially employed as migrant workers, came to establish themselves as inhabitants of Tarquinia. The characteristics of this group are conveyed through the representation of one archetypal figure, the *contadino* or agricultural worker. The life of this figure knows no disruption; it is characterized by domestic order and unceasing work in the fields. The *contadino* does not own the land he works but is happy to respect existing hierarchies. Indeed, 'nobility of manners, religion and happiness with his station in life' are the 'divinities' which he obeys. The reactionary simplifications present in such a fabled account are obvious.

Another prose piece, 'Alessandrone', is cast as a popular narrative; it relates the events which befall the arrogant leader of a group of agricultural workers. Alessandrone makes a great deal of money, but he parades his new-found wealth and is set upon and robbed. In a temporary fit of insanity, following this incident, he kills his innocent wife. The narration of the tale is informed by an intimate knowledge of the workings of Tarquinia's rural economy and punctuated with comments which express how Alessandrone is regarded by the inhabitants of the town. The tale exemplifies a piece of collective wisdom, that is to say, those who believe themselves to be above the laws of the town or flaunt its customs inevitably meet with retribution. As in the preceding piece, the subtext is that the successful individual should respect the status quo. The piece which follows on from 'Alessandrone' does not illustrate a moral lesson, but celebrates the appearance and narrates the deeds of a figure, Re Tarquinio, who is steeped in the lore of the town. Re Tarquinio is an interesting construction in so far as he is an archetypal 'italiano barbaro'; he has no knowledge or interest in the world that lies beyond his home town, he lacks any formal education, he distrusts anything mechanical, and he shows a closeness to the land which is reflected in his vigorous appetite both for food and for sexual activity. The narrator accentuates the peculiarities of the figure's physical appearance and the eccentricities of his clothing to imply the extent to which he has remained untouched by any notion of fashion and the degree to which he dislikes refinement. The details of his life are picaresque and he is characterized by his irrepressible good humour.

Immaginate un pezzo d'uomo alto quasi due metri, costretto in certi abiti lisi, corti, attillati, abbottonatissimi, in maniera da non poterne più uscire, con tanto di stivali che gli arrivano fino al ginocchio e un cappelluzzo da cacciatore delle Alpi, posato con mirabile equilibrio sopra una testa che, da qualunque parte la si guardi, è un capolavoro di scrinatura. (*Opere*, 404)

[Imagine a big fellow, almost two metres high, confined within very tight, worn and small clothes, clothes buttoned up so as to make it impossible to get out of them. He wears a pair of boots up to his knees and tiny hat in the style of an Alpine hunter, the hat is cleverly placed on a head which from every way you look at it is a masterpiece of someone's ability to use a pair of shears.]

Re Tarquinio may be the written version of Maccari's sketches of figures of village life which regularly appeared in the pages of *Il Selvaggio*. Yet despite his comic aspect, Cardarelli presents the figure as possessing an epic dimension and an inner nobility; he refuses to accept the inevitability of death and takes the suffering and shortcomings of life with stoicism. Throughout the prose piece it is implied that the character is the living embodiment of the rural spirit of the town. The death of Re Tarquinio would, Cardarelli writes, strike Corneto Tarquinia with the same effect as a natural disaster. Re Tarquinio is not the only figure to represent the simplicity and wisdom of popular traditions. The figure of the narrator's father reappears and, in the prose piece 'Il buffet della stazione', his life is the subject of a long and admiring account. In another piece which revolves around the evocation of an extended stay in Settignano, the narrator remembers his conversations with his host, Sor Ettore. The figure is described as a perfect example of the proud Tuscan: a stonemason by profession, he has an instinctive appreciation of art, speaks vividly of the events of the past, and is suspicious of modern or foreign intrusions.

The figures which appear in *Il sole a picco* are numerous and, more importantly, they are not isolated constructions. Characters like Sor Ettore or Re Tarquinio are presented as typically Italian. Whether or not they corresponded to certain types of Italians living in the 1920s, they certainly exemplified characteristics which believers in rural Fascism were keen to promote. As well as being the theorist of a certain type of 'italianità', Malaparte wrote pages of more creative prose populated by heroic figures who, as he saw it, embodied the values of the average Italian. For example, in the section of *Italia barbara* entitled 'Elogio del buon italiano' he presented Michelangelo in the following terms:

Nessuno è mai stato più italiano di Michelangelo, intendendo per italiano l'uomo per eccellenza, realista e pratico, metà sangue metà terra, pianta fino alla cintola, animale dalla cintola in su, una specie di centauro dei tre regni della natura, essere concreto che pensa come agisce . . . talvolta umano fino alla bestialità. (*L'Europa vivente*, 536)

[No one has ever been more Italian than Michelangelo, I mean by Italian a man above everything else, a man who is realistic and practical, half blood and half earth, a plant up to his waist and and an animal from his waist upwards, a kind of centaur made from elements of the three realms of nature, a concrete being who thinks and acts, sometimes human to the point of being bestial.]

Lack of refinement, earthy physicality, and a quasi-mythic status are elements which make Malaparte's Michelangelo and Cardarelli's Re Tarquinio appear as two faces of the same ideology. Another important practitioner of this kind of iconography was Ardegno Soffici. Both his *Ricordi di vita artistica e letteraria* (1930) and his *Taccuino d'Arno Borghi* (1933) offer a number of narrative portraits to add to the *strapaese* gallery of 'italianità'. In one prose piece he recalls a visit to the house of the ageing and toothless scholar Raffaele Del Rosso: he is irascible and eccentric, but his knowledge of ancient Tuscan culture is second to none, while his mode of speech is described as 'bizarre and marvellous'.[22] Similarly, when Soffici writes in remembrance of his friend and sometime tutor, Bino Binazzi, he places extraordinary emphasis

[22] Raffaele Del Rosso is further described as 'l'ultima immagine dell'italiano vero, all'antica' in 'Visita a un vecchio italiano', *Ricordi di vita artistica e letteraria*, in Soffici, *Opere*, 71–81.

upon the simplicity of his manners and the humility of his social position, as contrasted with the nobility of his countenance and speech. Binazzi is explicitly described as a saint of a timeless Tuscan tradition, while another of Soffici's friends, the peasant farmer Gosto, is the custodian of 'a true civilization'.

In the earlier *vociano* text, *Lemmonio Boreo*, Soffici had quite openly exploited the allegorical dimension of characters such as Spillo or Zaccagna to suggest how violent change might be effected. The figurations which appear in the *strapaese* texts, although invested with a wider array of attributes and, on occasions, with a historical reality, nevertheless show a commonality of characteristics which hints at their status as ideal types. These types establish a model of cultural identification: they supply a list of attributes to be recognized and emulated, while at the same time they imply a corresponding set of attributes which are to be disparaged or avoided. Their ideological significance, in other words, is to be found in the logic of their binary oppositions. Characters like Re Tarquinio or Bino Binazzi are exemplars of 'italianità' because they are untouched by any foreign influence. Indeed, all the figures of *Il sole a picco* are presented as belonging to what is referred to in Cardarelli's article 'Italia popolare' as 'that ancient people which carries the Etruscan and Roman traditions in its blood'. The celebration of national purity implies a dislike of what is international. Concomitantly, the persistence of timeless, rural traditions in the lifestyles and ways of thinking of archetypal figures implies a polemic against the introduction not only of the foreign but of the new. In such a scheme of things, the past is perpetuated in the present while providing a model for the future.

Within *strapaese* writing, the echoes of the aggressive autobiographies of the *vociani* are to be heard clearly. Although the narrator delineates other characters than the main protagonist, those characters share his place of origin and his sense of cultural belonging. In celebrating figures of a local community, the writer celebrates himself. It is immediately obvious, for example, that all *strapaese* heroes are male. The binary logic of exalting the male and excluding what is thought to be female is implicit in most writing associated with *L'Italiano* or *Il Selvaggio* and can indeed be deduced from the very titles of the two journals. In the work of Soffici that logic is, however, expressed in a way that is unpleasant to read but useful to expose. In an extended meditation entitled 'Virilità e femminilità' he provides a list of all his pro-Fascist beliefs and systematically opposes each of these with what he describes as the feminine attitude. The piece contains a series of sentences such as the following:

La virilità essendo . . . carattere precipuo di ogni manifestazione vitale o disciplina spirituale del mondo greco, latino, eppoi italiano, lo spirito femminile è naturalmente opposto ed avverso a queste cose che sono nostre. Gran parte della cosidetta 'modernità', internazionalista, immoralista, anarchica, antisociale, irrazionalista, antiarchiettonica e decadente è mera espressione di femminilità.[23]

[Virility being the fundamental characteristic of every manifestation of energy or of every spiritual discipline of the world of the Greeks, of the Romans and then of the Italians, the female spirit is naturally opposed to these things that belong to us. Much of so-called 'modernity', which in character is international, immoral, anarchic, anti-social, irrational, anti-architectural and decadent is the mere expression of femininity.]

Both in the presentation of archetypal figures of 'italianità' and in the unequivocal expression of views such as the above, the writer does not respect the laws of logical argument but is quite prepared to declare a series of unexamined prejudices as articles of faith. It is in such a form of expression that the *squadrista* mentality shows itself.

The final point to emerge from a consideration of the non-rational elevation of figures deemed to embody national characteristics is the closeness such figures betray to a number of iconic descriptions of Mussolini. In Malaparte's chauvinistic collection of poems and marching songs, *L'Arcitaliano* (1928) the Duce figures as the natural leader of the people because he is the incarnation of their aspirations and traditions. In Soffici's *Ricordi di vita artistica e letteraria*, he is depicted as showing the noble, classical elements that we

---

[23] Quoted from the *Taccuino di Arno Borghi*, in Soffici *Opere*, iv. 349. The extent of the misogyny of Soffici and other *strapaesani* is an area which, given its obvious importance within orthodox Fascist writing, needs to be researched further. Soffici's ramblings in *Arno Borghi* also become both implicitly and explicitly racist.

are led to believe naturally distinguish the Italian people. Soffici's description of Mussolini accords to a striking degree with elements present in Cardarelli's portrait of the father quoted above. Soffici writes:

La luce invernale . . . rischiarava e ombreggiava gagliardamente quella sua testa rapata fra di plebeo e d'imperatore, testa dove perciò sono impressi i segni caratteristici della nostra razza terrestre a un tempo e divina, nella quale si coniugano, come in ogni organismo perfetto, la forza elementare e la grazia che viene dallo spirito. (*Opere*, vi. 96)

[The winter light . . . cast both light and shade over his shaved head. His head, both that of a man of the people and of an emperor, displayed the characteristic traits of our race which are both earthly and divine. In our race, as in every perfect organism, elemental force and spiritual grace are united.]

Such writing appeals to conceptions of race and civilization, while contributing to the cult of the leader. The reader is encouraged to believe in the myth of the new Fascist man, whose origins stretch back across the whole of Italian history.

The kind of writing which exalted a certain type of national figure and which presented a set of values supposed to be innately Italian naturally won official approval. As an example of *strapaese* writing, *Il sole a picco* was received enthusiastically in the Fascist press: Arnaldo Bocelli, writing in *Bibliografia fascista*, implied that the book was an expression of what he described as 'the conscience of Fascism', and three years later in the same journal Pietro Lissia defined Cardarelli's prose as 'full of the scent of the earth' and concluded his review with the sentence: 'Vincenzo Cardarelli and *Parliamo d'Italia* are naturally on the right side.'[24] In 1930 the prestigious literary prize the Premio Bagutta was awarded to Cardarelli for *Il sole a picco*. The extent to which the eulogistic portrayal of Tarquinia and its inhabitants in many prose pieces of *Il sole a picco* reinforced a reactionary myth of 'italianità', secured for Cardarelli an understandable degree of contempt among both contemporary opponents to Mussolini's regime and modern literary historians. Writing from prison Gramsci dismissively characterized Car-

[24] A. Bocelli, 'Il carattere della nuova letteratura', *Biografia fascista*, 3 (Mar. 1930), 194. P. Lissia, 'Parliamo dell'Italia', *Biografia fascista*, 5 (May 1933) 344–5.

darelli as 'a modern fossil'[25] and more recently Umberto
Carpi, when speaking of texts such as *Parliamo d'Italia*, has
spoken of Cardarelli as a detestable figure.[26]

Contradictions in Cardarelli's Writing

By examining sections of *Il sole a picco*, it is not difficult to
see how the neoclassicism of *La Ronda* could be married to
the ideology of *Il Selvaggio* to create an authentically pro-
Fascist form of literary production. Within that production,
elements of the *vociano* nationalism recur, as do some of the
views on the identity of rural Italy that had formed the
substance of Cardarelli's earlier appreciation of the work of
Charles Péguy. Yet what adds considerably to the interest of
Cardarelli's writing during the twenty years of Mussolini's
rule is the fact that it does not simply represent the trans-
position of an ultra-conservative ideology into pages of narrative or symbolic prose. The same can be said of the work of
a number of writers and artists who were deeply implicated
in the history of Fascism: for example, in the early 1930s
Malaparte himself wrote pages of subdued, reflective prose
(for example *Fughe in prigione*, 1936), while a good deal of
the painting of Mario Sironi combines troubling figurations
with monumental motifs. In Cardarelli's writings of the
1920s contradictions emerge between a neoclassical project
on the one hand and a decadent sensibility on the other,
between a desire to write prose expressing palingenetic
national myths and an impulse to explore introspective
themes, between writing that is highly compromised and yet
which still possesses claims to modernity.

The final prose pieces of *Il sole a picco* are not concerned
with the *strapaese* depiction of a microcosmic rural society.
Instead, they relate journeys made to different locations in
Italy and each of these locations becomes a fantastic space.
To achieve a notion of the fantastic, a number of interesting
compositional devices are employed: the writer disturbs the

---

[25] Gramsci's slighting definition of Cardarelli is now contained in *Letteratura e vita nazionale* (Turin: Einaudi, 1953), 182.

[26] Carpi, 'Cardarelli e Péguy', 23.

chronological order of his descriptions, merging past and present into a single atemporal moment; he avoids the localization, either in time or in space, of his first-person narrating voice, relying upon frequent breaks and shifts of perspective. On occasions he evokes only one aspect of the sensory data of a given scene. For instance, in the concluding paragaph of the piece, 'Le campane di Firenze', he mentions the likeness of the roofs of the town to a sea of burning bricks and then expands upon this comparison in each successive sentence, so that what begins as a realistic representation gradually assumes the attributes of a hallucination, as imaginary perception prevails over actual description. But some of the intricacies of this type of writing can best be brought out by isolating a paragraph from one of the most metaphorical and multifaceted prose pieces of the collection. The following extract is taken from 'Lago' (*Opere*, 456–9), a composition which evokes a visit undertaken in the past to the Lombard lakes:

Nasce il vento d'autunno sui monti, gravido di memorie. E cala giù furioso, funebre, inebriante, con l'umore della morte e della strage; e fa venir voglia di cantare. Spoglia le vigne rosseggianti dopo la vendemmia e le selve ingiallite. Così potess'io squassare i ricordi che ingombrano la mia mente come sotto l'impeto di quel vento esaltato . . . . Sopraggiungono di lì a poco, le lunghe piogge autunnali, simili a un gran pianto dirotto, interminabile, in cui par proprio che la natura si dolga e si lamenti di passare. . . . Quando più nessuno se l'aspetta, un sole freddoloso e mendico, più prezioso dell'oro vecchio e del vino stagionato, più smemorante del più fino liquore, torna poi, ogni mattina, a trovare le foglie gialle d'acacia . . . che il vento trascina lungo i viali come degli spettri, e pare non se ne voglia più andare. Così pallido, così antico, continua talvolta fino a Natale a risplendere sui monti che sono tutto un seccume e sui giardini sontuosi e disfatti come cimiteri.

[The autumn wind is born on the mountains, full of memories. And it sweeps down furiously; both agitated and funerary, it carries with it a feeling of death and destruction; it makes you want to sing. It strips the purple vines after the harvest and it divests the yellowed woods. If only I could rid myself of the memories that cloud my mind under the force of that exalted wind . . . . Soon afterwards the long autumn rains begin and they are like a great, endless weeping in which it seems as though nature itself suffers and laments at its passing. . . . When no one expects it any longer, a cold and impoverished sun, more precious than gold or matured wine and more pacifying than the finest liqueur returns every morning to find the yellow leaves of the acacia trees that the wind blows through the streets as if they were ghosts. So pale and so old, the sun continues sometimes until Christmas to shine on the bare mountains and on the gardens which, sumptuous but unkempt, are like cemeteries.]

The writing consciously strives towards a poetic register in its manipulation of elaborate patterns of sound and stress, but also it distinguishes itself conspicuously from the narrative use of prose in the way it exploits imagery. The extensive use of imagery serves the effect of simultaneously invoking two coherent yet intersecting and ultimately inseparable mental pictures. The first is grounded in physical reality; it portrays the final days of summer, the arrival of the autumnal winds, the coming of the rains, and finally the appearance of a pale winter sun. What is represented forms a part of an endlessly recurring cyclical process, and yet the emphasis of the writing is resolutely placed upon the notion of things coming to an inevitable point of extinction. The eschatological concerns of the piece are reinforced by the succeeding similes which accumulatively convey the sudden explosion of doleful anger, the sound of mourning, and the personified figure of an impoverished sun returning to haunt a despoiled world.

By depicting a physical reality yet at the same time adumbrating a metaphysical one, the narrator fulfils the role both of observer and of *voyant*: he suggests the idea of the spirit of the place while intimating the power that it exerts over its onlooker. More interestingly perhaps, the passage's sustained use of related similes has the effect of upsetting traditional distinctions between vehicle and tenor: or to put this point another way, it is far from clear whether the notions of mourning that recur throughout have been selected as the expressive medium through which to convey the feelings attendant upon the passing of summer or whether the transition from one season to another is used itself as a metaphor for the progression of sentiment caused by the imaginative contemplation of death and dying. The third sentence of the above paragraph, 'Così potess'io . . .', alerts the reader to the possibility that the writing may be a confused articulation of the narrating subject's inner vision of his own death. Thus the semi-supernatural apparitions of the passage may be symbols that speak of the inner life, or psychic projections that enable the self to contemplate mysteries beyond death. Aside from the obvious preoccupation with the theme of death, the particular nature of the interplay between the landscape and the self echoes the passage quoted earlier on Tarquinia, and in a less overt but more striking way recalls, in the vividness of its representation of impending rage and in its pained expression of submission, the troubled relationship between father and son that had dominated the concluding section of *Memorie della mia infanzia.*

The prose piece gains an added degree of complexity when the style and metaphorical constructions it uses are shown to be close to those of the second movement of Montale's famous lyric, 'Notizie dell'Amiata', written in anticipation of the Second World War.[27] What is certainly true is that Cardarelli's 'prosa d'arte' achieves its highest degree of modernity when the morbid elements of his imagination are allowed to predominate. In 'Insonnia' the piece that follows on from 'Lago', he constructs a nightmarish vision of the world of his waking reality, while in pieces such as 'Il mio paese' we encounter a narrative consciousness that identifies with the dead civilization hidden by Tarquinia and which communicates through the oneiric and the supernatural. Although there are important elements of *strapaese* writing within *Il sole a picco*, the work is far from being simply the literary elaboration of Fascist propaganda. Indeed, the text moves between the expression of chauvinism and the examination of the self's more private obsessions. Such a movement points initially to Cardarelli's desire to conform to a self-proposed model of a Fascist intellectual. In 1926 he had written to Soffici declaring that, concerning support for Mussolini's regime, he was 'an unshakeable pillar',[28] and throughout the twenty years of Fascist rule he sought to

[27] Published in *Le occasioni*, (Turin: Einaudi, 1939). For a comparison between 'Lago' and 'Notizie dell'Amiata', see C. Burdett, 'The Success and Failure of Cardarelli's Neoclassical Project', *The Italianist*, 15 (1995), 128–49.

[28] He wrote: 'In fatto di fede nel fascismo io sono una rocca che non crolla.' The letter was addressed to Soffici and dated 24 Sept. 1926. See *Epistolario*, ii. 134.

identify the narration of his personal story with the legitimizing myths of Fascism. Although he may have sought a role
for himself both as the high priest of Italian neoclassicism
and as a prominent exponent of nationalistic ideas, his texts
failed to create either an unequivocal ideology or a robust
self-image. Works like *Il sole a picco* show the ambiguities
which emerge when autobiography is used as a vehicle to
convey a series of political beliefs. The desire to create a
Fascist literary self is one that becomes more difficult as the
medium for its expression becomes more complex.

5

THE CLASSICISM OF CARDARELLI'S POETRY

Cardarelli's Poetry and the Writing of the Time

Publications such as *Il Selvaggio* and *L'Italiano*, together with the myths they broadcast concerning Italy's classical heritage and the supposedly untainted traditions of the Italian people, represented only one part of cultural production between the wars. Throughout the 1920s and the early 1930s Mussolini sought to avoid confrontation with the liberal literary élite. Despite the publication of Croce's 'Manifesto of Anti-Fascist Intellectuals' in 1925 which had immediately followed Giovanni Gentile's pro-Fascist manifesto, the regime successfully won the consent of a large number of intellectuals. The cultural review which Giuseppe Bottai had established in 1923, *Critica fascista*, became a respected journal and published the opinions of an impressive range of writers and critics. Many of those who were opposed to the ideology of Fascism were prepared to remain silent in the belief that literary endeavour need have no connection with politics.[1] Many writers of the period were willing to contribute to journals, such as *Solaria*, the expressed intention of which was to defend the autonomy both of literature and of the intellectual.

Solaria was started at the beginning of 1926 under the editorship of Alberto Carocci and was published over a ten-year period. The review seemed to support a distance between the world of literature and that of politics, promoting the notion of an 'ideal city' divorced from urgent social realities. Such a stance recalled the position which *La Ronda* had earlier taken. Indeed, *Solaria* attracted the names of writers, such as Giuseppe Raimondi and Filippo Burzio, who

---

[1] On the tendency of intellectuals to remain 'au dessus de la mêlée', see Lino Pertile, 'Fascism and Literature' in D. Forgacs (ed.), *Rethinking Italian Fascism* (London: Lawrence & Wishart, 1986), 162–85.

had been directly involved in editing the earlier journal. In one of the first issues of *Solaria* a long article was dedicated to a discussion of the role which *La Ronda* had fulfilled, and the author of the article described Cardarelli as having offered a 'profound example of the dignity of the writer'.[2] But the similarities between the two journals ended with the apparent division they both perceived between culture and politics. If many of the *rondisti* proved eager converts to Fascism, the same was not true of those who participated in *Solaria*. The Florentine journal sought to encourage a high level of debate about a whole range of European authors including Gide, Valéry, and Joyce. The informed debate concerning European literature, while it encouraged a level of censure from the pro-Fascist press, attracted the interest of many of the more innovative writers of the period. Although *Solaria* did not publish poetry after 1931, Giuseppe Ungaretti, Eugenio Montale, and Salvatore Quasimodo all wrote for the review. Carlo Emilio Gadda and Giovanni Comisso published some of their first writings in *Solaria*, and later contributors to the journal included Natalia Levi (later Ginzburg), Elio Vittorini, and Giacomo Noventa. Throughout its existence, moreover, *La Ronda* had sought to define and promote 'la prosa d'arte', but by contrast *Solaria* cast doubt on the validity of the *vociano* attack on the novel and helped to encourage the success of the genre in the 1930s. Contributors to the journal showed an interest in the narrative works of Italo Svevo and Federico Tozzi, while works by Gianna Manzini and Pier Quarantotti Gambini were either published by journal's press or reviewed positively in its pages.[3]

The attempt of *Solaria* to create a pure space for literary debate came under increasing strain as censorship became tighter in the 1930s. The journal managed to attract its enemies and was in fact closed down in 1936. One of the reviews which proved hostile to *Solaria* was the other major Florentine publication of the time, *Frontespizio*. Started in 1929 under the editorship of Piero Bargellini, *Frontespizio*

---

[2] R. Franchi, 'Vincenzo Cardarelli', *Solaria*, 2 (Feb. 1926).

[3] For a more extended account of the character of *Solaria*, see Manacorda, *Storia della letteratura italiana tra le due guerre 1919–1943*, 177–219.

aimed to be the mouthpiece of Catholic intellectuals who had welcomed the formal alliance of Church and state that had taken place with the signing of the Lateran accords. In the course of its ten-year life, the journal presented Fascist Italy as a vehicle for spreading Catholic civilization. It preached against modernization while supporting Mussolini's colonial ambitions. Papini and Soffici, while they did not publish often in the journal, remained, in the words of Giorgio Luti, its 'hidden gods'.[4] It was no coincidence that *Frontespizio* shared elements both with the *strapaese* movement and with some of the journals that had been important in the years before the outbreak of the First World War, such as *Leonardo* and *La Voce*. In contrast to the sophistication which characterized *Solaria*'s interest in literary questions, the tone of *Frontespizio* was often bigoted and irrational. The journal liked to assume an anti-European stance and, in terms which were clearly anti-Semitic, it attacked *Solaria* for the appreciation it showed for the work of leading European intellectuals. In 1936, for example, Bargellini spoke of the 'attack of all areligious and immoral literature against Catholic and Fascist Italy' and he went on to state that 'Anyone who loves Proust cannot love Italian serenity and virility'.[5]

In its early years *Frontespizio* succeeded paradoxically in attracting the collaboration of several poets who were later to establish themselves as leading voices in what was to become known as hermetic poetry. By the mid-1930s all these writers had, however, migrated to other journals. The term 'hermetic poetry' defines the most significant movement of twentieth-century Italian verse. The movement, which never printed a statement of its aims and which always remained eclectic in character, is generally seen to have grown out of some of the positions which *Solaria* had established in the late 1920s. Hermeticism certainly had its physical centre in Florence in the early 1930s and found expression in later journals including *Letteratura* and *Campo di Marte*. The idea that literature, consciously divorced from ordinary reality, represented an autonomous space for the

[4] Luti, *Cronache letterarie tra le due guerre 1920–1940*, 172.
[5] Ibid. 175.

self to investigate its deepest beliefs was central to hermeticism. The written self thus became the site for the main-
tenace of values which a conformist and oppressive political
culture seemed increasingly to threaten. It is to some extent
ironic that Ungaretti, a committed Fascist, provided one of
points of reference for hermetic poetry with his volume *Il
sentimento del tempo* (1933). Other expressions of the movement included Carlo Betocchi's *Realtà vince il sogno* (1932),
and Alfonso Gatto's *Morto ai paesi* (1937), and many of the
poems contained in Salvatore Quasimodo's two collections
Acque e terre (1930) and *Oboe sommerso* (1932) can be said
to be close in sensibility to mainstream hermeticism. The
poetry of Montale, especially in *Le occasioni* (1939), is, however, regarded as the major expression of the movement.

Initially those poets who seemed to adopt a common form
of expression and inspiration were referred to as practitioners of 'la poesia pura'. The term hermeticism was used
only later. It referred to the difficulty in understanding the
complex idiom that poets associated with the school used.
The cultivation of obscurity was part of a desire to elude
simple and reductive meanings. The use of allusion and
semantic ambiguity was heightened by a deliberate weakening of any connection between concrete reality and the
purity of the written word. All those poets most directly
linked to the school were aware of the practices of French
symbolist poetry and cultivated an array of mysterious personal symbols, while they consciously blurred distinctions
between the real and the oneiric. The obscurity of the
hermetic idiom served most obviously to define the movement, but there was also a degree of thematic cohesion.
Works by different poets displayed a concentration on
regional and memorial themes; the self of much hermetic
verse was presented as an example of the human condition;
it was engaged in an existential drama and many poems
hinted, without necessarily proposing any religious sentiment, at a transcendental reality that could be glimpsed only
through moments of magical or mystic intuition. Literature
for the hermetics was understood as being one with internal
life and, in the view of Luperini, the movement had its most

cogent explanation in the essay written by Carlo Bo and entitled, 'Letteratura come vita'.[6]

Throughout the 1920s Cardarelli published poems in different literary journals.[7] In 1934 he brought out a collection of forty-nine poems with the title *Giorni in piena*. Of these poems, fourteen had already appeared in his first volume of prose and poetry *Prologhi* and another nine had been published together with the prose pieces of *Il sole a picco*, but the remaining poems all appeared in a printed volume for the first time. Two years after the publication of *Giorni in piena*, he brought out a revised edition of his poetry, adding seven more compositions and giving it the bare but grand title of *Poesie*.

If the hermetic poets aimed to discover a complex linguistic equivalent to highly elusive states of being, then the linguistic texture of much of Cardarelli's poetry has been described as discursive.[8] It is undeniable that the sentiment conveyed in *Poesie* follows an arrangement which is close to that of conceptual reasoning. Cardarelli made no attempt to deny the affinity of his poetry with descriptive writing. In the preface to *Giorni in piena* he argued that his verse did not exclude 'logical rigour' and that it aimed 'rapidly to reach its conclusion without delays or digressions'. He also claimed that he felt his poetry to be made up of ideas, concepts, and poetic situations rather than pure language. The emphasis which he laid on syntactical lucidity tended also to mean that his poetry, often subservient to an intransigently logocentric structure, reduced imagery to a minimum. A criticism which has often been levelled against his poetry is that it achieves a solemn, classically rhetorical register only by imitating earlier examples. Almost all of his lyrics follow

[6] Luperini, *Il Novecento*, 607. The essay by Bo appeared in the September 1938 issue of *Frontespizio*. It was the final piece of writing which Bo published in the journal and it can be read as an attack against the editor of *Frontespizio*, Piero Bargellini.

[7] For an exhaustive survey of the initial dates of publication of Cardarelli's poems, together with the names of the literary journals in which they first appeared, see Martignoni's edition of Cardarelli works, pp. 1161–6.

[8] In the view of many critics, Cardarelli's poetry has strong affinities with prose. Writing on *Poesie*, Montale singled out the 'tono prosastico' of the volume and suggested that 'la sua musicalità si sosteneva appena impercettibilmente sopra il livello della buona prosa d'arte'. *Sulla poesia*, 307.

traditional metrical patterns; they owe their structure primarily to different combinations of lines of seven and eleven
syllables, and many lyrics employ a lexicon that consciously
echoes the phrasing of Leopardi's *Canti*.[9]

The circumscribed role that is accorded to the image in
Poesie inevitably means that the collection has nothing like
the suggestiveness, the conceptual density or the formal
intricacy of the hermetic experiments which were contem-
poraneous with it. Cardarelli was himself conscious of this
divide. In a late evaluation of his career, he claimed that he
was regarded essentially as a prose writer and that as far as
poetry was concerned he had 'to concede primacy to Ungaretti and Montale'.[10] In the same evaluation he confessed
that he found much recent hermetic poetry 'difficult and
confusing', and he wrote that 'where Ungaretti is adored my
work has no place'.[11] On his death in 1959 Montale wrote an
obituary for the *Corriere della sera* with the title 'An Isolated
Voice'. The obituary pointed to Cardarelli's obsession with
creating an elevated picture of himself in his works, his
over-dependence on Leopardi, and the intransigence of his
neoclassicism. The piece contained no reference to any
influence which his poetry may have had on the hermetic
school, and it ended by saying that, although many readers
would be inclined to discard Cardarelli's poetry, the poems
could be considered in a way that was perhaps not altogether
fruitless.[12]

Despite the abstract and discursive nature of Cardarelli's
verse and despite the fierce criticism which it has received

[9] The debt which Cardarelli's verse owes to the earlier Leopardian example has
been comprehensively examined by Gilberto Lonardi in '"Autunno": Osservazioni
sul Leopardi di Cardarelli', *Studi novecenteschi*, 4 (Dec. 1982), 249–91. Martignoni
has rightly insisted that the extent of Cardarelli's *leopardismo* is not as extensive as is
widely assumed. In 'Vincenzo Cardarelli tra mito e moralità', she writes: 'Va detto e
ripetuto che quella levigata neoclassicità a cui si lega (quanto indelebilmente?) la
sua condanna critica, si può limitare di fatto a una serie quantitativamente e
qualitativamente modesta di poche liriche, le stancamente leopardiane degli anni
Trenta.'

[10] The confessional statement of Cardarelli is printed in *Lettere non spedite* (Rome:
Astrolabio, 1946). See *Opere*, 870.

[11] Ibid. 850.

[12] Montale's essay on Cardarelli first appeared under the title, 'Vincenzo Cardarelli: Una voce isolata' on 16 June 1959 in the *Corriere della sera*. It was later
reprinted in *Sulla poesia*.

because of its formal characteristics, his poetry does present an interesting object of study for a variety of reasons. To begin with, it represents a different facet of the same record of subjectivity that extends to include his prose writings and his statements in support of Fascism. Yet, if the *strapaese* writings had given life to various symbolic incarnations of 'italianità', by contrast the poetry creates a series of more complicated self-figurations. The morbid, obsessive nature of the verse is at odds with the robust, reactionary language of texts like *Parliamo dell'Italia*: while the prose writings speak of the rebirth of the Italian nation and the flourishing of its traditions under Fascism, the poetry cultivates an interest in mortality and in wholly private themes. It may well have been Cardarelli's intention to present himself as a Fascist intellectual, but the evidence supplied by his poetry suggests that he was not wholly in step with the brutal certainties of Italy in the late 1920s and early 1930s. Indeed, one of the most interesting things to emerge from a study of *Poesie* is that its affinities are not with writings that were sympathetic to the regime, but with more oppositional voices. In particular, some of his poems demonstrate a clear thematic closeness to celebrated examples of hermetic verse. It is striking how close a similarity may exist between the literary self of a convinced supporter of Mussolini and that of poets like Montale who were hostile to every aspect of Fascism. There is no space here for a comprehensive evaluation of Cardarelli's later verse. However, it is worth looking at some of the techniques which are central to his poetry's construction of the self and specifically at the allusions which are made to ancient myth. Subsequently, the areas that prove most interesting are the self's interest in monumentality and in mortality. The final aspect worth examining is the way in which the literary self interacts with other figurations which are present within the poetry. Both the difference and the curious similarity that exists between *Poesie* and collections of verse written by poets belonging to the hermetic school can be brought out by comparing individual poems with others written by Ungaretti, Quasimodo, and, most importantly, by Montale.

The Representation of the Self and the World of Myth

In *Poesie* Cardarelli does not construct a tenuous or fluc-
tuating self. He does not endeavour either to leave wide
margins of silence or to conceal the essence of a literary self
in a coded and enigmatic language. Instead he modulates
his poetic voice in such a way as to create a self-image that is
lucid and stable to the point of seeming almost static. In
Poesie there is no complex interplay between differing representations or constructions of the same self, but a voice
which remains constant from one poem to another as it
explores closely related psychological states. Patterns of
imaginative experience emerge, similar networks of self-
defining images recur, and the same set of personal obsessions figures in modified form from one poem to another,
prompting Gianfranco Contini to reflect: 'Cardarelli's poetry is a repertory, a historiography of *idées fixes*. Its inspiration is methodological in character.'[13] Unlike the poetic
voices of Umberto Saba or Attilio Bertolucci, the self of
Cardarelli's later poetry is isolated from a domestic setting.
Throughout, the verse avoids a casual or conversational
mode of expression and, in the words of Franco Fortini, the
poetry is animated by 'an intense desire to ennoble the
self'.[14]

Poesie divides into several groups of poems and in each
group a variety of textual strategies is employed to elevate
the status of the speaker. For example, a number of
poems either evoke different seasons of the year or the
atmosphere that pervades different localities.[15] All these
poems either use or depend upon personification and its
corollary, apostrophe, and all therefore rely upon a highly
rhetorical mode of address which draws attention to the role
which the speaking voice is keen to assume. In one lyric,

[13] Contini's observation appeared in his review of *Giorni in piena*, 'La verità sul
caso Cardarelli', first published in *Solaria* (May–June 1934), and later reprinted in
a collection of his criticism, *Esercizi di lettura*, 34–42.
[14] Fortini, 'Vincenzo Cardarelli', 134.
[15] Several poems had appeared in *Il sole a picco*. They are 'Santi del mio paese',
'Autunno veneziano', 'Alba', 'Sera di Gavinana', 'Amore', 'Distacco', 'Liguria',
'Settembre a Venezia', and 'Ottobre'.

'Sardegna', the speaker uses a declaratory voice to address the spirit of the island; in another, 'Autunno veneziano', the cold and damp atmosphere of Venice anthropomorphically becomes the 'breath' of the city whose 'face' emerges like that of Medusa; in the poem 'Autunno', the self who speaks is in communion with a set of fantastical personas as it judges and interprets the significance of the passage of time. The poem reads:

> Autunno. Già lo sentimmo venire
> nel vento d'agosto,
> nelle pioggie di settembre
> torrenziali e piangenti,
> e un brivido percorse la terra
> che ora, nuda e triste,
> accoglie un sole smarrito.
> Ora passa e declina,
> in quest'autunno che incede
> con lentezza indicibile,
> il miglior tempo della nostra vita
> e lungamente ci dice addio.

[Autumn. We already felt it coming | in the wind of August, | in the rains of September, | both torrential and weeping | and a shudder ran through the earth | which now, bare and sad, | welcomes a lost sun. | Now passes and declines, | in this autumn which advances | with unbelievable slowness, | the best time of our life | and slowly it says farewell]

In 'Autunno' abstractions, or more precisely inanimate phenomena, are transformed into active supernatural beings. The coming of autumn is represented by the drama enacted by the three personifications: autumn is invested with attributes indicative of the divine, its momentous arrival being foretold both by the mournful sound of weeping and by the shudder which runs through the earth. The other two figures in the initial part of the poem are less grandiose: the earth assumes the guise of a lover who embraces the weakened figure of the sun. A funereal motif is present in this poem, as it is in most of those poems which in some way derive their inspiration from the passage of the seasons. It is not surprising that the season which Cardarelli prefers in his later poetry is autumn.[16]

[16] In this respect, these poems differ from those of *Prologhi* where the season which most nearly corresponded to the sensibility of the speaking voice had been

Other compositions belonging to *Poesie* revolve around the problems which prey upon the self. In such poems the same conspicuous dependence on personification is present, obsessions being transformed into anthropomorphic projections in a way that recalls Baudelaire's *Les Fleurs du mal*. Already in one prose piece included in *Il sole a picco*, 'Insonnia' (*Opere*, 478–81), Cardarelli had dramatized abstractions, such as sleep or solitude, into monstrous presences which delighted in tormenting the experiencing subject. In *Poesie*, the lyric 'Alba' is constructed as a series of incantatory formulas addressed to a supernatural agent capable of bestowing favours upon a suppliant subject, while the poem 'Insonnia' presents a conflict between the subject and its predatory fears. It begins with the lines:

> Talvolta a me par di vederlo il Sonno,
> mostro enorme, impalpabile,
> starmi sopra, già pronto ad inghiottirmi,
> e son sua preda in quello stesso istante.

[Sometimes I think I can see Sleep, | an enormous, impalpable monster, | hovering above, and ready to devour me,| and in that moment I am its prey.]

The conversion of abstractions into menacing supernatural figurations is matched by an interest in finding figures for the self in the ancient past. In the prose writings of the 1920s, the Etruscan and Roman civilizations were presented as the source of Italian identity. The subtext of those writings had been that the Fascist revolution would serve to lead Italy towards a discovery of its true cultural heritage. The evocation of the ancient past in the poetry is not accompanied by a political subtext. A more troubled notion of the past predominates: Cardarelli uses mythical themes and characters in his poems to represent a self that struggles, but fails, to affirm a stance of stoical grandeur. For

summer. In 'Ottobre' Cardarelli overtly casts off this epoch of his life, with the lines: 'Un tempo, era d'estate, | era a quel fuoco, a quegli ardori, | che si destava la mia fantasia. | Inclino adesso all'autunno | dal colore che inebbria, | amo la stanca stagione | che ha già vendemmiato'. It is worth noticing here the closeness of this lyric to Quasimodo's 'Autunno' of *Oboe sommerso*, the opening lines of which read: 'Autunno mansueto, io mi posseggo | e piego alle tue acque a bermi il cielo, | fuga soave d'alberi e d'abissi.'

example, in one poem the Greek hero Ajax is presented as a proud but isolated figure, cursed by an adverse fate and involved in a fruitless search for stability. 'Ajace'[17] is clearly inspired by Ugo Foscolo's famous lyric 'A Zacinto', but in Cardarelli's poem the plight of the mythical hero recalls that which afflicts the self in other overtly autobiographical poems. If 'Ajace' is unable to attain any certainties, then Cardarelli writes in 'Viaggio':

> Oh senza sosta io vissi,
> ed esule dovunque.
> Nessun'arte imparai, niuna certezza
> mi assiste
> nel punto di salpare ormai per sempre.[18]

[Oh without rest I lived | and as an exile everywhere, | I learned no art, no single certainty | sustains me | at the moment of setting sail forever.]

Another characteristic of the autobiographical fables contained in prose collections like *Il sole a picco* is that they present a series of rural communities that are not susceptible to the passage of time, but they stand instead as living emblems of an unchanging identity. In *Poesie*, however, the attempt to immobilize time is experienced as a source of torment. One of the most thematically homogeneous sections of the collection contains the lyrics 'Alla terra', 'Ballata', 'Passaggio notturno', 'Partenza mattutina', and 'Ritorno al mio paese', all of which were written between November 1932 and January 1934. In these lyrics Cardarelli's home town of Tarquinia appears and functions as a multi-determined symbol: it is associated with childhood and is used as a signifier for past time, it represents the fixity of recollection, and finally it functions as an image of a land of the dead. In 'Ritorno al mio paese', Cardarelli conveys the notion of the fixity of time by conjuring up an internal image of his home town that is paradoxically both unsettling and reassuring:

---

[17] 'Ajace' was first published in April 1933 in *La Gazzetta del Popolo*.
[18] A comparison could be made between the lines of Cardarelli's lyric and those with which Montale's 'Casa sul mare' in *Ossi di seppia* ends: 'Il cammino finisce a queste prode | che rode la marea col moto alterno. | Il tuo cuore vicino che non m'ode | salpa già forse per l'eterno.'

Qui tutto è fermo, incantato,
nel mio ricordo.
Anche il vento . . .
Quel vento antico, quelle antiche voci,
e gli odori e le stagioni
d'un tempo, ahimé, vissuto.

[Here everything is still, under a spell, I in my memory. Even the wind . . .
I That ancient wind, those ancient voices, I the perfumes and the seasons I
of a time, alas, that has been lived.]

Elsewhere the town appears both as a concrete locality
and as an abstract symbol and it is this disparity which is
explored. In 'Passaggio notturno' the speaking voice passes
through Tarquinia. The moment of passing is fleeting, the
town obscured from sight by darkness, and it seems to the
consciousness of the poem that the place as it is imagined
and as it is in its everyday reality are merged into a
single entity. If 'Passaggio notturno' revolves around varying
notions of time, then so too does 'Partenza mattutina'. The
difference between the two poems is that in the latter the
picture of Tarquinia that is supplied by sensory perception
fails to match the image of the town which exists as a
recollection within the mind of the perceiver. The intuition
of the divergence between the internal and external perception of the same object forces the experiencing subject to
recognize the unreality of the past, and to acknowledge that
the endeavour to control the action of time by venerating a
personal symbol of immutability has met with failure. The
final lines of 'Partenza mattutina' read:

Sconosciuto, inatteso,
eccomi in via di nuovo
per quella stazioncina solitaria
in cui vissi bambino, a cui ritorno,
e tutto il mio passato mi frana adosso.
Inorridisco al suono
della mia voce.

[Unknown, unexpected, I here I am going away I from that small, solitary
station I where I lived as a child and to which I return, I and the whole of
my past slides over me. I I am horrified at the sound I of my voice.]

In the prose writings of *Memorie della mia infanzia* and *Il
sole a picco*, Tarquinia had functioned as a symbol of the

resting-place of the ancient Etruscans. In *Poesie* Tarquinia becomes not so much the burial site of the Etruscans but a land inhabited by the dead. The notion of a place that is sacred to the memory of Etruria that operates in the prose is transformed into something altogether more disturbing in the poetry. In 'Ritorno al mio paese' Cardarelli evokes Tarquinia as a town of ghosts where all that changes is the appearance of the living. In another poem, 'Ballata', he thinks obsessively of the past only to intuit the 'silent agitation of memories and shades'. In other lyrics the suggested association between Tarquinia and an afterworld is made more strongly. In the lyric 'Nostalgia', the remnants of Etruscan civilization, its tombs and the funereal objects which remain, are used to invoke a space that exists beyond life:

> Alto su rupe,
> battuto dai venti,
> un cimitero frondeggia:
> cristiana oasi nel Tartaro etrusco.
> Là sotto è la fanciulla
> bellissima dei Velcha,
> che vive ancora nella Tomba dell'Orco.
> È il giaciglio gentile
> della Pulzella
> poco discosto.

[High on rocks, I battered by the wind, I the leaves of a graveyard flourish: I a Christian oasis in the Etruscan steppe. I Underneath lies the beautiful I girl of the Velcha, I who still lives in the Tomb of the Orco. I The gracious resting place I of the maiden I is not far off.]

In the very way that the verse is phrased, the endurance of some form of psychic life beyond death is postulated. The Etruscan necropolis is, of course, the resting-place of the dead, but it also assumes the attributes of a spiritual location to which it is possible, through death, to gain access. 'Nostalgia' plays with the suggestion that death offers the key to restoring a primary state of satisfaction. The speaking voice yearns for an end to the consciousness of living, for a cessation of all activity, and for a return to inorganic existence. The poem continues:

Oh poter seppellire
nella città silente
insiem con me la favola
di mia vita!
Non esser più che una pietra corrosa,
un nome cancellato,
e riposar senza memoria in grembo
alla terra natìa come se mai
me ne fossi scostato.

[Oh to be able to bury | in the silent city | together with me the story | of my life! | To be only an eroded tombstone, | a cancelled name, | and to rest without memory in the womb | of the earth as if I had never | gone away.]

What is perhaps most interesting about 'Nostalgia' and the poems which are close to it in *Poesie* is the degree to which they are similar to compositions in Quasimodo's *Oboe sommerso*. If the speaking subject of *Poesie* is beset with the insistent clamour of the dead and if an association is made between Tarquinia and an eternal place of rest, then similarly Quasimodo's Sicily is presented as a place of refuge, seemingly beyond time and inhabited mysteriously by the subject's ancestors. The major difference between the respective tendencies to locate the afterworld in a definite place of origin is that in the poetic universe of *Oboe sommerso* the figures of Christian mythology are present, while Cardarelli's subjectively conditioned notion of Tarquinia is created by ancient and pagan figurations. Yet the aspiration for the eternal, the confusion between an ancient and a personal past, and the creation of legendary landscapes are essentially the same.

In *Poesie* the subject not only aspires to the eternal, but attempts to immobilize the flow of time. Such an attempt leads to an increasingly anguished sense of temporal progression. Yet, if there is one instance when the obsessive sentiment of time's advance is suspended, it is at the moment of parting when the traveller imagines the state of consciousness enjoyed by those who remain in one place. The transitory notion of stability which is then experienced forms the substance of two poems of the collection. The lyric 'Viaggio' begins with the lines:

Come felice, stabile,
si mostra il mondo a lui che lo contempla
con l'animo d'un esule, con occhi
di morituro.

[How happy, stable, | the world shows itself to he who contemplates it |
with the soul of an exile, with the eyes | of one who is dying.]

The impression of fixity thus achieved is compounded by
the peculiarly Cardarellian notion that the material world is
least threatening when it is on the point of being absorbed
by memory. The inclination is to make the present dissolve
immediately into the past, the hermetic implication being
that a passive memory of a place is more stable and solid
than its concrete reality.

The Monumentality of the Self

The poems examined so far show Cardarelli's propensity to
use the ancient past together with the world of myth to
create an image of the self; this literary self becomes still
more interesting when its obsession with mortality is further
investigated. Two of the starkest, but also most semantically dense, lyrics of *Poesie* are entitled 'Carattere' and 'Alla
morte'. Both poems are assertive statements which reveal a
range of connotative meanings when analysed. The voice
which speaks in 'Carattere' expresses the desire not to suc-
cumb to the temptations of life, and to suppress that part of
the self which is inclined to do so. The poem articulates a
number of inhibiting moral imperatives. By enunciating
these authoritative statements, the speaking subject attains
an intellectual distance from the self and seeks to gain a
degree of autonomy not only from the external world but
also from the action of time. The opening to the poem
reads:

Vivo di sogni e di speranze pazze.
Nella mia libertà sepolto
vedo passare i giorni,
sempre nuovi per me, sempre diversi.
Giorni che io vivo e perdo

come chi si costringe
in oscura caverna
a castigar la sua brama di luce.

[I live on dreams and absurd hopes. | Buried in my freedom | I see days pass, | they are always new and different to me. | Days that I live and lose | like someone who lives | in a dark cavern | and tries to punish his need for light.]

In these lines the concept of constriction is semantically linked with the seemingly contradictory notion of freedom: the subject is 'buried in his freedom'. He enjoys a certain autonomy and yet he defines his existence in terms with sepulchral overtones. But the self shudders at the awareness of its constricted existence, and its reaction is to immerse itself in the flow of time. The ideas of stability and self-possession with which the poem opens are quickly transformed into images of uncertainty and frenzied agitation. 'Carattere' continues:

Poi per le strade uscendo sul crepuscolo
lo incalza il disperato desiderio
di rincorrer quell'ora che gli sfugge.
Sempre avrò amore al mondo e brevi gioie.
E noie, disgrazie, mai mi parranno
meno precarie e meno tollerabili.
Ché non c'è nulla di continuo e certo
nella mia vita, fuor che il vario inganno
della fortuna e le malìe del tempo.

[Then going out on the streets around dusk | assailed by the desperate wish | to pursue that elusive hour. | I shall always experience love for the world and brief moments of joy. | And irritations and misfortunes will never seem | less precarious or less tolerable. | There is nothing continuous and certain | in my life, apart from the changing deception | of fortune and the spell of time.]

Cardarelli prefers concepts to images and this preference is apparent in the above lines. Thematically what these lines convey is a shift from the recognition of a sense of order to a heightened perception of precariousness. The enunciated self attempts to interact meaningfully with an outside reality which remains hopelessly beyond its grasp. In the poem the self is placed between the possibility of an imposed state of immobility and a multiplicity of happenings which escape the dominance of its reasoning. The perception of the instability both of the self and of the real gives rise to a sense of imprisonment within a meaningless repetition of events. In 'Carattere' the self's realization of the uselessness of all endeavour is communicated through metaphors which imply the inevitability of death. The final lines of the poem read:

> E nelle pene estreme aridi ho gli occhi.
> Mi chiude nello sdegno un dio la bocca.
> Il non potere e il non volere insieme
> fanno un tale groviglio entro il mio petto
> come radici d'una vecchia pianta
> che non crolla per impeto di vento
> e solo il fulmine potrà schiantare.

[And in moments of extreme pain, my eyes remain dry. I A god seals my mouth in contempt. I Powerlessness and lack of will together I are so entrenched within my breast I that they are like the roots of an ancient tree I which cannot be felled by the wind I and which only lightning can destroy.]

The final section of the poem amounts to a declaration of stoicism in that any emotional response to the contingencies of existence is excluded. But if the language that is being used in this latter part of the poem is examined closely, then a subtext becomes apparent. The terms which are being used to represent the self ('aridi ho gli occhi', 'mi chiude . . . la bocca', 'il non potere e il non volere,' 'una vecchia pianta che non crolla') all suggest that the stoicism of the self represents a kind of death. The exclusion of emotion gives a statuesque rigidity to the speaking subject.

However, it is at the moment in which the poem most explicitly recognizes the vulnerability and powerlessness of the subject that the self's identity is most powerfully affirmed.[19] It is through the realization of its inevitable extinction that the self is able to grasp a notion of its own identity. By acknowledging its mortality, the subject succeeds in delimiting its destiny and manages to impose a structure

[19] My observations on the relation of identity to mortality are informed by Piotr Hoffman's discussion of Heidegger's ideas in the essay, 'Death, Time, History: Division II of *Being and Time*', in Charles Guignon (ed.) *The Cambridge Companion to Heidegger* (Cambridge: Cambridge University Press, 1993), 195–214.

on its experiences. The self gains an impression of the determinacy of the past. By seeing itself as finite and limited, the subject can also see itself as concrete and determinate. The poem thus constitutes itself as a monument to the self in the sense that Gianni Vattimo has defined.[20] Like a funerary monument, the poem is not constituted simply as a replica of real life but is already a formula of life constituted so as to give a trace of memory of an individual existence, thus already acknowledging the mortality of the subject it commemorates. It is a formula that does not offer a challenge to time but owes its being to an acknowledgement of temporality.

Contini characterized Cardarelli's lyrics as being 'so many epic moral portraits, even when they seem most descriptive'.[21] The observation, while defining the central quality of the poetry, does not point to the fact that these acts of self-definition depend on the contemplation of the annihilation of the self. Throughout his career Cardarelli claimed an affinity between his own verse and that of Baudelaire. Such an affinity is most obvious precisely in those lyrics which address the question of ultimate extinction. The extract quoted earlier from 'Nostalgia', which alludes first to the physical reality of burial and then expresses the wish for oblivion, is syntactically and conceptually closely related to Baudelaire's 'Le Mort joyeux',[22] while other poems plunder the stock of imagery that is used in *Les Fleurs du mal*.

The very extent to which much of Cardarelli's poetry relies upon anthropomorphism presents further evidence of the presence of *Les Fleurs du mal* within *Poesie* as a whole. Personification is a poetic device that is very much in evidence in the second lyrical contemplation of death, the poem 'Alla morte', which repays analysis. In 'Alla morte'

[20] See Gianni Vattimo, 'L'infrangersi della parola poetica' in his *La fine della modernità* (Milan: Garzanti, 1985), 73–86.

[21] Contini, 'La verità sul caso Cardarelli', 38.

[22] Baudelaire's poem opens with the lines: 'Dans une terre grasse et pleine d'escargots | je veux creuser moi-même une fosse profonde, | Où je puisse à loisir étaler mes vieux os | Et dormir dans l'oubli comme un requin dans l'onde.' In his analysis of Cardarelli's poetry, Frederic Jones provides a number of other instances of the conscious recuperation of lines from Baudelaire. See 'Vincenzo Cardarelli and the Ideal of Modern Classicism', in his *The Modern Italian Lyric*, (Cardiff: University of Wales Press, 1986), 298–333.

the images of dying which are summoned up depend on symbolist figurations of death: through metaphor, the attributes of the *femme fatale* of late nineteenth-century writing are transferred onto the abstract notion of death. 'Alla morte' begins:

> Morire sì,
> non essere aggrediti dalla morte.
> Morire persuasi
> che un siffatto viaggio sia il migliore.
> E in quell'ultimo istante essere allegri
> come quando si contano i minuti
> dell'orologio della stazione
> e ognuno vale un secolo.
> Poi che la morte è la sposa fedele
> che subentra all'amante traditrice,
> non vogliamo riceverla da intrusa,
> né fuggire con lei.

[To die, yes, I not to be assailed by death. I To die persuaded I that such a journey is for the best. I And in that moment to be happy I as when one counts the moments I of the clock in the station I and every one lasts for a century. I Since death is the faithful companion I who replaces the faithless lover, I I don't want to receive her as an intruder, I or flee with her.]

The initial attraction of death is troubled by the recognition of its potential horror. The closing lines of the poem read:

> Al pensier della morte repentina
> il sangue mi si gela.
> Morte, non mi ghermire,
> ma da lontano annunciati
> e da amica mi prendi
> come l'estrema delle mie abitudini.

[At the thought of a repentant death I my blood freezes. I Death, do not seize me, I but announce yourself from afar I and as a friend take me I as though you were the last of my habits.]

The tone of supplication or command adopted by the experiencing subject indicates the extent to which he is either seduced or terrified by the personified figure of death.

The poem, while indebted to Baudelaire, also displays a number of parallels with Ungaretti's 'Inno alla morte', which dates from 1925 and appears in *Il sentimento del tempo*. The two poems certainly share the same structure, in that they are both meditations on an abstract concept which assumes different meanings depending on the conscious imagining of the subject. Both lyrics are examples of the 'poesia alta' where the self, confronting an inevitable existential situation, addresses a mysterious second person. Cardarelli's mode of address relies on traditional symbolic concepts of death; his verse is syntactically ordered and obeys the logic of conceptual thought. By contrast Ungaretti's verse, working through ellipsis and allusion, cultivates more personal emblems. Death is invoked in a series of striking epithets or oxymorons, as in the lines:

> Morte, arido fiume...
> Immemore sorella, morte,
> L'uguale mi farai del sogno
> Baciandomi.
> Avrò il tuo passo,
> Andrò senza lasciare impronta.

[Death, arid river... I Heedless sister, death, I You will make the equal of dreams I Kissing me. I I shall have your step, I I shall go without leaving a trace.]

Despite the difference in expression, death appears in both lyrics as alternatively chilling and attractive. Both lyrics communicate an attitude of resolution in the face of potential regret. The final lines of 'Alla morte' express a terror of repentance, while in 'Inno alla morte' Ungaretti writes:

> Abbandonata la mazza fedele
> Scivolerò nell'acqua buia
> Senza rimpianto.

[Having thrown away my trusty staff I I shall slide into the dark water I Without regret.]

Though exploring the same thematic ground as 'Alla morte', Ungaretti's lyric cultivates greater ambiguity. The self of Cardarelli's poem remains separate from the figuration which is invoked, while Ungaretti's subject fuses with the anthropomorphic projection of death. 'Inno alla morte' finishes with the lines:

Mi darai il cuore immobile
D'un iddio, sarò innocente,
Non avrò più pensieri né bontà.

Colla mente murata
Cogli occhi caduti in oblio,
Farò da guida alla felicità

[You shall give me the still heart | Of a god, I shall be innocent, | I shall
have neither thoughts nor goodness. | With my mind walled | With my
eyes having fallen into oblivion, | I shall act as the guide of happiness.]

Though the two lyrics differ greatly in their use of imagery,
they share the same declarative style. The comparisons that
can be drawn from an analysis of two thematically similar
poems could be extended. It is true that Cardarelli and
Ungaretti were not unaware of the development of each
other's writing. Ungaretti was the only poet to publish verse
in *La Ronda*, and he was sympathetic to the journal's call for
order and to its intention to promote a classically inspired
form of literature. In the years that followed the demise of
the journal, he cultivated his own form of *leopardismo*, seeing
Leopardi not as a model of stylistic perfection but as a
philosopher of time and memory. In the 1920s, when Ungaretti was employed as the Parisian correspondent for *Il popolo
d'Italia*, Cardarelli counted on him to have some of his work
published in translation in France. Unfortunately, the relationship between the two writers deteriorated around this
time and, rather than helping his former friend, Ungaretti
did much to ensure that few of his prose pieces were received
positively in France.[23] Aside from the occasional thematic
closeness between the two writers' work, another aspect of
their lives which bound the two figures curiously together
was that they were both strong supporters of Fascism and in
return they both won recognition and a degree of financial
support from the regime. In the view of both writers Mussolini offered an authentically popular form of government,
one which reminded Italy of its past in antiquity and which
promised an ever deeper cultural revolution. Both writers
were blind to the political repression and violence that
accompanied the maintenance of Fascist power.

[23] For a history of the relationship between the two poets see *Cardarelli and
Ungaretti*, ed. Galateria and Napoletano, 56–63.

The Self and the Other

Poems like 'Alla morte' and 'Carattere' are interesting because of the way in which they create a self in the face of mortality. But an intriguing question that arises from the analysis of *Poesie* is how verse that is manifestly concerned only with the existence of the speaking subject can conceive of alterity. The earlier and more experimental collection of poetic fragments, *Prologhi*, had set out to destroy any notion that the self existed in relation to others. In *Poesie* there is a series of lyrics which address a second person.[24] Although the aggressive desire to annihilate the Other is subject to greater control in these lyrics, it is by no means absent. The level and kind of interaction which occurs in *Poesie* between the subject and a second person can best be examined by looking at one poem in particular. The lyric 'Passato' presents an interesting case, first because it is more reliant on metaphor than many of the compositions in *Poesie*, which tend to explore deductively an image or idea that is suggested in the initial sentence. 'Passato' is also a good poem to examine because it shows a remarkable closeness to two famous poems of Montale's collection, *Le occasioni*. 'Passato' first appeared in 1931 and Montale's two poems were first published in roughly the same years: 'La casa dei doganieri' in 1930 and 'Bassa marea' in 1933. By comparing 'Passato' with two lyrics from *Le occasioni* it is possible to gain a perception of two kinds of poetry which, while on the whole distinct, do have some revealing points of contact. It also becomes clear that, despite Cardarelli's professed hostility towards hermetic poetry and despite Montale's slighting obituary of Cardarelli, a two-way traffic of influence did exist between the writers.

Both 'Passato' and 'Bassa marea' are constructed as apostrophes and both speculate on the mortality of the second person. In 'Passato' the addressee is given no physical or psychological characterization and therefore remains

---

[24] The poems, printed one after another in each edition of *Poesie*, are 'Amore', 'Distacco', 'Io non so più qual era', 'Attesa', 'Abbandono', 'Passato', 'Crudele addio', and 'Rimorso'.

scarcely above the level of an abstraction. By contrast, the addressee of 'Bassa marea' is a figure who was once known to the speaking voice but who died while still young. In *Le occasioni* she is known as Arletta. Both poems begin by evoking the notion of borders being crossed and of the barrier between the living and the dead being partially broken down. 'Passato' begins:

> I ricordi, queste ombre troppo lunghe
> del nostro breve corpo,
> questo strascico di morte
> che noi lasciamo vivendo,
> i lugubri e durevoli ricordi,
> eccoli già apparire:
> melanconici e muti
> fantasmi agitati da un vento funebre.

[Memories, these too long shades | of our poor bodies, | this train of death | that we leave as we live, | the lugubrious and lasting memories, | watch as they appear: | the melancholy and mute | shades animated by a funereal wind.]

The opening lines of 'Bassa marea' rest essentially on the same conceit as those of 'Passato'. The major difference is that while the setting of Cardarelli's lyric is metaphysical, Montale exploits the sights of the Ligurian landscape to suggest a traffic across existential borders. He writes:

> Varcano ora il muro
> rapidi voli obliqui, la discesa
> di tutto non s'arresta e si confonde
> sulla proda scoscesa anche lo scoglio
> che ti portò primo sull'onde.

[Crossing over the wall | is the rapid oblique flight [of birds], the descent | of everything does not stop and confused | against the steep incline of the shore | is the cliff that first bore you across the waves.]

In the opening sections of both poems the accent is on the ambiguity of place; memory is the site where a nearing of opposing worlds can occur. The fleeting images of the remembered dead flicker in 'Passato', while in 'Bassa marea' the emphasis on a crossing of boundaries is expressed through a notion of descent with clear Dantean overtones.

However, in both 'Passato' and 'Bassa marea', it is the

apparition of the object of memory which accenuates the intensity of the moment of contact between separate worlds. Cardarelli's poem continues:

> E tu non sei più che un ricordo.
> Sei trapassata nella mia memoria.
> Ora sì, posso dire
> che m'appartieni
> e qualchecosa fra di noi è accaduto
> irrevocabilmente.

[And you are no more than a recollection. | You have passed into my memory. | And now yes, I can say | that you belong to me | and something between us has happened | irrevocably.]

By becoming no more than a memory, the love-object makes its own journey into the abstract underworld which is brought to life by the experiencing subject. The attributes which characterize the world of the dead are transposed onto the remembered presence, making that presence both spectral and mysterious. In a precisely analogous fashion, the characteristics of Arletta in 'Bassa marea' are infiltrated by the locality to which she belongs:

> Viene col soffio della primavera
> un lugubre risucchio
> d'assorbite esistenze; e nella sera,
> negro vilucchio, solo il tuo ricordo
> s'attorce e si difende.
> S'alza sulle spallette, sul tunnel più lunge
> dove il treno lentissimo s'imbuca.

[There comes together with the spring wind | a lugubrious undertow of absorbed existences; and in the evening, | only your memory, like a dark creeper | flickers and resists. | It rises over the parapets, and over the more distant tunnel | where, with extreme slowness, a train disappears.]

If this section of 'Bassa marea' is read in conjunction with the lines which I quoted earlier from 'Passato', then the extent of the semantic and linguistic overlap between the two poems comes most clearly into focus. The 'soffio della primavera' becomes the 'vento funebre' of 'Passato'; the 'lugubre risucchio | d'assorbite esistenze' is reworked to become 'i lugubri e durevoli ricordi'; if the memory of the love-object flickers among other shades in 'Passato' then in

'Bassa marea', 'il . . . ricordo s'attorce e si difende'. It is well known that in 'Bassa marea' Montale appropriates elements from Browning's 'Two in the Campagna', and it would seem that allusions to Browning's verse go together with echoes of Cardarelli's 'Passato'.

However, it is not only the degree of intertextuality which is striking. Although there are elements of echoing or repetition, there is also a dialogue between 'Passato' and 'Bassa marea': the difference between the two poems is as interesting as the similarity. The difference is to be found in the subject's interaction with the past. The speaking voice of 'Passato' willingly addresses the other as a memory, or as a mental stimulus existing uniquely within its own psychical life, over which it enjoys complete control. The act of remembering in 'Passato' is associated with the act of self-assertion and, despite the fact that the poem was written many years after the publication of *Prologhi*, it nevertheless retains features of the same speaking self. In 'Passato', the object of memory is a prisoner of the self who remembers. The land of the dead to which the shade belongs is a realm over which the self, like a chthonic deity, holds sway. There is a sadistic tone to the enunciation: 'Non sei più che un ricordo. | Sei trapassata nella *mia* memoria' (You are no more than a recollection | you have passed into *my* memory). As in the much earlier 'Adolescente' the type of possession attained by the self amounts to the destitution of the addressee. The spectral is not something which haunts the self, but something over which the self exerts its dominance.

In Montale's lyric there is the same traffic between the worlds of the living and the dead, but the recuperation of a memory trace is experienced as an altogether more disconcerting phenomenon. In 'Passato' the addressee remains passively the object of the speaker's gaze. By contrast, in 'Bassa marea' the uncanniness of the memory is foregrounded. At one level, the love-object is familiar, and since she belongs to the conscious sphere of the subject's imagining, controllable. But at another level her apparition is alien: the memory, rather than flickering uncertainly, dominates the Ligurian landscape, eludes the control of the speaker, and alters the relation between subject and object. The remembering subject is destabilized by the power of the apparition.

'Passato' is close in sensibility not only to 'Bassa marea', but also to Montale's 'La casa dei doganieri', a lyric in which the presence of Arletta is evoked through the contemplation of a desolate customs house, inhabited only by the thoughts of the dead. In both 'La casa dei doganieri' and 'Passato' the attributes of the imagined locality are transferred to both the speaker and the addressee, and it is in this transference of attributes that self and Other temporarily merge. In spite of the desolate nature of the objective correlative in 'Passato', the self's confrontation of the finiteness of existence engenders an enhanced sense of possession of the past, together with an affirmed sense of identity. There is no such consolation in 'La casa dei doganieri'. It is the liminal, unstable quality of the point of contact which forms the substance of the poem. The self is alienated from the object of remembrance, but also, importantly, from the self. The contingency of the point of contact is stressed at the beginning by the impossibility of the Other recognizing its existence. But the receptivity of the self to the memory of the Other is equally becoming weaker in 'La casa dei doganieri':

> Tu non ricordi la casa di questa
> mia sera. Ed io non so chi va e chi resta.

[You do not remember the house of this my evening |And I do not know who stays or who goes.]

The mythical land of the dead in Cardarelli's poem is a region of the self. In 'La casa dei doganieri', however, the dilapidated locality is also a metaphor of the self and as such it conveys the impression of a consciousness no longer able to distinguish between life and death.

The comparison between 'Passato' and two of the lyrics from *Le occasioni* betrays a connection between Montale and Cardarelli that was in reality quite strong. There is evidence to suggest that Montale was attentive to the return to classicism for which Cardarelli militated between 1919 and 1923 in the pages of *La Ronda*. It is a fact that he later wrote that the journal offered 'a lesson in dignity that it was absolutely

necessary to follow'.[25] There are other points of contact
which could be explored. For example, in his prose text of
1920, *Memorie della mia infanzia*, Cardarelli invests the figure
of his father with the attributes of an implacable deity who
plays upon the memories of the son. Both thematically and
lexically the representation of the father-figure is akin to the
symbolic presentation of the sea in Montale's cycle of poems,
'Mediterraneo'. The prose piece 'Lago' belonging to *Il sole a
picco* of 1929 is inherently similar, in its presentation of
impending catastrophe, to another of *Le occasioni*, 'Notizie
dall'Amiata'.[26]

When compared with the work of Cardarelli, the voices of
poets like Ungaretti, Quasimodo, and Montale do assert
their own essential characteristics. The formal divide remains strong between one poet whose use of imagery is
confined to the exploitation of archetypal symbols and
others whose poetry merges unrelated areas of experience
and reality in ways that are new, unexpected, or disconcerting. Yet the various coincidences of expression between
the work of Cardarelli and the hermetics reveals a complex
relationship. In the view of the majority of critics the hermetic poetry of the 1930s served as a form of resistance on
the part of intellectuals who wished to remain distant from
the politics of the regime. It is surprising, therefore, to find
that some of the principal motifs of hermetic verse are
common to the poetry of a figure like Cardarelli who made
every effort to define himself as a Fascist intellectual and
who was not above writing elegies to Fascist icons.[27]

The relationship of the self of *Poesie* to the figure of the

---

[25] The observations of Montale are reported in the article by Giuseppe Cassieri,
'I cinquant'anni della *Ronda*', *L'Approdo letterario*, 46 (Apr.–June 1969), 89–104.

[26] It is worth noting that in the opening to his lyric, 'Nostalgia', Cardarelli seems
clearly to echo the first lines of the second movement of 'Tempi di Bellosguardo',
again contained in *Le occasioni*. Montale's lines read, 'Derelitte sul poggio | fronde
della magnolia | verdibrune se il vento | porta dai frigidari'; Cardarelli's poem
begins with the words, 'Alto su rupe, | battuto dai venti, | un cimitero frondeggia: |
cristiana oasi nel Tartaro etrusco.' For a longer discussion of the parallels of this
kind see C. Burdett, 'Montale and Cardarelli: A Two-Way Traffic of Influence', in
proceedings of conference on Montale, July 1996 (Hull: Hull University Press,
forthcoming).

[27] See e.g. the poems entilted 'Camicia nera' and 'Canzone di marcia' in
Cardarelli, *Opere*, 113–16.

speaker in other texts and articles is equally complex. In his prose writings for *L'Italiano*, *Il Tevere* and other journals, Cardarelli was not shy of arrogating to himself the role of the interpreter of his country's history and traditions. He was an enthusiastic apologist for the Fascist recreation of Italian national identity, and he later proved a keen supporter of colonial expansion. Considering the kind of rhetoric that he was regularly able to deliver, it is strange to find that his poetry serves as the locus for investigating questions of contingency and precariousness. The self of *Poesie* is troubled by the evidence of encroaching mortality. The dynamics of the collection depend upon the progressive erosion of apparent certainties. While the declarative openings to many lyrics seem to suggest a conception of poetry as grand art, the development of themes of doubt and anxiety hint that the poetry fails to achieve the art which it posits. The very absence of imagery may indicate a deletion of life. Any analysis of Cardarelli's poetry reveals the extent to which his notion of classicism and his belief in a resurgent Italy were not as solid as he may have professed to believe. Indeed, the depth of his interest in mortality and the more than occasional closeness of his poetry to the verse of poets like Montale demonstrates the contradictory nature of many of the statements he was keen to make both on politics and on aesthetics. It is the conflict between his written intentions and his actual practice, between his identity as a Fascist intellectual and the enunciated self of his writing, that provides much of the interest of his work.

6

IN PRAISE OF THE REGIME:
THE TRAVEL-WRITING OF THE 1930s

Italy in the 1930s: The Totalitarian State

By 1930 the foundations of the Fascist state had largely been laid, but throughout the decade the regime increased its attempts to regiment the lifestyles and thought processes of ordinary Italians. Under the supervision of Achille Starace (party secretary from 1931 to 1939), the PNF played an important role in enlisting support for Mussolini and his policies. The Lateran accords of 1929 facilitated the support of the Catholic Church for elements of Fascism, including anti-Communism and the policy of rurality. A series of initiatives was introduced to standardize the behaviour and speech of Italians: these ran from the vaguely comic, such as the well-known attempt to abolish the use of 'lei' in the second person, to the more overtly sinister. In the early 1930s there was an attempt to fuse the work which the Opera Nazionale Balilla sought to accomplish with the education offered in primary and secondary schools. From 1929 schoolteachers were required to take an oath of allegiance to the regime if they wanted to follow their profession, and by 1930 a number of Fascist textbooks were in use. The purpose of fusing the Opera Nazionale Balilla (which from 1937 was to become the Gioventù Italiana del Littorio) with the schools and of restricting what should be taught and by whom was to create, in the words of Philip Morgan, 'a nation of warriors, physically fit, mentally agile, disciplined, courageous and obedient, committed believers and fighters in the cause of the nation'.[1] The emphasis on creating a new type of Italian who would be ready to play a part in the aquisition and the later running of a colonial empire focused on the cultivation of supposedly masculine virtues,

---

[1] Morgan, *Italian Fascism*, 111.

while leaving the regime with the problem of what role or type of association it could propose for women.

The regime also sought to strengthen its regulation of the working lives of Italians. From 1929 onwards the Great Depression was interpreted explicitly by Mussolini as indicating the terminal decline of the Western capitalist system. What distinguished Italian Fascism both from the American model of production and from Soviet collectivism was the corporativist framework which had begun to operate seriously in the 1920s. The global economic crisis of the early 1930s gave an additional impetus to corporativism. By 1935 almost all areas of agricultural and industrial production were regulated through a series of different corporations which had the power to regulate both prices and economic relations. With the war in Ethiopia and the sanctions which the League of Nations imposed, the Italian economy struggled to move towards complete autarky. The endeavour, coupled with the stagnancy of trade across the world, left industry dependent on the permanent intervention of the state. In 1933 the government agency IRI (the Institute for the Reconstruction of Industry) was set up with the specific purpose of supporting ailing industrial and banking concerns. The agency grew rapidly in importance. The government programme of large-scale public works continued throughout the 1930s with the building of stations, courthouses, hospitals, and other public buildings. Although state expenditure on public works was limited by the demands of failing industries, the Fascist programme of urban renewal succeeded in changing the physical aspect of many Italian cities. In the latter part of the 1930s huge amounts of government money were spent in Italy's newly acquired colonial empire. The Fascist economy never, however, managed to generate enough money to allow military spending of a level that would allow Mussolini to achieve the ambitions of his foreign policy.

If the regime was to succeed in fostering the idea that the individual should be entirely subordinate to the will of the nation and that such subordination should express itself through active involvement in the organizations of the Fascist state, then clearly massive use of propaganda was necessary. Cinema was developed as a means of spreading ideas and images which could be associated with Fascism, although, as has often been noted, the most successful films of the period were escapist and optimistic dramas that steered clear of addressing any substantive issues.[2] The radio grew in importance as an effective means of spreading propaganda, although it never managed to gain the same influence in diffusing ideas that the daily newspapers enjoyed.[3] Over a period of years the editorial staff of all the major newspapers from the *Corriere della sera* downwards had been replaced by figures who were either sympathetic to the aims of the regime or who were active proponents of Fascist ideals. Curzio Malaparte, for example, had briefly enjoyed the editorship of *La Stampa* between 1929 and 1931. In 1933 control of the Ministry of Press and Propaganda passed directly to Mussolini's son-in-law, Galeazzo Ciano. His objective was to ensure a uniformly pro-Fascist press. To this end, the ministry supplied a constant stream of directives to the editors of most newspapers informing them of what areas it was legitimate to write about and of the interpretation to be given to certain news stories. It was the clear intention of Mussolini's government to regulate all cultural activity for its own specific ends. In May 1937 this particular arm of government was renamed the Ministry of Popular Culture.

The major feature which distinguished the second decade of Fascist rule from the first was the pursuit of a more aggressive foreign policy. Mussolini's political movement had come to power determined to reverse the effects of the Versailles peace settlement in which Italian ambitions in Africa and the Adriatic had been humiliatingly thwarted. At the same time as he consolidated the power of his regime at home, he looked to extend Italy's sphere of influence in Albania, to keep a watchful eye on the possibility of a formal and threatening union between Austria and Germany, and to secure territorial gains to the east of the Mediterranean. The expansionist foreign policy that he intended to follow

---

[2] See Geoffrey Nowell-Smith, 'The Italian Cinema under Fascism', in D. Forgacs (ed.), *Rethinking Italian Fascism*, (London: Lawrence & Wisgart, 1986), 142–62.

[3] On this point see Danilo Veneruso, *L'Italia fascista* (Bologna: Il Mulino, 1981), 199.

was the natural corollary of the renewal of Italian national life that Fascism claimed it had accomplished. The under-lying purpose of the increasing regimentation of Italian society and the increasing importance given to propaganda and education was to prepare Italy not only for imminent colonial enterprises but also for the possibility of a larger conflict in which the provisions of Versailles could be over-turned. Ethiopia provided the first occasion for Fascist Italy to extend its borders significantly.

Italian claims to parts of Ethiopia dated back to the first Ethiopian war of 1894–6, but a concrete indication of renewed Italian colonial interest in the country was pro-vided, ironically enough, with a pact of friendship that the two countries signed in August 1928. The major obstacle to an Italian annexation of the country lay, however, in the potential reactions of the other colonial powers of the region, Britain and France. By early 1935 Mussolini had largely overcome French objections to Italian expansion, although his failure to reach a compromise with Britain convinced him of the need for military action. The war in Ethiopia began in October 1935, and huge military force was used in the interests of securing rapid victory. At the height of hostilities over 400,000 soldiers were engaged in the campaign. The conquest of the country was officially declared complete in May 1936. International reaction had taken the form of sanctions imposed by the League of Nations. The sanctions failed to alter the course of Italian foreign policy and merely accentuated the regime's attempts to achieve economic self-sufficiency through corporativism. Within Italy, the colonial adventure had been accompanied by the massive dissemination of propaganda. Isnenghi has explored the way in which the annexation of the country was reported towards the end in the *Corriere della sera*.[4] The Italian operation was not presented as an act of force but as a civilizing mission, and the objections of other European countries and the League of Nations were portrayed as a shameful obstruction. While the army of Haile Selassie was the object of unrelenting denigration, the indigenous

[4] Isnenghi, 'Il radioso maggio africano del *Corriere della sera*', in his *Intellettuali militanti e intellettuali funzionari*, 92–151.

population was generally portrayed as welcoming Italian troops and willing to follow its newly installed colonial masters. Finally, Italy was portrayed as at last taking up the rightful heritage of imperial Rome.

With the help of the press and the propaganda ministry, Mussolini was undoubtedly successful in encouraging mass support for his exercise in colonialism. Indeed, a number of historians have seen May 1936 as the apex of the popularity of Italian Fascism. The conquest of Ethiopia was not, however, the end of Mussolini's ambitions but the first step in building a much larger empire. The myth of the cultural reconstruction of Italy on which Fascism was founded came increasingly to depend on the successful expansion of its borders. The Italian economy was geared towards the aims of the regime's foreign policy, while the Italian people were continually subjected to efforts to mobilize their support for territorial expansion. The Spanish Civil War followed quickly on from the formal end of hostilities in Ethiopia, and from its outset Italy supplied men and equipment to Franco's Nationalists. The conviction, meanwhile, that the power of France and Britain in the Mediterranean represented an obstacle to greater Italian expansion in the area led to the rapprochement with Nazi Germany that lay directly behind the eventual collapse of Italian Fascism.

Italian Writers and the Question of Travel

In his monograph *Abroad: British Literary Travelling Between the Wars*,[5] Paul Fussell has shown the extraordinary extent to which British writers between the wars wrote as travellers. He has argued that the impulse to travel was for some caused by experiences suffered in the trenches, while for others it arose out of a pronounced dissatisfaction not only with the British climate but with the country's institutions. Writers such as D. H. Lawrence, Robert Byron, and Evelyn Waugh were inspired to seek and write about the cultures of distant countries. In the process they not only journeyed to the

---

[5] Oxford: Oxford University Press, 1980.

same places that Italian writers visited, they wrote about Italy and even the effects of Italian colonialization. For example, Lawrence's *Etruscan Places* was published in 1932, while *Waugh in Abyssinia* appeared in 1936. The genre of travel writing may have flourished in Britain between the wars, but it also enjoyed considerable success in Italy. Many writers were engaged by newspapers and periodicals to write down their impressions on visits to near and distant locations. Ungaretti, as correspondent for *Il popolo d'Italia* in Paris, wrote not only on the French capital but also published records of his journeys to Holland and Belgium.[6] In 1932 Giovanni Comisso's evocations of his journeys to the east were published in the volume *Cina–Giappone*. In the early 1930s Mario Soldati and Giuseppe Antonio Borgese narrated excursions to the United States,[7] while in the late 1930s Alberto Moravia, employed as a correspondent for *La Stampa*, journeyed both to Mexico and to China. Working for a number of journals (including *La Stampa*, *Mediterraneo*, and *Lavoro fascista*), Corrado Alvaro published records of journeys undertaken both within Italy and abroad. When Italy had successfully concluded its invasion of Ethiopia in May 1936, Guido Piovene and Ugo Ojetti, writing in *Corriere della sera*, recorded their impressions of ordinary Italians celebrating the foundation of the Italian empire and launched into eulogies of Italy's new identity as a colonial power.

The majority of writers who had been associated with *La Ronda* wrote elegant descriptions of their journeys. In 1928 Riccardo Bacchelli published under the title of *La ruota del tempo* a collection of short and for the most part elegiac writings on aspects of the Italian landscape. Throughout the 1930s he continued to write similar pieces for *Corriere della sera*. In 1931 Bruno Barilli collected his impressions of travels in Africa in the volume *Il sole in trappola*. In 1934 Antonio Baldini published his observations on the character

---

[6] Ungaretti's travel writing is collected in *Il deserto e dopo* (Milan: Mondadori, 1961).

[7] Giuseppe Antonio Borgese published *Escursioni in terre nuove* (Parma: Guanda, 1931) and *Atlante americano* (Florence: Ceschina, 1936), while Mario Soldati wrote *America primo amore* (Florence: Bemporad, 1935).

of Parisian life in *La vecchia del Bal Bullier*. But it was Emilio Cecchi who established himself as the most important writer on travel in the inter-war years. For Cecchi travel represented the occasion for the scholarly investigation of other cultures. In 1931 he made an extensive journey through southern California into Mexico, writing a series of short prose pieces which appeared throughout 1931 in the *Corriere della sera* under the rubric 'Lettere dal Messico'. Five years later, during a visit to Greece from July to December 1934, he published another series of articles for *Corriere*. Between 1937 and 1938 he returned to the United States and Mexico to send a series of lengthy articles on the two countries back to the same newspaper, and in 1939 these observations were published in book form under the provocative and openly hostile title of *America amara*. Indeed, Cecchi's impressions have been described as offering the semi-official picture of the United States and as appearing totally biased to anyone who reads them after the collapse of Fascism.[8]

In 1939 Carlo Emilio Gadda published a collection of articles he had written on travels within Italy, *Le meraviglie d'Italia*. In his preface to the collection he explicitly thanked Cecchi for the interest he had shown in the preparation of the work. In *Le meraviglie* Gadda's prose bears a number of formal similarities with that of Cecchi. Another practitioner of the genre of travel writing in the inter-war period was the former *rondista* Alberto Savinio, although his collection of journeys through Milan and northern Italy, *Ascolto il tuo cuore, città*, was not published until 1944.[9] Savinio's travelogue is interesting because it is so regularly interspersed with references and allusions to the work of other travel writers. In his book he speaks of Baldini's infatuation with Paris, refers to the 'fantastic beauty' of Barilli's narration of his African journey, and describes outings to different parts of Italy in the company of Cardarelli, Cecchi, and Broglio. He even meets and speaks to some of the figures which

---

[8] Donald Heiney, *America in Modern Italian Literature* (New Brunswick: Rutgers University Press, 1964), 35.

[9] The edition from which all quotations are taken is *Ascolto il tuo cuore, città* (Milan: Adelphi, 1984).

Cardarelli had described in *Il sole a picco*. For Savinio, those writers who were employed by *Corriere della sera* and by other journals to write about their journeys to different locations represented a clearly identifiable élite, or, to use his term in *Ascolto il tuo cuore, città*, a 'closed civilization' (p. 29).

The fact that many of the pieces of travel literature published in the inter-war period were by writers who had known one another over a lengthy period and indeed had worked for the same journals and newspapers certainly tended to increase the formal and semantic homogeneity of their writings. In most prose pieces which take travel as their subject, the journey is woven into elegantly constructed, elaborate sentences. It is rare that such prose compositions accommodate reported speech or conversation. The travellers who narrate their journeys keep their own company. In *Le meraviglie d'Italia* Gadda refers to the growing tourist industry in Italy but he does so disparagingly[10] and in general the travellers of the inter-war period are highly conscious of the literary quality both of their journeys and of their writing. Unsurprisingly, the travel texts of the time do not mention controversial political events of the recent past. The reference which Savinio makes to the burning down of the offices of *Avanti!* (p. 100) represents one notable exception to this rule; another is the reference which Gadda makes in *Le meraviglie d'Italia* to the armoured cars of American design that he sees on display at the fair in Milan in 1936 (p. 182). The deliberate avoidance of political speculation, which can be traced directly back to the aesthetic of *La Ronda*, is masked by the narrator's concentration on the imaginative exploration of visual and auditory phenomena.

It is not, however, the formal characteristics of such writing or its emphasis on aesthetics that command most interest. The majority of Italian travel writers of the 1930s wrote texts which in their choice of places to visit and in their selection of details displayed a clear intention to support the nationalistic premises on which Fascism was based. If many British travellers between the wars were inspired to travel because of a strong dislike of their country of origin, the

---

[10] Carlo Emilio Gadda, *Le meraviglie d'Italia* (Turin: Einaudi, 1964), 174.

opposite was true for many Italian writers who wrote as
travellers. Many texts of the period manipulated notions of
history and geography in order to construct a series of
national stereotypes and a utopian idea of the Italian nation.
Cardarelli's claim that he and the writers of the *Ronda* (as
'lovers of Italy') did their best to 'represent and exalt' their
country points to the propagandistic function that his prose
and that of others indirectly served.[11] Isnenghi has referred
to a whole category of writers who composed elegant descriptions of aspects of Italy as the 'essayists [*elzeviristi*] of the
regime' and has convincingly argued that their writings
played a part in furthering the notion that Italy, as an ancient
colonial power, was entirely within its rights in forcefully
extending its sphere of influence.[12]

The travel writing of the 1930s, while disseminating a
series of ambiguous notions of how Italians may have seen
themselves and their country, also functioned as a means of
creating negative perceptions of other countries, peoples,
and economic systems. For example, Emilio Cecchi published accounts of his journeys to non-European destinations
in the pages of *Corriere della sera* thus reaching an audience
of over 300,000 readers. His views, while not obviously cast
as propaganda, often served to characterize a potentially
menacing Other. A separate but related point is that the
most prominent travel writers were all male. The recording
of impressions of different countries or of different regions
within the same country entails a parallel delineation of the
identity of the traveller. What any modern-day reader finds
in Italian travel writing of the Fascist period are constructions of an overtly masculine identity that is not redefined
but reinforced by the experience of travel. By looking at the
two travel texts which Cardarelli wrote in the late 1920s and
1930s it becomes possible to examine more closely some of
the internal properties and wider implications of a genre
which was highly successful during the years of Mussolini's
rule. Cardarelli's texts, like those of many other writers,

---

[11] In an open letter addressed to Riccardo Bacchelli and published in *Il Resto del
Carlino* on 15 June 1932, Cardarelli wrote: 'Amanti della nostra terra l'abbiamo
esaltata e raffigurata nella nostra povera prosa.'

[12] Isnenghi, *Intellettuali militanti e intellettuali funzionari*, 144.

move between two poles. On the one hand, the writer, in a
variety of concealed ways, seeks to convey a series of negative
stereotypes of foreign peoples. On the other hand, he seeks
to delineate a particular version of 'italianità', usually by
putting together the sum of different regional characteristics. In Cardarelli's writings, as in all travel writing of the
period, political comment is presented as the registration of
purely empirical data.

Cardarelli's Journey to Russia

It was as a correspondent for *Il Tevere* that Cardarelli sent
a series of dispatches on Russia back to Italy. His reports
were published between November 1928 and April 1929.
He had gained the position of foreign correspondent only
temporarily and it was not one which he retained for long.
The regular correspondent for the *Il Tevere* in Russia, Ettore
Lo Gatto, returned to take up his post in April 1929.[13] On a
number of counts the possibility of writing on Russia was
certainly an interesting one. First, many Western intellectuals, from André Gide to Bernard Shaw, had journeyed to
Russia in the ten years that had elapsed since the Communist
revolution, with a desire to see for themselves what such a
vast economic and sociological experiment could produce.
Secondly, Italy had come close to experiencing a left-wing
coup in the immediate post-war period and now under
Fascism considered itself a bulwark against the 'red threat'.
Thirdly, before becoming an arch-conservative, Cardarelli
himself had been a sympathizer of the extreme left. Unfortunately, however, the series of articles which he wrote on
Soviet Russia proves disappointingly anecdotal: the articles
convey little sense of the importance of the newly created
alternative model for society and they do not reflect on the
cost in human lives of collectivization or enforced industrialization. What the articles do provide are impressions on the

[13] Cardarelli's notes on Russia were, with a number of alterations, later published
in *Viaggio di un poeta in Russia* (Milan: Mondadori, 1954). For a history of the
writing and publication of the volume, see Martignoni's edition of Cardarelli's
works, pp. 1101–2.

daily lives of ordinary inhabitants of Leningrad and Moscow, considerations on the architectural sites of the two cities, and a highly subjective idea of the country and its inhabitants. Owing to their superficiality these observations tell us little of the deep structures of Russian society, but they do serve to indicate the notion the traveller has of his place of origin and the regime by which it is governed.

When reporting his journey to Russia, Cardarelli makes it clear to his reader that he is travelling to a vast territory that belongs to the Orient and which cannot therefore be understood with reference to the same paradigms which govern understanding of western European countries. As he charts his progress across Czechoslovakia and Poland, he claims that he moves away from familiar places that serve to denote a common conception of Europe and towards something that is altogether more menacing. The unease which he feels as a traveller reaches its highest degree as he crosses the 'infernal landscape' of the industrialized parts of Poland, uttering the words 'Addio civile Europa' (*Opere*, 750). When he stops off briefly in Warsaw, he is assailed by the sense of the fragility of a Westernized model of civilization that is threatened by the nearness of a contrasting world. The language which he uses to describe his stay in Warsaw is permeated with military terminology and metaphors: Warsaw, although undermined by the obvious presence of 'an overbearing enemy', is the extreme 'outpost' of Western civilization; over the eastern side of Poland there is an atmosphere of 'an alarming ceasefire, a strange calm' (p. 754). Indeed, the atmosphere of impending danger is something which the traveller detects even as he crosses the border into Russia itself, a country which he argues has always faced the threat of hoards of Mongols, of Tartars, of 'horrendous invaders' (p. 762). The way in which he concentrates on describing feelings of apprehension in his journey into the unknown suggests that his impressions, and those of other travellers to Russia in the 1920s and 1930s, may well have exerted a powerful influence on the imagination of Dino Buzzati, whose internationally famous novel, *Il deserto dei Tartari*, appeared in 1940.

The emphasis on a sense of misgiving as the traveller

approaches his destination also indicates an attitude of mind which rather than being open to the experience of otherness seeks confirmation of its prejudices. As he is about to cross the border into Russia, Cardarelli admits to a fear that he is about to enter the sinister realm of the GPU (Ghepeù, Cardarelli's term for the Russian secret police), that he may be set upon or that he may disappear without trace. When he does arrive, first in Moscow and then in Leningrad, the comments that he makes about the Russians themselves reveal the extent of his xenophobia. Many of the articles which he sent back to *Il Tevere* revolve around speculation on the racial characteristics of the inhabitants of Russia's two main cities. To begin with the traveller is disconcerted by the heterogeneity of the population of Moscow, which he sees as a microcosm of the whole of Russia. He has difficulty in discerning the place of origin of the people he meets in the city, which he describes as 'the most beautiful zoological garden in the world' (p. 776). As he encounters more of Moscow's inhabitants, he begins to construct a stereotype of Russians as both vaguely menacing and absurd. He is struck by the degree of superstition evident in people's adoration of icons that are both religious and profane. He remarks that only in Russia could people erect portraits to 'such a repellent face as that of Karl Marx' (p. 821). He reflects that a highly developed sense of superstition is accompanied by an 'intellectual obtuseness' (p. 808) and a spirit of material-ism that makes the Russians peculiarly unreceptive to any real understanding of the precepts of Communism. The Russians also conceal a number of violent instincts that are partially revealed by their fanatical anti-Semitism.

The pattern of disavowal evident in the characterization of the Russians is most obvious when their modes of sexual interaction are described as scarcely human, and when the writer, reflecting on various incidents of irascibility that he has witnessed, refers to the whole Russian people as 'highly infantile'. In the same passage he observes:

È dubbio se questo popolo abbia il senso della lealtà, della fedeltà, dell'onore come noi l'intendiamo. Se ci sia da fidarsene. Se sia possibile costruire in Russia qualche cosa di sicuro, di assoluto, di moralmente bello, senza ricorrere alla frusta. Promiscuità, confusione, indistinto della vita russa. Mescolanza del sacro e profano. Pericolosa innocenza. (*Opere*, 820)

[It is doubtful whether this people has a sense of loyalty, faithfulness or honour as we understand these terms. One can ask whether it is possible to trust them and whether it is possible to build something in Russia which is certain, absolute and morally beautiful without resorting to coercion. Promiscuity, confusion, indistinctness make up life in Russia. A mixture of the sacred and the profane. A dangerous innocence.]

The racist assertion of this passage is that there is a correlation between the heterogeneity of the Russian people and a weak or impure sense of morality. As well as offering this syllogistic piece of reasoning, the passage also makes an implied contrast between the Italian and the Russian peoples: if the Russians lack the ability to understand concepts such as loyalty and honour, then such concepts are fundamental to Italians; if Russian life is characterized by promiscuity, then Italian life is by contrast pure; if in Russia a new political synthesis can be achieved only through coercion, then in Italy it can be attained through consent.

The xenophobic nature of Cardarelli's description of the Russians is matched by his characterization of the Communist regime. He deliberately avoids conducting a serious examination of the ideological basis of the revolution and the material effects which it has created. He makes no comparison between the setting up of soviets and the attempt to establish factory councils in Italy during the 'biennio rosso'. Instead, he chooses to observe minor and frequently comic details. He notices, for example, how many of the newly formed institutions of the regime have been housed in some of the most splendid palaces in Leningrad. He sees how many women wear a red scarf and interprets this as a sign that Communism is merely a passing fashion. While prepared to accept the evidence that the Communists have been successful in causing the level of illiteracy to fall, he uses the observation as the springboard to launch an attack on the figure of Lenin. Observing the amount of newly printed material, he writes:

Su queste montagne di pubblicazioni illustrate e colorate del più edenico ottimismo si eleva l'immagine ammonitrice e accattivante del dittatore coi suoi occhiettti mongoli, le sopracciglia da Mefistofele, e il suo eterno berretto di giramondo e di proletario. Quest'uomo rude, dalle idee rudi, ha trasformato la Russia in un brefotrofio. (*Opere*, 806)

[On these mountains of publications, illustrated with the most optimistic colours, the striking and admonishing figure of the dictator rises, with his small Mongol eyes, his Mephistophelian eyebrows and his cap that gives him the air of both a traveller and a working man. This rough man with his rough ideas has transformed Russia into a charitable hospital for orphans.]

The portrait of Lenin as a vaguely threatening orator who during his lifetime was able to peddle a series of half-baked ideas is accompanied by a network of statements which serve to suggest that Communism is destined to wither in Russia. It is the contention of the travel writer that the regime, in seeking to change the whole of Russian society, is engaged in a hopeless task. It is suggested that Communism, unlike Italian Fascism, does not have the backing of the masses who are unable to understand its philosophy and unable to adapt to its rules. The leaders of the Russian revolution are accused of showing enormous naivety in believing that 'their simplistic little doctrine' (p. 814) could be imposed upon a backward-looking agrarian population. The drive towards industrialization in the Russia of the late 1920s is interpreted as a means of concealing the illegitimacy of the origins of the Communist regime. Everywhere that the traveller looks he sees evidence of the scarcity of resources: he notices large groups of people queuing for every commodity; he complains about the slowness of the rail network and he observes 'the miserable wooden mausoleum' in which Lenin is buried (p. 764).

Cardarelli returned from his brief journey to Russia in the spring of 1929, but the early 1930s marked an increasing Italian interest in Russia. The journal *Critica fascista* ran a column on the differences between Communism and Fascism from 1931. Gaetano Ciocca travelled to the country the following year and published his observations in *Giudizio sul bolscevismo* (1933). Between 1933 and 1934 Piero Bardi published a series of reports on Russia in the journals *L'Ambrosiano* and *Il lavoro fascista*. In 1934 Corrado Alvaro was sent to Russia as a correspondent for *La Stampa* and a year later his reports were published in book form under the title

I maestri del diluvio: Viaggio nella Russia sovietica (1935).[14] Alvaro's text provides a much more ample study of the phenomenon of Russian Communism: on his visit to Novgorod he documented the concrete results of industrialization and, in his journeys into the Russian countryside, he formed an opinion of aspects of collectivization. Unlike Cardarelli he was prepared to acknowledge that Communism had brought an increase in material well-being for the average Russian citizen. He did, however, remain preoccupied by the failure of the Russian state to account for the desires of the individual, and throughout he used the Russian experiment as a means of constructing an apologia for Fascist Italy.

Travelling in Italy

The reports which Cardarelli wrote on his trip to Russia showed the extent to which he was prepared to use another place as the ground from which to create a highly positive vision of Italy. The observations he had published on Russia were complemented by his next travelogue. In 1939 he published *Il cielo sulle città*, a collection of writings which had previously appeared in newspapers from *La Gazzetta del Popolo* to *Il Tevere*. *Il cielo sulle città* narrates journeys made in Italy, or more precisely in the northern half of the Italian peninsula. Cardarelli declared that the localities in Italy which he wrote about were all places with which he had a strong personal connection. In the course of his book he also set out to define an identity for himself as a particular type of traveller. He wrote of himself as someone who, through economic necessity, was frequently impelled to travel but who feared the experience since it always entailed an acute form of introspection. He suggested that travel represented the gateway to an unwelcome journey inwards. He claimed to be unsuited to travel, and yet he implied a peculiar awareness of all its psychological implications; he

---

[14] For a more detailed analysis of Italian writing on Russia during the inter-war period, see the introduction by Marcello Flores to Alvaro's *I maestri del diluvio* (Massa: Memoranda Edizioni, 1985), pp. v–xviii.

claimed to be a poor traveller, yet he maintained that he always bought a third-class ticket; he also claimed that his heightened sense of the meaning of travel endowed him with a certain nobility (*Opere*, 635).

In the 'capitoli' which make up *Il cielo sulle città*, there are many instances where the narration of memories and fragments of autobiographical information predominate over the description of given localities. However, although in the text Cardarelli returns to the sites of his past, the book is not exclusively concerned with the internal landscape of the self. The text is made up of five sections each having as their subject a region or place in Italy: 'Etruria', 'Aspetti di Roma', 'Viaggio nelle Marche', 'Palude e laguna', and 'Lombardia'. What becomes apparent in the narration of the journeys to each of these different locations is a desire to turn space into time. What Cardarelli does in his travelogue is to try to recreate an idea of a glorious Italian past. In common with the majority of the travel texts which were written at the time, such a vision of the past is driven by the ideological principles of the present. As he moves in his text from one region to another, the traveller does so as a pilgrim paying homage to a series of holy sites. On his visit to Urbino he talks of a return to the origins of a civilization and of a journey to one of the 'sacred fonts of Italian beauty' (p. 608). In other places he enjoys a mystic encounter with the ancient spirit of a locality and he traces a line of descent from the Etruscans through the Romans to the Italians of the present day.

By seeking a form of intense contact with the visible remains of the ancient past, Cardarelli shows himself to be very much a traveller of his time. A number of other writers in the inter-war period posited themselves as imaginative interpreters of the mysteries of Italian history. Both Cecchi and Alvaro travelled to ancient sites of worship in the south of the country and sought to discover the arcane messages of the Sibilla Cumana. In the narration of his journey to Abruzzo in *Le meraviglie d'Italia* Gadda was fascinated not only by the irrigation works accomplished by the Romans, but attempted to see the dramatic landscape of the region through the mythological conceptions of its original inhabitants. More adventurous endeavours to search for the sites of the foundations of Italian civilization included Cecchi's journey to Greece in 1936 and Giovan Battista Angioletti's journey through Europe in 1934. In his own work, Savinio was keen to defend Italy's Greek and Roman heritage even to the point of claiming that Milan was essentially a Greek city. He compared the façades of certain famous buildings to the faces of ancient gods and goddesses and pointed to the perpetuation of ancient society through the unchanging traditions of the city's artisans.

The sacred nature of the traveller's task of unravelling the mysteries of the past is, in many texts of the period, foregrounded by the apparition of spectral guides and by frequent references to scenes from Dante's *Commedia*. The awe that Savinio experiences in his visits to Padua and Venice is enhanced by the fact that he encounters the figurations of Renaissance and medieval painting (*Ascolto il tuo cuore, città*, 71–7). Both Cecchi and Gadda, when visiting different cemeterial spaces in Italy, find themselves in silent conversation with the dead.[15] For Cardarelli the encounter with the materiality of the past is most intense when he travels through Etruria. In his writing on this part of Italy, he attempts to chart the history of the region's first inhabitants. Etruria is seen as the 'spiritual mould of Rome', the Etruscans' colonization of large stretches of central Italy is interpreted as a necessary antecedent to the imperial ambitions of the Romans, and it is affirmed that 'all the Etruscans accomplished was in essence no more than a homage to the Italian soil' (*Opere*, 530). The aggressive colonial endeavours of Mussolini's Italy clearly influenced the historical information that Cardarelli was willing to supply. In his self-appointed role as the interpreter of Etruscan civilization, he deploys a series of devices to communicate a sense of awe at the achievements of the ancient people. In one passage he narrates the discovery, made in 1823, of the tomb of an Etruscan warrior:

---

[15] Cecchi 'Collina di Firenze' in his *Corse al trotto* (Florence: Bemporad, 1936), reprinted in his *Saggi e vagabondaggi* (Milan: Mondadori, 1962), 528–34. Gadda, 'Sostando nella Necropoli Comunale', in his *Le meraviglie d'Italia*, 105.

Quella tomba, fresca di venticinque secoli di clausura assoluta, suscitava
gli stessi sentimenti che se fosse stata arredata e murata il giorno innanzi.
... Tutto parlava il grande linguaggio funebre degli Etruschi, nelle forme
più commoventi e dirette. Vi si vedevano spoglie bruciate devotamente o
distrutte, spezzate, quasi con disperazione o trasandatezza nell' adempi-
mento del rito. (*Opere*, 524)

[The tomb, fresh from its twenty-five centuries of absolute seclusion,
aroused the same sentiments as if it had been furnished and walled up the
day before. . . . Everything spoke the grand, funerary language of the
Etruscans in the most moving and direct fashion. One could see offerings
that had been burnt with devotion or destroyed, broken with desperation
or negligence during the course of the funeral.]

What the passage goes on to evoke is the ghostly semblance
of a man who had lived twenty-five centuries earlier, or as
Cardarelli puts it, 'the awakening of a spirit in its sepulchral
dominion'. The description of the Etruscan tomb, which
moulds the past and present together in an eerie mixture, is
only one instance of the travel writer claiming to illuminate
the origins of the nation's identity by visiting the sites of its
past. It is interesting, however, that Alvaro in his *Itinerario
italiano* also saw the central regions of the Italy of the 1930s
as being animated by the spirit of the Etruscans. In the
chapter, 'Gli Etruschi e la civiltà popolare', he went so far as
to affirm that Etruria was 'a small popular civilization in the
larger national civilization' (p. 32).

The similarities between the writing of Cardarelli and
Alvaro on the Etruscans point to the common matrix of the
travel texts of the period. As these Italian travellers journeyed through their own country, they travelled not only
to a series of identifiable localities but also through a field
of other representations which helped to determine their
understanding of those very localities. Thus in *Il cielo sulle
città* Cardarelli refers, at times deliberately, to the work of
archaeologists, ethnographers, or travellers who had pre-
ceded him. Like many of his fellow 'elzeviristi' he also
appropriates and develops a number of officially propagated
discourses on history and cultural identity. Nowhere is
this more obvious than in the frequent use of words such
as 'civiltà', 'spirito', and 'popolo' and in the repeated
contention that characteristics attributed to Italy's original

inhabitants have endured through time down to the present. Indeed, it is not difficult to see how in many instances Cardarelli, whether consciously or not, provides a genealogy for certain cultural attributes deemed by the regime to be the intrinsic properties of Italians. A good example of this tendency is to be found in the concentration on martial attitudes and modes of behaviour.

An important aim of the Fascist regime was to alter radically the way in which Italians perceived themselves, their country, and the role of Italy in an international context. In order to compel widespread support for the militaristic nature of the regime and its colonial ambitions, every effort was made to demonstrate that the aggressive values that the regime sought to propagate belonged authentically to an established Italian tradition. The cult of the Duce presented Mussolini as inspiring not only a mystical sense of devotion but a willing resistance on the part of the people to all of the many enemies of the Fascist nation. Organizations such as the Gioventù Italiana del Littorio served to inculcate a militaristic sense of patriotism with slogans such as 'credere, obbedire, combattere'. A great deal was made of the Italian victory in the First World War and those soldiers who had fallen in battle became the heroes of the regime. In Cardarelli's writing and in that of others, a number of textual strategies are employed to suggest what is posited as the intrinsically bellicose nature of the Italians. For example, the travel writer often works on a specious correlation between the physical appearance of an urban or rural landscape and the mental characteristics of its inhabitants. When Cardarelli visits Ancona he lists the occasions on which the city resisted attempts at invasion and sees the triumphal arch erected by Trajan as the symbol of the city. He writes:

Ancona esprime a meraviglia la formidabile reazione di questa razza di agricoltori sul mare e più che città marinara, è una fortezza, una vecchia fortezza repubblicana e papale. Città dura, fierissima, costruita non soltanto con vigore, ma con veemenza, o, per meglio dire, col disprezzo della forza stessa. (*Opere*, 595)

[Ancona expresses perfectly the formidable reaction of this race of farmers of the sea and more than being a coastal city it is a fortress, an old republican and papal fortress. It is a hard, extremely proud city which has been built not only with vigour but with vehemence, or, better, with a contempt for force itself.]

The description of Ancona evokes an image of a civil but aggressive people; its warlike instincts are appropriately represented by the town's coat of arms, which depicts a charging warrior waving his broadsword. More generally, the notions which lie at the heart of the fictitious spirit of the people of the Marche revolve around the unquestioning allegiance to ancient loyalties, pride in the past, collective action, and, above all, force. From the description of aspects of the architecture in Ancona, Cardarelli succeeds in creating a stereotype of the soldier–citizen. Elsewhere in *Il cielo sulle città* he describes the countryside of Lombardy as being 'heroic and primordial', while after listing the military glories of the Estense rulers of Ferrara he defines the rulers as 'hard and inexpressive men' whose responsibility it was to reconquer their own state against foreign enemies. It is in his description of Ferrara that he makes an explicit link between the actions of rulers in the distant past and more recent examples of violence. Recounting the history of a palace originally built to accommodate Ludovico il Moro, he describes how the building was, after the First World War, taken over by a group of homeless delinquents, thus becoming in his words a 'fortress of Bolshevism'. He then relates how this 'fortress' was stormed by the Fascists and how such an event has already acquired the aura of legend (p. 620).

For other writers travel was a means of seeking contact with the Italian people and of producing a series of representations of their way of life and ideals. In Alvaro's prose, for example, the agricultural worker and the artisan emerge as heroes as he tours the industrial areas of central Tuscany, and visits the mines of Massa and Carrara and the fishing villages of the Argentario. When he reaches the former city-states of the north-east, he claims that the inhabitants of these places have for centuries colonized other lands both within Italy and beyond. He refers to the settlements established in Ethiopia by people from Treviso; he also speaks enthusiastically about the movement of people from the Po delta to inhabit the newly established cities in the reclaimed Pontine marshes. He concludes his observations on the renewed sense of colonial adventure brought by Fascism by stating that there are too many people living in cities like Ferrara and that 'men need to act; if they don't they will act against themselves and against their civil inclinations' (*Itiner-ario italiano*, 145). In Alvaro's work, the apologia for Musso-lini's foreign policy is constructed around an image of the past as the locus of the true nature of the Italian people. In a similar fashion Savinio is prepared to denigrate other civil-izations which do not have the same expansionist history as Italy. He is also prepared to make a number of assertions, such as the following, on the ideal type of Italian:

Non illudiamoci: a tanti secoli dalla fine del predominio della forza bruta, l'ideale dell'uomo, pur del più ingobbito e ingoffito dalle fatiche buro-cratiche, del più pedindolcito dalla vita sedentaria, rimane l'uomo d'arme. (*Ascolto il tuo cuore, città*, 283)

[Let's not delude ourselves: so many centuries after the end of the reign of brute force, the ideal type of a man, even for those most bowed by bureaucratic labours and most softened by a sedentary life, remains the man of arms.]

As well as glorifying the mentality and activities of ordinary people, much Italian travel writing of the 1930s aimed to reinforce the cult of the great man. A familiar topos of the journeys of the period is the pilgrimage that is made to the birthplaces or tombs of illustrious figures. In the case of those writers who had earlier been committed *vociani*, it is worth noticing the transition from a form of writing that sought to aggrandize the self to a kind of composition which accommodated the admiration of monumental figures. Re-ferring to Weininger's ideas on genius, Savinio spoke, in *Ascolto il tuo cuore, città*, of the necessity of building monu-ments to distinguished men and he applauded the recent erection of a statue to the boxer Primo Carnera (p. 89). In both Cecchi's collections of prose and in the work of Ojetti, the visit to localities inhabited by the spirit of the illustrious dead provides the occasion for several prose pieces. In *Il cielo sulle città*, Cardarelli sees the whole of Urbino as testimony to the grandeur of Federico da Montefeltro, and while in the marches he travels as a pilgrim to Recanati, the hallowed birthplace of Leopardi. In the piece 'Visita a Recanati' the narrator travels from Ancona to Recanati as the sun is setting, in the company of a silent guide. As the speaker and his guide move nearer to Recanati, the intuition of the unseen presence of Leopardi becomes stronger; as they pass the cemetery shortly before the entry into the village, the narrator has the impression of brushing against Leopardi's tomb and of being shaken by his presence.

Cardarelli's literary excursions to areas in northern Italy are interesting in their threading together of autobiographical themes and propagandistic writing, but the main body of his travel text concerns Rome. In the seven short chapters of *Il cielo* included in the section 'Aspetti di Roma', (*Opere*, 540–65, 993–1000) a short history of the capital is charted. The method adopted to tell the city's history amounts to sewing together elements of historical fact, fragments of legendary stories, and strongly intuitive notions. One means by which the writer animates the city's past is to gaze at the outlines the town's buildings make against the sky; he implies that the changing physiognomy of the city through the ages reveals how its inhabitants have attempted, according to their differing belief systems, to come to terms with the evidence of infinity.[16] Thus, much of the history of Rome supplied by the text is in the form of imaginative interpretations of different architectural fashions. For example, the narrator sees the seventeenth century as being terrified by a sense of emptiness which it attempted to combat by constructing whole streets where 'the sky is enclosed like a river between two banks' (*Opere*, 547). On other occasions, the writer draws a contrast between his awareness of his own ageing and the evidence of the transformation which the city is presently undergoing.

While it is possible to read extracts from Cardarelli's writing on Rome as elegant pieces of imaginative speculation, the more closely they are examined the more a coherently pro-Fascist form of rhetoric emerges. Cardarelli was

---

[16] In a letter written to a friend, explaining one of the core concepts of the book, he had written: 'Tutto il mio libro è fondato su questo concetto: che la città ha un modo ben definito, chiuso, che vede l'orizzonte, la natura, il paesaggio, ossia l'infinito, attraverso archi, porte, in fondo alle strade.' The letter was addressed to Ernesto Braghetti and dated 24 Oct. 1937. See *Epistolario*, iii. 1041.

later to claim that the pieces which openly praised the achievements of the regime were the most transitory aspects of the text and could be omitted from post-war editions,[17] but those very pieces are integral to the argument his book develops. An idea that recurs is that architecture represents the language through which a nation expresses a vision of itself. Such an idea leads to chauvinistic declarations about the architectural superiority of Italy over other nations: the French are, for example, deemed to be guilty simply of aping the achievements of the Romans in their taste for grandiose monuments (p. 555). When speaking of a specifically Italian history of architectural fashions, the writer works on a contrast between the building projects of the regime and those which typified Umbertian Rome, the period between 1878 and 1900. The nation state of the earlier period is defined as 'sad and excessively bureaucratic' (p. 558). The project of its rulers was essentially to associate the whole of Italy with the Piedmontese monarchy. The timidity of the interventions of the period are deprecated, as is the length of time which was spent on the erection of the monument to Victor Emmanuel II.[18] But Cardarelli goes further, accusing Umbertian Rome of representing a 'narrow-minded, prohibitive and bourgeois spirit' (p. 556), a spirit which, he contends, was reflected in the passion of the time for wrought iron gates designed to keep the people at bay.

The attack on the building practices of the earlier time prepares for an extended eulogy of the radical changes to the physical aspect of Rome that occurred in the twenty years of Fascist power. The degree to which Rome was irrevocably altered in the inter-war years is well known. Architects from different schools were willing to participate in competitions for the construction of public buildings: for example, architects such as Adalberto Libera, Angiolo Mazzoni, and Giuseppe Pagano aimed to marry the principles of rationalism with those of Fascism; serious consideration

[17] See Cardarelli, *Opere*, 1090.
[18] In the same piece Cardarelli went on to proclaim that the prolonged existence of cheap hotels in the vicinity of the monument represented 'an affront to patriotic sentiment', *Opere*, 995. For an analysis of reactions to the building of the monument, see John Dickie, '*La macchina da scrivere*: The Victor Emmanuel Monument in Rome and Italian Nationalism', *The Italianist*, 14 (1994), 261–86.

was accorded to Henrik Christian Andersen's project for a 'World Centre for Communication'; Marcello Piacentini assumed the task of restructuring central Rome with the specific intention of elaborating, through metaphors of space, the lineal descent of Fascist Italy from ancient Rome. It was Mussolini's desire to make Rome appear 'marvellous to all the people of the world: vast, ordered, mighty, as it was in the first empire of Augustus'.[19] In the endeavour to produce a palingenetic vision of the newly founded Rome, many of the supposedly undistinguished buildings which cluttered sites near to ancient monuments were removed. Following Piacentini's ideas, two grand avenues were to move out from Piazza Venezia and cut through the centre of Rome so as to reveal the city's ancient splendour. The first of these avenues, Via dell'Impero, was inaugurated in 1932 with enormous pomp and ceremony. The new road had been achieved only at the cost of destroying centuries of urban building. By 1936 Piacentini and his team had set to work on the Via della Concilizaione, the grandiose approach to Saint Peter's which was designed to symbolize the reconciliation of the Church with the state that had taken place formally with the signing of the Lateran accords. Among a string of other projects designed to testify to the glory of the Fascist state, the late 1930s saw the construction of la Città Universitaria and the Città del Cinema.

The vandalism which accompanied the project of isolating the vestiges of ancient Rome may today be the object of near-universal condemnation, but Cardarelli in his interpretation of the history and spirit of Rome, welcomed the 'action of the pickaxe' (p. 555). Indeed, in his study of the building projects sponsored by Mussolini in Rome, Antonio Cederna has cited him as one of the most fervent supporters of the *sventramenti* that occurred as a necessary consequence of the Fascist taste for architectural statements of grandeur.[20]

[19] The quotation is taken from the address which Mussolini delivered on 31 Dec. 1925 on the appointment of the first governor of Rome. It is reported in Richard A. Etlin's extended analysis of the development of Italian architecture, *Modernism in Italian Architecture, 1890–1940* (Cambridge, Mass.: MIT Press, 1991), 392.

[20] *Mussolini urbanista* (Bari: Laterza, 1979). The text is quoted by Martignoni in Cardarelli, *Opere*, 1088.

The degree to which Cardarelli was prepared to defend the interventions of the regime in the heart of the capital derived in part from his faith that Mussolini was reacting against the prohibitions on the movement of people that had distinguished earlier periods. In his opinion, if Umbertian Rome had been the spacial expression of an exclusive bourgeois ideology, then the projects of the Fascist epoch were a bold statement of popular sentiment: the projects represented an act of appropriating for the people a number of sites which had previously been the preserve of a privileged élite. The building programme which Mussolini had initiated expressed not the desire of one class to defend itself against another, but the true language of the nation.

The second reason why Cardarelli was impelled to write with such enthusiasm about the 'high civil and historical necessity' (p. 996) of the renovation of Rome was his appreciation of an ill-defined and subjective notion of classicism. Even before the advent of Fascism, it had been his contention that artists and writers should act to define an aesthetic which would not seek to explore the new but glorify the past through imitation. The perpetuation of the language of the past was in his view legitimized by the feeling that the Italian people were instinctively sceptical of experimentation while willing to place their trust in the expression of traditional concepts. The architecture produced by Piacentini and others provided the spatial analogue of the concept of 'popular classicism' which he had advocated in the pages of *La Ronda*, and it is hardly surprising that he should have been one of the staunchest supporters of the imperial redefinition of Rome. Indeed, in the piece 'Il destino di Roma' (pp. 561–3, 995–7), he was prepared to argue, in perfect consonance with the discourse of the regime, that Fascism provided Rome with the chance to regain its character as an ancient city after centuries of decay. He appreciated the identity of the capital as the centre of a newly acquired empire and claimed that the monumental architecture which celebrated the colonizing state performed an inspiring educational role. It served as the impetus for Italians to acquire 'the taste for a noble and vigorous Romanness'.

The act of transforming the city is, in *Il cielo sulle città*, presented throughout as the effect of the will of Mussolini. Not only is the achievement of having swept away the spirit of Umbertian Rome attributed to him, but Cardarelli sees his declaration of wishing to move towards the people as being expressed in the drive to open the approach to St Peter's. Mussolini, described as a 'modern Caesar', is credited with having resurrected the remains of ancient Rome and made the whole of the city into a monument to Italian glory. More specifically, the Duce is the object of a panegyric for his success in at last creating the proper environment to surround the monument to Victor Emmanuel II. In Cardarelli's vocabulary, the monument becomes an altar to the nation, inspiring a religious devotion and a 'fear of God' (p. 995) in those who visit it. In the same piece in which he celebrates the creation of a site fitting for the monument to the Italian nation state, he goes on to speak about the building of the two avenues which will spread out from Piazza Venezia and of the work that 'raising the tone' of the capital has involved. He writes:

Opera necessaria e propriamente romana, che dimostra l'impulso civile del fascismo e la sua grandiosa e popolare visione della storia e della vita moderna. Opera che spiega, infine, come il romano autentico, vincendo qualche segreto rimpianto, abbia subito preso confidenza con la Roma di Mussolini, mentre si tenne sempre un po' in disparte dalla Roma umbertina. Chi avesse qualche dubbio in proposito pensi al successo di via dell'Impero, al giubilo dei romani il giorno in cui venne aperta la nuova strada augurale, che potrebbe anche dirsi via del Consenso. (*Opere*, 996–7)

[A necessary and essentially Roman project which demonstrates Fascism's civic sentiments and its grandiose and popular vision of history and modern life. A project which explains finally why the authentic inhabitant of Rome should, after overcoming some initial regret, have placed his trust in Mussolini's Rome, after having remained somewhat distant from the Rome of the Umbertian period. Anyone who has any doubt about this matter should think of the success of Via dell'Impero, of the joy of the Romans when the avenue was opened, an avenue which could be called Via del Consenso.]

In a passage such as this there is little attempt to define the meaning of the concepts that are used. The writing, while apparently constructed as a persuasive argument, works through assertion rather than through exemplification. The argument hinges upon the idea of what is 'truly Roman' and yet no definition of that is forthcoming. The lack of exemplification extends to the concept of history which underscores the writing. Not only here but in the whole of *Il cielo sulle città*, history emerges as a kind of a patchwork where some periods attain greater authenticity, and therefore validity, than others. Such a notion of temporal duration works implicitly to justify the monumental expression of Fascist power: the erasure of the material evidence of certain times is deemed unimportant, while the link between the ancient past and the present is made to appear self-evident. The partial and irrational telling of the nation's history is most obvious in the suggested parallel between the inhabitants of Mussolini's Rome and the ancient Romans. The two epochs are bound together by a common appreciation of grandeur. The inauguration of Via dell'Impero is presented as though it were the celebration of a successful Roman conquest. At the same time as it is suggested that the Italians of the present are the incarnation of the ancient Romans, an idea of the nature of Fascism is put forward: Mussolini's regime is authentically Italian; it serves to encourage heroic and martial values; it is the popular expression of the will of the masses and its actions are motivated by a sense of civic responsibility.

It is interesting to contrast the articles on Rome which appear in *Il cielo sulle città* with those which Cardarelli had written for *Avanti!* before both his engagement in the Florentine avant-garde and his subsequent conversion to the cause of reaction. Rather than being interested in revealing the squalor of the lives of the less fortunate inhabitants of the city, his later prose presents Fascist Italy as an effectively enacted utopia. While working as a correspondent for *Avanti!*, he had written on the plight of people living in the villages south of Rome. In *Il cielo sulle città* he returned to the same site but to write of the Pontine marshes as being a place which demonstrated to the world Italy's claim to be a 'great nation'. In his view, not only had Mussolini's draining of the marshes shown the ability of the Italians to colonize successfully, it represented, as families from different areas came to settle in the region, 'a grandiose return to the soil' (p. 999). Cardarelli was certainly not alone in paying homage both to the Duce and to the Fascist state through his observations on the changing physiognomy of Rome and its outlying areas. The authorized travellers of the period did not journey in order to criticize the sites which they saw, but to discover evidence of the successful working of the state. When journeying to Aquila in the company of a civil engineer, Gadda admired the work of land reclamation that had recently been accomplished (*Le meraviglie*, 76). Ojetti, in the prose piece 'Stelle sull'Impero', created a mythic picture of ancient Rome based on watching Mussolini address a huge crowd of Roman citizens.[21] In his visit to Rome at the start of his journey throughout the Italian peninsula, Alvaro spoke of the foundation of a new capital and of the awakening of 'a cult of youth, beauty, courage and force' (*Itinerario italiano*, 22). Elsewhere he claimed that 'glory was the great drug of the Italians' and that the race, imbued with the martial virtues of ancient Rome, 'must have its say' (p. 88).

The ways in which a certain type of travel writing served to support the regime were manifold. The texts of the period all tended to construct a history of Italy which led directly to the birth of the Fascist state. In such a history, the glories of the ancient past were stressed so as to confer an aura of grandeur on the present. Moreover, the bellicose aspects of the country's past were brought into relief in a way that provided a convenient historical context for contemporary advenures in Africa and elsewhere. But as well as rewriting Italian history, many travel texts of the 1930s sought to define the Italian people as a spiritual community that automatically shared the ideals of the Fascist state. The attempt of the regime to force ordinary Italians to identify their interests with the expansion of the nation-state found support from writers who saw the trace of collective design on all lasting monuments. To a degree the narration of journeys to different parts of Italy represented an ideal form of propagandistic literature. By concentrating on evoking

---

[21] See Isnenghi, *Intellettuali militanti e intellettuali funzionari*, 139–40.

the surface aspect of buildings or places, writers could point to the palingenesis of the nation without asking awkward questions about the relation between the visually apparent superstructure and its underlying economic and ideological base. The ease with which the sign was accepted as proof of a series of unexamined mythologies was a given of this type of writing. It is one of the ironies of the genre that, while writers like Cardarelli were expressing their boundless enthusiasm for the architectural innovations introduced by Mussolini in the capital and elsewhere, Italy was on the verge of catastrophe.

CONCLUSION

The Collapse of Fascism

The conquest of Ethiopia, while it had met with considerable support within Italy itself, did enormous damage to Italian relations with Britain and France. The extension of the newly founded Italian empire would now face more resolute opposition. Italian involvement in the Spanish Civil War further alienated the two established colonial powers, while those Italians who had been attracted to Fascism from the left were alienated by Mussolini's support of the Spanish Nationalists. The developments of the mid-1930s forced Italy to look elsewhere for political friendships and increasingly in the direction of Germany. In 1934 Hitler had made his famous visit to Italy. In 1936 Ciano's appointment to the position of Foreign Minister signalled an opening to a closer unity between the two countries. In the years which followed, the growing closeness between Italy and Germany worked to the advantage of the latter. Mussolini facilitated the recognition of Hitler as a statesman and on occasions acted as his mediator. In autumn 1937 he visited Germany in the belief that the country would be the sure victor in any eventual conflict and that it was in Italy's interest to attach its fortunes to a powerful ally of this kind. In 1937 Italy signed the anti-Comintern pact, while the alignment with Nazi Germany was marked by the introduction of the racial laws in November 1938. In May 1939 Italy signed the Pact of Steel.

The rapprochement with Germany was conceived as a way to enlarge Italy's empire, but it was to prove the policy which lay most directly behind the fall of Fascism. The Duce underestimated Hitler's intentions and gravely miscalculated the potential of German expansionist designs to coincide with his own. The urgency of Germany's desire to invade Poland, regardless of the probable consequences of such action,

came as a revelation to both Mussolini and Ciano. Although
Italy had taken the opportunity to annex Albania in April
1939, it was manifestly not ready to become involved in a
major conflict. When war broke out in September 1939, the
country initially declared its 'non-belligerence'. As Hitler
pursued a successful campaign on the eastern front, Italy's
neutrality presented a problem for a militaristic regime
which claimed to have awakened the authentically warlike
spirit of the Italians. The annexation of Austria in March
1938 also meant that Hitler was that much closer to the
Italian border. The rapidity with which the German army
advanced into France in the spring of 1940 finally convinced
Mussolini that Italy could take part in a conflict that was
likely to be short and from which Italy could make huge
gains.

On 19 June 1940 war against France was declared and,
in October of the same year, an invasion of Greece was
mounted. However, Italy's actions both in Greece and later
in Africa proved disastrous. The war revealed a lack of
communication between different sections of the army; an
astonishing lack of military equipment, made worse by the
slowness with which the economy moved to a war footing; a
shortage of fuel and means of transport; a dependence on
German aid. Mussolini's strategic planning was poor, and
the war extended unnecessarily over several fronts. Morale
both within the army and within the civilian population was
weakened by Allied air raids, worsening shortages, and by
the absence of any compelling reason for Italian involvement in the conflict. Party propaganda was unable to
mask the extent of the military defeats which Italy suffered
or to shore up support for the regime. By early 1943 both
the king and important figures within the PNF itself were
urgently considering an alternative to Mussolini. In July
1943 Allied troops landed in Sicily. On 24 July the meeting
of the Fascist Grand Council that decided on Mussolini's
dismissal from office was held. On 8 September 1943 Italy
surrendered to the Allies. German occupation and civil war
followed.

Shortly after the end of the Second World War Cardarelli
published, under the title of *Lettere non spedite* (1946), a

small collection of letters that he had written, but not posted, both to close friends and casual acquaintances during the conflict. The collection presented a picture of the privations he suffered in the war years and it provided some interesting admissions concerning his perception of himself. He wrote to one reader of his poetry that he was no more than a 'poor and troubled minor writer who cannot claim any acquaintance with Glory or Fame' (*Opere*, 888). In a letter to a closer friend, he spoke of the damage which had been caused to Tarquinia and he drew an analogy between the town and the rapidity of his own physical decline. He wrote:

In un attimo tutto è crollato. Per me come per tanti altri. Ma io sono caduto forse peggio di tutti. Sono tornato vecchio, cadente, in un luogo abbandonato a diciannove anni, bellissimo nel ricordo, orribile e sinistro nella sua presente realtà. (*Opere*, 915)

[In a moment everything has collapsed. For me as for so many others. But I have fallen perhaps more than most. I have returned old and decrepit to a place that I left at the age of 19, a place that is extremely beautiful in memory, but horrible and sinister in its present reality.]

Lettere non spedite was the last work of new material which he published. From 1946 until his death over ten years later, he continued to live off the generosity of his friends and to publish new editions of old poetry and prose. The texts *Solitario in Arcadia* (1947) and *Il viaggiatore insocievole* (1953) were collections of minor prose pieces and journalistic writings, many of which had been written in the years before the war. Towards the end of his life, he lived exclusively in Rome and, afflicted by an illness that left him partially paralysed, he rarely journeyed further from his rented room than to the Café Strega in Via Veneto. He died in the summer of 1959.

Fascism, Literary Culture, and the Case of Cardarelli

It is difficult to define Italian Fascism exactly: the movement was a synthesis of different, and to some extent contradictory, currents; it proved a flexible political ideology that altered to accommodate different groupings and changing circumstances; it effectively created a disparity between its own rhetoric and the impact which it exerted on the lives of ordinary Italians.[1] Yet, though it lacked the theoretical elaboration of other political doctrines, Fascism did have its own belief system, its own vision of a future, its own myths, and its own goals.[2] The origins of what constituted Fascist ideology were to be found in the avant-garde culture of the years before the First World War and the ever-growing nationalist revolt against the Italy of Giolitti. It was the First World War which weakened the institutions of Liberal Italy and allowed Fascism to develop as a social and political force. The 'biennio rosso' allowed the movement to harness the anti-Socialist feelings of the agrarian middle classes and to attract a level of support which substantiated its claim to represent the only power that could restore order.

The political implications of Fascist ideology became clearer after the march on Rome. First, the structure of the Liberal state was altered radically: the dominance of one party replaced parliamentary democracy and a highly repressive apparatus was established. Though depriving the individual of democratic freedoms, the regime maintained that it was Italy's authentic mode of government and that it was the expression of the will of the people. Secondly, Fascism attempted to subordinate every aspect of the private to the public: the press, the education system, the leisure industry were all subject to massive state intervention. Thirdly, Fascism presented itself as a lay religion: it celebrated its own anniversaries and its own heroes; it cultivated the mystique of leadership; it promoted complete dedication to the idea of the nation. As an ideology which expressed itself more through aesthetics than through theory,[3] it manipulated all areas of the media to diffuse modes of thought and behaviour which defined the new identity of Italians.[4]

[1] Much recent scholarship has concentrated on examining the ways in Fascism was experienced by ordinary Italians.
[2] The work of historians such as Gentile in *Le origini dell'ideologia fascista*, Sternhell in *The Birth of Fascist Ideology*, or Griffin in *The Nature of Fascism* has done much to show the origins and development of a recognizably Fascist ideology.
[3] The expression is from Gentile's reworking of Benjamin's famous phrase in *Le origini dell'ideologia fascista*; 21.
[4] On the subject of the massive dissemination of propaganda, Isnenghi has

Fourthly, though denying the political philosophy of democracy, Fascism accepted the economic basis of capitalism.
The interventions of the state in the running of the economy, from corporativism to the drive for autarky, did not
fundamentally alter the system of production.

   Italian Fascism developed as a result of the First World
War and from its outset it associated militarism with patriotism. The cultivation of martial symbols and values went hand
in hand with the propagation of myths of palingenesis.
Military rhetoric permeated every aspect of Fascism. The
domestic policies of the regime depended on the mobil-
ization of the masses and were designated as campaigns.
Mussolini's aggressive foreign policy depended on the
assumption that Fascist Italy was permanently at war: the
country had to struggle to assert its identity as a nation, to
defend itself against the hostility of its enemies, and to regain
its status as a colonial power. The notion that Italy was
both under threat and compelled to assert its power enforced a chauvinistic appreciation of Italian culture and
a corresponding hostility to that which was considered foreign. The inhabitants of the countries which Italy sought to
colonize were not the only victims of the myth of Italian
cultural and racial superiority. The intolerance towards sectors of the Italian population itself, an intolerance which
culminated in the racial laws of 1938, displayed the consequences of Fascist ideology.

   The relation of literary culture to Fascist politics has not
been fully explored. Some writers were certainly opposed to
Fascism from the outset. The example of Gobetti is a case in
point. Other writers may have been initially attracted to the
movement and have come to revise their opinions later.
Several prominent literary figures, such as Malaparte, who
had done much to promote the rise of Fascism, did their
best to define new identities for themselves in the wake of
the Second World War. Many writers were aware of the
vulgarity and violence of Fascism, but assumed a stance of
detachment. Yet, many members of the Italian literary community were not only sympathetic to Fascism, but actively

defined the Fascist regime as 'una macchina mitopoeitica'. *Intellettuali militanti e
intellettuali funzionari*, 39.

helped to define its values and contributed to the elaboration of its mythologies. Adamson, Carpi, and others[5] have pointed to the role of the pre-war avant-garde in disseminating ideas which would later be appropriated by Fascism. The writers of *La Voce* encouraged a moral revolution and claimed that the world of culture should act to renovate the world of politics in Italy. They saw their task as forming the consciousness of a new élite and their masculinist poetics announced the advent of the new man. Papini, Soffici, and especially Boine poured scorn on the principles of the Enlightenment.

A writer like Cardarelli, who began his career as a sympathizer of the reformist left, demonstrated the powerful attraction that a grouping such as *La Voce* could exert. He played his part in popularizing the work of figures associated with rightist thought in France and he was keen to express his belief in the power of the will and in the myth of national rebirth. The views which he expressed, like those of Slataper or Boine, demonstrated that a profound belief in the necessity of radical change could accompany an impatience and hostility towards Futurism. Like most of the *vociani*, his sense of self-belief had clear misogynous overtones. His awareness of modernist thought, his longing for order and discipline, his fragmentary conception of the self were typical of the generation of writers who were drawn first to *La Voce* and subsequently towards Fascism.

The return to classicism advocated by *La Ronda* can be viewed as simply the expression of the conservative instincts of a number of writers who had witnessed the civil turmoil caused by the First World War. However, the position adopted by the *rondisti* was mirrored by that assumed by other formerly avant-garde writers and by some of the most celebrated painters of the time. The Catholicism of Papini, the 'maturity' of Soffici, the rediscovered traditionalism of Carrà and De Chirico all represented concrete indications of a reactionary climate of thought. Though not explicitly identified with Fascism in its early stages, the advocates of

[5] See e.g. the recently published work edited by Marino Biondi and Alessandro Borsotti, *Cultura e fascismo*, and Mario Isnenghi's latest collection of essays, *L'Italia del Fascio* (Florence: Giunti, 1996).

literary reaction were willing to ignore acts of *squadrista* violence and were prepared to acknowledge a certain commonality between their goals and the proposed restoration of political order. They welcomed the shift which Fascism made between 1920 and 1921 to the right, while the way in which their conservatism developed after the march on Rome showed that they were more than fellow-travellers of the regime.

During the years which *La Ronda* was published, Cardarelli had arrogated to himself the role of the high priest of Italian classicism. In the years which followed, he was keen to declare his understanding of the will of the Italian people and to reinterpret Italian history in the light of the Fascist revolution. He was an inspirational figure for both *Il Selvaggio* and *L'Italiano*. The idylls he wrote of a pre-industrial society and his construction of a timeless stereotype of 'italianità' had their analogues in the writings of Soffici and Malaparte. Indeed, the similarities between the works of these three writers point to a common intellectual affinity with Fascism that had different ramifications. The emphasis upon a regressive model of regional identity is accompanied in Soffici's writings with the overt expression of xenophobia and anti-Semitism. In Malaparte, the notion of the purity of the rural world went hand in hand with the exaltation of *squadrista* violence. In all three cases, the revolt against the modern world carried connotations of an opposition to rationalism, equality, and democracy. In the writings of all three authors, history was rewritten as fable. Considering the pernicious consequences of the chauvinistic ideology which each writer helped to foster, a certain amount of guilt can undoubtedly be attached to each one of them.

Despite the xenophobia of his attacks on journals like *900* and his support for some of Mussolini's most regressive policies, Cardarelli did not write simple eulogies of the regime in a style which Italian critics refer to as 'fascistese'. His adhesion to Fascism was not the result of opportunism, but of a deeply rooted elective affinity. The works of his later period, rather than simply transposing Fascist thinking into creative writing, refer in complex ways to concepts such as the inheritance of Rome or the utopia of the past. The metaphors he used to construct his vision of Italy's new identity formed part of the same language that he employed to evoke the self of his texts. The evolution of his written persona reflects the evolution of aspects of Italian Fascism: in the texts which belong to the period of the Florentine avant-garde, the self is assertive, but fragmentary; it develops in the texts which were written after the First World War to become a monumental figure which speaks on behalf of its region and nation. The self bears clear similarities with other figurations that belong to different currents of pro-Fascist writing and painting. It reflects the attempt of an individual consciousness to interact with external suprapersonal forces. Paradoxically, however, the self of the poetry has affinities also with the self of some hermetic verse. Indeed, Cardarelli's work provides an interesting link between those writers who were associated with the worst excesses of *strapaese* culture and those who, through journals like *Solaria*, struggled to maintain the autonomy of the literary subject. The emphasis on mortality that is a distinguishing feature of *Poesie* also points to the morbidity of the desire to dwell in the past or to exist in a time defined by myth.

The travelogues which a number of prominent writers wrote in the 1930s show the coincidence of their vision of reality with that propagated by the regime. At the same time as the names of towns and streets throughout Italy were being altered, they were discovering the physical evidence of the past's grip on the present. Writers like Cardarelli, Savinio, and Alvaro appreciated the neoclassical architecture of Piacentini and others; they shared the conceptions of geography and history that were beginning to appear in school textbooks; they disseminated the same stereotypes as the regime, and they placed the same emphasis on a masculine model of Italian virtue. However, in the same years that the *rondisti* journeyed through Italy, writers like Vittorini or Giame Pintor were beginning to elaborate less inward-looking visions of imagined communities. In particular, they created a liberating idea of the United States and began to reject the stylistic constrictions of the 'prosa d'arte'. The travel writing in the 1930s presents a series of highly interesting documents which need to be examined further. While

Mussolini's ultra-nationalistic regime was recreating an identity for Italians through mythic notions of the past and through Manichaean stereotyping, writers were replicating or implicitly challenging such a notion of Italy through encounters with other cultures and ways of understanding reality.

The collections of writings which Cardarelli published, whether at an early or later stage of his career, did not enjoy a wide audience. His works achieved nothing like the circulation figures of popular writers such as Guido da Verona, Salvatore Gotta, or Liana Negretti. It was not the writers of *La Ronda*, but the realistic novelists of the 1930s who reached a growing public. But Cardarelli's writings, and those of many of his associates, often appeared initially in the cultural sections of newspapers such as the *Corriere della sera* or *Il Tevere* and were, therefore, exposed to important sections of the population. The *rondisti* considered themselves to be the custodians of high culture, and the support they were willing to offer the regime served its part in legitimizing Fascism. *La Ronda* proved, moreover, the breeding ground for a literary genre, 'la prosa d'arte', which made a virtue of the avoidance of serious political comment. The ideas on classicism promoted by the *rondisti* had their formal analogue in the later painting of Carrà and De Chirico, and in the architecture of Piacentini. Finally, Cardarelli and his closest colleagues represented a strain of anti-modern thought which coincided with a Fascist policy of rurality and which was reflected in much of the literary production of the time. The complacent and conservative tone of the writings of the *rondisti*, together with the series of prejudices they exhibited, are irredeemably unattractive. The works these writers produced do, however, remain central to our understanding of the literary culture of Fascist Italy.

BIBLIOGRAPHY

ADAMSON, W., *Avant-Garde Florence* (Cambridge, Mass.: Harvard University Press, 1993).

ALVARO, C., *I maestri del diluvio: Viaggio nella Russia sovietica*, ed. M. Flores (Massa: Memoranda Edizioni, 1985).

—— *Itinerario italiano*, ed. M. Onofri (Milan: Bompiani, 1995).

AMENDOLA, G., *La volontà è il bene* (Rome: Libreria, 1911).

ANDREOLI, A., *Leo Longanesi* (Florence: La Nuova Italia, 1980).

ASOR ROSA, A., *Storia d'Italia dall'Unità a oggi*, 3 vols., vol. ii: *La cultura* (Turin: Einaudi, 1975).

BALDACCI, L., 'Movimenti letterari del Novecento italiano', in *Dizionario della letteratura italiana contemporanea* (Florence: Vallecchi, 1973).

BANFI MALAGUZZI, D., *Il primo Rebora* (Milan: Mondadori, 1964).

BIONDI, M., and BORSOTTI, A., (eds.), *Cultura e fascismo: Letteratura, arti e spettacolo di un ventennio* (Florence: Ponte alle Grazie, 1996).

BOCELLI, A., 'Il carattere della nuova letteratura', *Bibliografia fascista*, 3 (Mar. 1930), 194–201.

BOINE, G., *Carteggio: G. Boine–E. Cecchi (1911–1917)* eds. M. Marchione and S. Scalia (Rome: Edizioni di Storia e Letteratura, 1972).

—— *Il peccato. Plausi e botte. Frantumi. Altri scritti*, ed. D. Puccini (Milan: Garzanti, 1983).

BORGESE, G. A., *Escursioni in terre nuove* (Parma: Guanda, 1931).

—— *Atlante americano* (Florence: Ceschina, 1936).

BRADBURY, M., and McFARLANE, J., (eds.), *Modernism: A Guide to European Literature 1890–1930*, 2nd edn. (London: Penguin, 1991).

BURDETT, C., 'The Success and Failure of Cardarelli's Neoclassical Project', *The Italianist*, 15 (1995) 128–49.

—— 'Montale and Cardarelli: A Two-Way Traffic of Influence', in proceedings of conference on Montale, July 1996 (Hull: Hull University Press, forthcoming).

CARDARELLI, V., *Prologhi* (Milan: Facchi, 1916).

—— *Viaggi nel tempo* (Florence: Vallecchi, 1920).

—— *Favole e memorie* (Milan: Bottega della Poesia, 1925).

—— *Il sole a picco* (Bologna: L'Italiano, 1929).

—— *Parliamo dell'Italia* (Florence: Vallecchi, 1931).

—— *Giorni in piena* (Rome: Novissima, 1934).

—— *Poesie* (Rome: Novissima, 1936).

—— *Il cielo sulle città* (Milan: Bompiani, 1939).

—— *Lettere non spedite* (Rome: Astrolabio, 1946).

—— *Solitario in Arcadia* (Milan: Mondadori, 1947).

—— *Il viaggiatore insocievole* (Bologna: Cappelli, 1953).

CARDARELLI. V., *Viaggio di un poeta in Russia* (Milan: Mondadori, 1954).
—— *Lettere d'amore a Sibilla Aleramo*, ed. G. Cibotto and B. Blasi (Bloomington, Ind.: Indiana University Press, 1974).
—— *Opere*, ed. C. Martignoni (Milan: Mondadori, 1981).
—— *Epistolario*, ed. B. Blasi, 3 vols. (Tarquinia: Ebe, 1987).
—— *Pagine sparse*, ed. C. Martignoni (Rome: Bulzoni, 1988).
—— *Autunno, sei vecchio, rassegnati*, ed. C. Martignoni (Lecce: Manni, 1988).
—— *Cardarelli e Ungaretti: Lettere a Corrado Pavolini (1926–1930)*, ed. M. Galateria and F. Bernardini Napoletano (Rome: Bulzoni, 1989).
—— *Assediato dal silenzio: Lettere a G. Raimondi*, ed. C. Martignoni (Montebelluna: Amadeus, 1990).
CAROCCI, G., *Giovanni Amendola nella crisi dello stato italiano* (Milan: Feltrinelli, 1956).
CARPI, U., *La Voce: Letteratura e primato degli intellettuali* (Bari: De Donato, 1975).
—— *Giornali vociani* (Rome: Bonacci, 1979).
—— 'Cardarelli e Péguy', *Il Cristallo*, 2 (Aug. 1984), 17–24.
CASSIERI, G., anthology of *La Ronda* (Florence: Landi, 1955; 2nd edn. Turin: RAI, 1969).
—— 'I cinquant'anni della *Ronda*', *L'Approdo letterario*, 46 (Apr.–June 1969), 89–104.
CASTELNUOVO FRIGESSI, D. (ed.), *La cultura italiana attraverso le riviste: Leonardo, Hermes, Il Regno*, 2 vols. (Turin: Einaudi, 1977).
CASTRONOVO, V., *La stampa italiana dall'Unità al fascismo* (Bari: Laterza, 1984).
CECCHI, E., *Corse al trotto* (Florence: Bemporad, 1936)
—— 'Ricordo di Vincenzo Cardarelli', *L'Approdo letterario*, 7 (July–Sept., 1959), 8–12.
—— *Saggi e vagabondaggi* (Milan: Mondadori, 1962).
—— *Taccuini*, ed. N. Gallo and P. Citati (Milan: Mondadori, 1976).
CEDERNA, A., *Mussolini urbanista* (Bari: Laterza, 1979).
CICCHETTI, A., and RAGONE, G., *Le muse e i consigli di fabbrica: Il progetto letterario della Ronda* (Rome: Bulzoni, 1979).
CLARK, M., *Modern Italy 1871–1982*, 7th edn. (London: Longman, 1991).
CONTINI, G., *Esercizi di lettura* (Turin: Einaudi, 1974).
CORRADINI, E., *Scritti e discorsi 1901-1914*, ed. L. Strappini (Turin: Einaudi, 1980).
DE FELICE, R., *Mussolini il rivoluzionario*, 2nd edn. (Turin: Einaudi, 1995).
DEI, A., *La speranza è nell'opera* (Milan: Il Saggiatore, 1979).
DI BIASE, C., *La Ronda e l'impegno* (Naples: Liguori, 1971).
DICKIE, J., '*La macchina da scrivere:* The Victor Emmanuel Monument in Rome and Italian Nationalism', *The Italianist*, 14 (1994), 261–86.

ETLIN, R. A., *Modernism in Italian Architecture, 1890–1940* (Cambridge, Mass.: MIT Press, 1991).

FORTINI, F., 'Vincenzo Cardarelli', in id. (ed.), *Ventiquattro voci per un dizionario di lettere* (Milan: Il Saggiatore, 1968, 133–6.).

—— 'La scansione di Vincenzo Cardarelli', in id. (ed.), *I poeti del Novecento* (Bari: Laterza, 1977, 83–6).

FRANCHI, R., 'Vincenzo Cardarelli', *Solaria*, 2 (Feb. 1926).

FUSSELL, P., *Abroad: British Literary Travelling Between the Wars* (Oxford: Oxford University Press, 1980).

GADDA, C. E., *Le meraviglie d'Italia* (1939; Turin: Einaudi, 1964).

GENTILE, E., *La Voce e l'età giolittiana* (Milan: Pan, 1972).

—— *L'Italia giolittiana*, 2nd edn. (Bologna: Il Mulino, 1990).

—— *Le origini dell'ideologia fascista* (Bologna: Il Mulino, 1996).

—————— *The Sacralization of Politics in Fascist Italy* (Cambridge, Mass.: Harvard University Press, 1996).

GENTILI, A., 'Per un ritorno alla "parabola" poetica di Cardarelli', *Tuttitalia*, 7 (June 1993), 26–37.

GRAMSCI, A., *Letteratura e vita nazionale* (Turin: Einaudi, 1953).

GRIFFIN, R., *The Nature of Fascism* (London: Routledge, 1991).

GUERRI, G. B., *L'Arcitaliano: Vita di Curzio Malaparte* (Milan: Leonardo, 1990).

GUZZETTA FAVA, L., '*La Ronda* cinquant'anni dopo: Ideologia e letteratura', *Lettere italiane* (Jan.–Mar. 1971).

HEINEY, D., *America in Modern Italian Literature* (New Brunswick: Rutgers University Press, 1964).

HEWITT, A., *Fascist Modernism: Aesthetics, Politics and the Avant-garde* (Stanford: Stanford University Press, 1993).

HOFFMAN, P., 'Death, Time, History: Division II of *Being and Time*', in C. Guignon (ed.), *The Cambridge Companion to Heidegger*, (Cambridge: Cambridge University Press, 1993), 195–214.

ISNENGHI, M., *Il mito della grande guerra* (Bari: Laterza, 1973).

—— *Intellettuali militanti e intellettuali funzionari* (Turin: Einaudi, 1979).

—— *L'Italia del Fascio* (Florence: Giunti, 1996).

JONES, F., 'Vincenzo Cardarelli and the Ideal of Modern Classicism' in id., *The Modern Italian Lyric* (Cardiff: University of Wales Press, 1986), 298–333.

LISSIA, P., 'Parliamo dell'Italia', *Bibliografia fascista*, 5 (May 1933), 344–5.

LONARDI, G., '"Autunno": Osservazioni sul Leopardi di Cardarelli', *Studi novecenteschi*, 4 (Dec. 1982), 249–91.

LUPERINI, R., *Il Novecento: Apparati ideologici, ceto intellettuale, sistemi formali nella letteratura italiana contemporanea*, 2 vols. 4th edn., (Turin: Loescher, 1994).

LUTI, G., *Cronache letterarie tra le due guerre 1920–1940* (Bari: Laterza, 1966).

LYTTELTON, A., *The Seizure of Power: Fascism in Italy 1919–1929* (London: Weidenfeld & Nicolson, 1973).

MALAPARTE, C., *Opere complete*, ed. E. Falqui, 4 vols. (Florence: Vallecchi, 1961–71).

MANACORDA, G., *Letteratura e cultura del periodo fascista* (Milan: Principato, 1974).

—— *Storia della letteratura italiana tra le due guerre 1919–1943* (Rome: Riuniti, 1980).

MARTIGNONI, C., 'Alle radici della prosa d'arte cardarelliana', *Letteratura italiana contemporanea*, 5 (Jan.–Apr. 1984), 161–87.

—— 'Per una storia dell'autobiografismo metafisico vociano', *Autografo*, 2 (June 1984), 32–47.

—— 'I *Frammenti* di Boine: aforisma, autobiografia, divisione dell'io', *Autografo*, 15 (Dec. 1988), 21–34.

—— 'Vincenzo Cardarelli tra mito e moralità', *Poesia*, 3/26 (Feb. 1990), 35–42.

MAURI, P., 'Il dito alzato del poeta Cardarelli', *La Repubblica*, 14 June 1979.

MENGALDO, P. V., *Poeti italiani del Novecento* (Milan: Mondadori, 1990).

MONTALE, E., *Le occasioni* (Turin: Einaudi, 1939).

—— 'Vincenzo Cardarelli: Una voce isolata', in *Sulla poesia* (Milan: Mondadori, 1976), 307–10.

MORGAN, P., *Italian Fascism* (London: Macmillan, 1995).

MUSSOLINI, B., *La Doctrine du fascisme*, vol. ix of the *Édition définitive des œuvres et discours de Benito Mussolini* (Paris: Flammarion, 1935).

NOWELL-SMITH, G., 'The Italian Cinema under Fascism', in D. Forgacs (ed.), *Rethinking Italian Fascism* (London: Lawrence & Wishart, 1986), 142–62.

O'GRADY, D., *Off Licence* (Dublin: Dolmen Press, 1968).

PAPINI, G., *Tutte le opere*, 10 vols. (Milan: Mondadori, 1958–66).

—— *Un uomo finito* (Florence: Vallecchi, 1960).

—— and PREZZOLINI, G., *Storia di un'amicizia*, 2 vols. (Florence: Vallecchi, 1966).

PÉGUY, C., *Notre jeunesse* (Paris: Gallimard, 1957).

PERTILE, L., 'Fascism and Literature', in D. Forgacs (ed.), *Rethinking Italian Fascism* (London: Lawrence & Wishart, 1986), 162–85.

POZZI, G., 'Vincenzo Cardarelli', in *La poesia italiana del Novecento: Da Gozzano agli Ermetici* (Turin: Einaudi, 1965), 117–30.

PREZZOLINI, G., *Amendola e La Voce* (Florence: Sansoni, 1974).

—— *La Voce 1908–1913: Cronaca, antologia e fortuna di una rivista* (Milan: Rusconi, 1974).

RAGGHIANTI, C. L. (ed.), anthology of *Il Selvaggio* (Vincenza: Neri Pozza Editore, 1959).

RAGONIERI, E., *Storia d'Italia dall'Unità a oggi*, 3 vols., vol. iii: *La storia politica e sociale* (Turin: Einaudi, 1976).

RAIMONDI, G., *I tetti sulla città* (Milan: Mondadori, 1977).

RAMAT, S.,'L'Ecce homo e alcuni esemplari di scrittura autobiografica in Italia', in id., *Protonovecento* (Milan: Il Saggiatore, 1978), 254–60.

RIMBAUD, A., *Œvres complètes* (Paris: Bibliothèque de la Pléiade).

ROMANÒ, A., *La cultura italiana del Novecento attraverso le riviste. La Voce (1908–1914)* (Turin: Einaudi, 1960).

RUSSO, L., *I narratori* (Milan: Mondadori, 1951).

SANGUINETI, E., *Poesia del Novecento* (Turin: Einaudi, 1969).

SAVINIO, A., *Ascolto il tuo cuore, città* (Milan: Adelphi, 1984).

SERRA, R., *Epistolario*, ed. L. Ambrosini, G. De Robertis, and A. Grilli (Florence: Vallecchi, 1934).

—— *Scritti*, ed. M. Isnenghi (Turin: Einaudi, 1974).

—— *Esame di coscienza di un letterato*, ed. B. Tonzar (Pordenone: Edizioni Studio Tesi, 1994).

SLATAPER, S., *Ibsen* (Florence: Sansoni, 1944).

—— *Epistolario*, ed. G. Stuparich (Milan: Mondadori, 1950).

—— *Appunti e note di diario* (Milan: Mondadori, 1953).

—— *Scritti letterari e critici*, ed. G. Stuparich (Milan: Mondadori, 1956).

SOFFICI, A., *Opere*, ed. E. Falqui, 7 vols. (Florence: Vallecchi, 1959–68).

SOLDATI, M., *America primo amore* (Florence: Bemporad, 1935).

SOREL, G., *Reflections on Violence*, ed. T. E. Hulme (New York: Huebsch, 1914).

STERNHELL, Z., *The Birth of Fascist Ideology: From Cultural Rebellion to Political Revolution*, trans. David Maisel (Princeton: Princeton University Press, 1994).

VALLI, D., *Vita e morte del frammento in Italia* (Lecce: Milella, 1980).

VATTIMO, G., *La fine della modernità* (Milan: Garzanti, 1985).

VENERUSO, D., *L'Italia fascista* (Bologna: Il Mulino, 1981).

VIVARELLI, R., *Storia delle origini del fascismo*, 2 vols. (Bologna: Il Mulino, 1991).

WEININGER, O., *Geschlect und Charakter*, trans. as *Sesso e carattere* by G. Fenoglio (Turin: 1912).

INDEX